# Baseball
## Between the Wars

# Baseball and American Society
### *Series ISBN 0-88736-566-3*

1. Blackball Stars
   John B. Holway
   ISBN 0-88736-094-7
   CIP 1988

2. Baseball History, Premier Edition
   Edited by Peter Levine
   ISBN 0-88736-288-5   1988

3. My 9 Innings: An Autobiography of 50 Years in Baseball
   Lee MacPhail
   ISBN 0-88736-387-3
   CIP 1989

4. Black Diamonds: Life in the Negro Leagues from the
   Men Who Lived It
   John B. Holway
   ISBN 0-88736-334-2
   CIP 1989

5. Baseball History 2
   Edited by Peter Levine
   ISBN 0-88736-342-3   1989

6. Josh and Satch: The Life and Times of Josh Gibson and
   Satchel Paige
   John B. Holway
   ISBN 0-88736-333-4
   CIP 1991

7. Encyclopedia of Major League Baseball Team Histories
   Edited by Peter C. Bjarkman
   Volume 1: American League
   ISBN 0-88736-373-3
   CIP 1991

8. Encyclopedia of Major League Baseball Team Histories
   Edited by Peter C. Bjarkman
   Volume 2: National League
   ISBN 0-88736-374-1
   CIP 1991

9. Baseball History 3
   Edited by Peter Levine
   ISBN 0-88736-577-9   1990

10. The Immortal Diamond: Baseball in American Literature
    Peter C. Bjarkman
    ISBN 0-88736-481-0 (hardcover)   CIP forthcoming,
    1992
    ISBN 0-88736-482-9 (softcover)   CIP forthcoming,
    1992

12. Baseball Players and Their Times: Oral Histories of the
    Game, 1920–1940
    Eugene Murdock
    ISBN 0-88736-235-4
    CIP 1991

13. The Tropic of Baseball: Baseball in the Dominican
    Republic
    Rob Ruck
    ISBN 0-88736-707-0
    CIP 1991

14. The Cinema of Baseball: Images of America, 1929–1989
    Gary E. Dickerson
    ISBN 0-88736-710-0
    CIP 1991

15. Baseball History 4
    Edited by Peter Levine
    ISBN 0-88736-578-7   1991

16. Baseball and American Society: A Textbook of Baseball
    History
    Peter C. Bjarkman
    ISBN 0-88736-483-7 (softcover)   CIP forthcoming,
    1992

17. Cooperstown Symposium on Baseball and the American
    Culture (1989)
    Edited by Alvin L. Hall
    ISBN 0-88736-719-4
    CIP 1991

18. Cooperstown Symposium on Baseball and the American
    Culture (1990)
    Edited by Alvin L. Hall
    ISBN 0-88736-735-6
    CIP 1991

19. Baseball Between the Wars: Memories of the Game
    by the Men Who Played It
    Eugene Murdock
    ISBN 0-88736-821-2
    CIP 1992

20. Pitchin' Man: Satchel Paige's Own Story
    Leroy Satchel Paige as told to Hal Lebovitz
    With a New Foreword by John B. Holway
    ISBN 0-88736-836-0
    CIP 1992

21. Cooperstown Symposium on Baseball and the American
    Culture (1991)
    Edited by Alvin L. Hall
    ISBN 0-88736-810-7   1992

22. My Greatest Memory in Baseball—Nostalgic Letters
    from Hall of Famers and Other Diamond Legends
    Edited by Peter C. Bjarkman
    ISBN 0-88736-804-2   CIP forthcoming, 1992

23. My Life in the Negro Leagues: An Autobiography
    Wilmer Fields
    With an Introduction by John B. Holway
    ISBN 0-88736-850-6
    CIP 1992

24. Biographical Encyclopedia of the Negro Leagues
    James A. Riley
    ISBN 0-88736-839-5   CIP forthcoming, 1992

25. Encyclopedia of Defunct Major League Teams
    Frederick Ivor-Campbell
    ISBN 0-88736-709-7   CIP forthcoming, 1993

26. The Hilldale Club: The History of a Negro League
    Baseball Team, 1910–1932
    Neil J. Lanctot
    ISBN 0-88736-864-6   CIP forthcoming, 1993

# BASEBALL
# BETWEEN THE WARS:

## MEMORIES OF THE GAME BY THE MEN WHO PLAYED IT

### EUGENE MURDOCK

Meckler

Westport • London

**Library of Congress Cataloging-in-Publication Data**

Murdock, Eugene Converse
      Baseball between the wars : memories of the game by the men who
played it / Eugene Murdock.
          p.  cm.  --  (Baseball and American society ; 19)
      Includes index.
      ISBN 0-88736-821-2  (alk. paper)  :  $
      1. Baseball players--United States--Interviews.  2. Baseball-
-United States--History.  I. Title.  II. Series.
GV865.A1M848   1992
796.357'0922--dc20
[B]                                                                                      92-5523
                                                                                              CIP

**British Library Cataloguing-in-Publication Data is available**



Meckler Publishing, the publishing division of Meckler Corporation,
      11 Ferry Lane West, Westport, CT 06880.
Meckler Ltd., 247-249 Vauxhall Bridge Road, London SW1V 1HQ, U.K.

Printed on acid free paper.
Printed and bound in the United States of America.

# Contents

Introduction

In an earlier book, *Baseball Players and Their Times: Oral Histories of the Game, 1920-1940* [Meckler, 1991], I wrote mini-biographies of 23 oldtime players I had interviewed in the 1970s. I used the interviews as a basis for the articles and then wove into them other materials, thereby providing the reader with a more rounded view of the players' careers. In this book I have stayed with the verbatim interview of 9 additional players with whom I talked. The three dot ellipses [...] are employed to save the space of another question. Thus, every time an ellipse appears, the reader can assume that another related question has been asked. I apologize for the frequent use of square brackets, but they appeared to be necessary for explanatory, clarifying, and correcting purposes. Even so a few errors are allowed to stand where there is a good story, though it may include mistakes in time and place. Let the reader be on guard and see if he can track down any such instances. I made post-inteview commentaries in a number of cases, but have included only one [Edd Roush] here. The interviews appear to end rather abruptly. This was not the case. We usually wrapped thngs up with autographing, looking at scrapbooks, and touring homes. A prefatory paragraph telling something about the circumstances attending the interviews, precedes each entry.

*   *   *

A majority of the interviews in this book were conducted on multi-interview trips. I did not do much of this when I first got into the business, but after awhile it became customary to group interviews together whenever my wife, Peg, and I planned trips of any length. Eddie Onslow and Walter Miller, both of whom lived relatively close to me, are the only "singles" in this book. Included here, in addition, are the results of one short-long trip, two long trips, and one very long trip. In February 1975 I traveled one weekend to Indianapolis where I interviewed Carmen "Bunker" Hill, Oral Hildebrand, and Dominic Dallesandro. In mid-March 1976 I spent a week traveling to Cincinnati, Chicago, and Sheboygan, Wisconsin, during which I talked with Waite Hoyt, Tony Piet, Red Faber, Bob Weiland, and Joe Hauser. In a two-week family trip through the South in August 1977 I met Kent Greenfield in Kentucky, Johnny Gill in Nashville, Joe Sewell, Riggs Stephenson, and Ed Wells in Alabama, and Elmer Riddle and Bob Smith in Georgia. The longest domestic trip Peg and I ever took was in the spring and summer of 1978 when we spent two months -- camping, sightseeing, and interviewing -- in the Southwest and West. Great interview

vii

opportunities awaited us, but unfortunately, many of them had to be missed because of the breakdown in the transmission system of our new Ford Fairmont in Palm Springs, California. This delay cut into our finances and available time and thus prevented possible interviews with Leo Durocher, Larry French, Johnny Rothrock, and Wally Berger in southern California and a host of oldtimers in the San Francisco area. Still I secured some good interviews in the West. Beginning with Ted Lyons in western Louisiana, I saw Nick Tremark, Bibb Falk, Jack Knott, and Mike Gazella in Texas, Thornton Lee and Charlie Grimm in Phoenix, Fred Fitzsimmons, Glenn Wright, and Louis Guisto in California, and Sylvester Johnson and Wes Schulmerich in Oregon. As I mentioned in the earlier book, I like to interview players of all levels of abilities. I like to talk to Hall of Famers, journeyman big leaguers, and lifetime minor leaguers. While most interviewers gravitate to the big names, I have found that a broad mix of player interviews -- talking with the not-so-greats as well as the greats -- provides a richer glimpse of the game than otherwise might be true. In this volume there are two Hall of Famers -- Waite Hoyt and Edd Roush -- and one who should be in the Hall, Riggs Stephenson. One, Eddie Onslow, spent practically his entire career in the minors, while the remaining seven, except for Roger Peckinpaugh and Bibb Falk, were average big leaguers. Peck and Bibb were well above the average level.

However all of this might be, we have here a grand collective history of baseball between World Wars I and II. As a boy who could never hit the ball out of the infield or throw from second base to first, I idolized these men and envied their athletic skills. It was a thrill for me, a senior citizen, to talk with them about their diamond exploits of many years before. I am not at all happy with the current status of baseball and the people who administer and play it. Perhaps the oldtimers would act like the moderns had they the opportunity. But they did not have that opportunity so we will ever know. As far as I could judge, they loved to play baseball, whatever the rewards. Edd Roush denied this, but he was the only one. To me, these men were the builders of a great American institution and I salute them for it.

# Roger Peckinpaugh

*Cleveland Heights, Ohio, July 9, 1973*

*"The Youngest 'Boy Manager'"*

Roger Peckinpaugh lived only about five blocks from my wife's parents in Cleveland Heights, Ohio, when I decided it was high time I got into baseball oral history. It was the summer of 1973. He was eighty-two years old, you know, and I was not sure what kind of shape he was in. I phoned one of his four sons, a practicing attorney in Cleveland, and inquired about the father. "Oh, he's doing all right," Walter Peckinpaugh replied. "Why don't you go and see him?" I did. Peck did not know me from Adam, of course, and was curious as to why I wanted to interview him. But once we got into the matter a warm rapport developed. He was an excellent interviewee and I listened with fascination as he described, among other things, Napoleon Lajoie's eight hits in the season-ending double-header in 1910, when Lajoie and Ty Cobb were vying for the American League batting title and the coveted Chalmers car. Also there was that memorable day in the Polo Grounds, August 16, 1920, when the Yankee's Carl Mays' underhand sinker pitch cracked Cleveland's Ray Chapman in the temple. Peck was the New York shortstop that day and witnessed the flight of the ball from the moment it left Mays' hand until it crushed Chapman's skull. Horrible as it was, this was baseball as it happened. Hearing it from an eyewitness thrilled me to the core and I was forever "hooked" on baseball oral history.

Note: An article based on this interview appeared in the *Baseball Research Journal* in 1975 and was reprinted in *Baseball Digest* of March, 1982, and *Insider's Baseball* (Scribners), 1983.

Q. Could you tell me a little about your family background, where you were born, and how you broke into baseball?

A. Well, I was born in Wooster, Ohio, a little town about 50 miles south of Cleveland. My folks moved to Cleveland when I was about four years old. We originally lived on the west side and then we moved to the south side, where I attended South High School. I played basketball and baseball there.

Q. When would that have been?

A. I think that was 1907. Then we moved to the east side where I attended East High School. I played in all the sports over there -- football, basketball, and baseball. That would be 1909. I was also playing sandlot baseball that year. A Cleveland Indians scout saw me play some sandlot ball and offered me a contract. In those days the rules weren't so strict, so I went to my principal, a man named Reynolds, at East High School, and asked him if I should take a shot at baseball or not. He said, "Why not? A couple years out of your life at this age won't matter, so give it a try!" He was a very sports-minded man. So I did give it a try. I jumped right out of East High School into the Cleveland organization the next year.

Q. Did you graduate from East High in 1909 and then join Cleveland in 1910?

A. Yes. Cleveland sent me to New Haven in the Connecticut State League in 1910 and I played the season there. The season closed around Labor Day.

Q. What was life like for a young man in the Connecticut League in those early days?

A. I thought it was fine. I was just a kid and having a great time... We traveled around mostly by interurban street car. Most of the towns, like Bridgeport, were pretty close. Only two towns were far enough away that we took the train. Well, with the season over in early September they brought me back here and I finished the season with Cleveland. That was a big thrill, playing shortstop next to Larry Lajoie, who was my boyhood idol. I was nineteen years old at the time. So that was a big thrill. With Bill Bradley at third on one side of me and Lajoie on the other. George Stovall was the first baseman. Tuck Turner was the regular shortstop and he was a big help to me.

Q. I met Turner once many years ago.

A. Yes, he was very nice. They had nice fellows on the team. Well, before the 1911 training season, they called me into the front office and gave me a choice. I think it was Ernest Barnard who spoke to me. He said I could go south with team for training and take my chances on making the team. Or I could go to Portland, Cleveland's affiliate in the Pacific Coast League. He said they wanted me very badly and I would be their regular shortstop. So I decided to go with Portland. Meanwhile I got married and we turned our trip out west into our honeymoon. Portland was training in southern California. I put in the whole season there. I played every game except perhaps the last series. We had already won the pennant and they had a long schedule, almost 200 games.

Q. How did you like it out there?

A. Oh, that was wonderful. We traveled up and down the coast by train. Although there were eight teams in the league, we made only three stops away from Portland. In Los Angeles there was the Los Angeles club and the Vernon club, which was a suburb. So we stayed in the one hotel for those two teams. Then up in Frisco, there was Oakland, San Francisco, and Sacramento. We stayed in a hotel on Market Street in Frisco for all of those games. As for Oakland we would play there on a Sunday morning, take the ferryboat across the bay to play in Frisco that afternoon. Then we would play the next three days there and on Thursday go back and play in Oakland. The big Frisco hotel, the St. Francis, was just being built then.

Q. Who was your manager at Portland?

A. Walter McCreedie. We won the pennant that year and several of the players went up to Cleveland the next year. A couple of pitchers, Bill Steen and Elmer Koestner. Then there was myself and a fellow they called "Raw Meat Bill" Rodgers... Portland was Cleveland's AA minor league team, New Orleans was their A team, and then they had New Haven.

Q. Now what about that double-header at the end of the 1910 season where Cobb and Lajoie were fighting for the batting title and the St. Louis team tried to help Lajoie win?

A. Well, the Chalmers Automobile Company was putting up a prize, one of their cars, for the leading batter in the American League. And Cobb and Larry were in a neck-and-neck race for the title right down to the end of the season. Now you know that Cobb was not too well liked by anybody, his own teammates or anybody else. But to me he was still the greatest ballplayer who ever lived. Cobb didn't play the last couple of games, as I recall it, so he wouldn't lower his average. It didn't seem possible for Larry to catch him. We had a double-header in St. Louis to finish the season. In the first three times up Larry lined out base hits. Then it occurred to somebody that if he got four more hits, maybe, he could beat Cobb out for the batting title. Of course, I was a kid doing what I was told. But the St. Louis third baseman started playing back and Larry beat out four straight bunts down the third base line. On one of those bunt hits, the third baseman had thrown belatedly to second base, since there was a man on first, but the throw arrived too late and the man was safe. We assumed that was a hit, but someone found out that the official scorer had scored it a fielder's choice. This meant Larry had to get another hit [chuckling]. And he wasn't likely to have another at bat. But by walks and things we got him up again. So he got another bunt hit. I think he wound up a fraction of a point or so behind Cobb, so the Chalmers people gave them both an automobile. I could be wrong about some of those things, but that's the way I remember it.

Q. So there really was something going on that the players were aware of in that second game?

A. Oh, yes, there had to be. Because later the manager was suspended and the third baseman was suspended.

Q. Then maybe it was kind of a joke thing, with no evil intent?

A. Oh, I think so. Nothing was at stake as far as the team standings go, and there was this feeling against Cobb, especially since he took himself out of the lineup for a couple of games at the end of the season so as not [to] let his average drop.

Q. Lajoie was getting older and was not very fast to begin with, so beating out all those bunts must have looked suspicious?

A. Oh, it did. But it wasn't a matter of throwing games; it was a matter of playing deep when everyone knew he was going to bunt. But nothing would have happened had not Larry gotten those three clean base hits.

Q. That was something I hadn't realized. I had thought he had beaten out about eight bunts throughout the two games. So there was no organized plot at the beginning of the first game then?

A. Oh, no. It all started after he got those base hits. The idea developed after we were well into the first game. One of those hits was a triple I think. But, of course, he was a great hitter and a wonderful chap personally.

Q. I understand that after retirement he didn't go to many games at all. That he seemed to lose interest in baseball.

A. Well, I don't know about that. After retirement he moved to Florida, around Lakeland, I think, and he became very interested in golf. I don't know that he lost interest in baseball, but a lot of players after retirement don't go to a lot of games. I don't go to many games, although I do watch them on television. My biggest gripe against baseball today is the length of the games. Nearly three hours every game. I can't understand it. In my time you could almost bank on a game not going over two hours... Yes, a lot of it is "over-managing," repeated trips to the pitcher's box and a lot of substitution. Connie Mack would do a lot of that by waving his scorecard. If I had to make a change I would just have the coach signal a change. All this walking out and back -- I suppose it's all right, but I don't think it's necessary.

Q. Why did Cleveland trade you to New York?

A. Well they had a young fellow coming up who was supposed to be a superstar -- Ray Chapman. He could hit and field and they thought he was going to be a great star. And there wouldn't be room for two shortstops on the team. I was expendable. Harry Wolverton, who had managed the Vernon club in the coast league the year I was out there, had been named manager of the Yankees. He had seen me play and wanted me, so he started the ball rolling. Then in the meantime Wolverton had been let out and Frank Chance came in. Although he was still with the Cubs, he lived on the West Coast and had seen my play and knew all about me. So he completed the deal. It was made, I think, on May 20, 1913. New York sent to Cleveland in exchange for me, Jack Lelivelt, an infielder and another player named Stumpf.

Q. How did you feel about leaving Cleveland?

A. Oh, fine, it didn't bother me at all. Because playing in your own town is always tough. And when I got to New York I got off to a good start. Of course, the New York club then was in last place -- they called it the "joy club." They didn't care and just went out to get nine innings in. Farrell --

Q. Did you know Frank Farrell, the owner?

A. He and his fellow owners were builders and they didn't care much about the team. It was a sideline with them. And it remained that way until the new owners, Jake Ruppert and Huston, came along. Meanwhile I was getting along pretty good. Then in 1914 Chance got mad at the owners, Farrell and the others, and he upped and quit in August of 1914. So he came to me and said that he had told the owners that they should make me the manager for the remainder of the season. And he whispered to me to ask for a little more money. He liked me. So the owners did that. They came out to see me and I probably never would have thought about asking for more money if Frank Chance hadn't told me to. And they weren't going to bring it up either. Finally, I asked for another $500, and after a little bargaining, I got it. So now I was manager of the New York Yankees.

Q. Yes, and the youngest manager in history; I think that's remarkable. How old were you then?

A. I was only twenty-three.

Q. Why didn't they keep you in 1915?

A. Oh, they figured I was too young and inexperienced. They brought in that veteran pitcher Bill Donovan.

Q. I thought that Ruppert and Huston bought the club that 1914-15 winter from Farrell and that the new owners wanted a new manager; I was thinking that was why they let you out and brought Donovan in.

A. No, Ruppert bought the club later. They just wanted a more experienced manager. [I'm afraid he's wrong on when Ruppert-Huston bought the club. It was in the winter of 1914-15. However, the new owners may well have replaced Peck with Donovan for the reasons stated. I can't prove any linkage between the new owners and Peck's displacement.]... No, it didn't upset me that I was replaced. I knew I was just in there temporarily. Then along came Ruppert and Huston and they began buying those players from Boston and we became a good team, winning our first pennant in 1921.

Q. Tell me about Babe Ruth.

A. Well, he was just a big, happy-go-lucky fellow that everybody had to like... Yes, he called everybody "kid," although he did call me "Peck" most of the time... I don't really know if he knew anyone's real name or not [chuckling]. He just loved to play baseball. I was only with him for two years, 1920 and 1921. He liked to play around and party at nights, but he was always there the next day ready for batting practice. He never looked like he ever had a hangover to me. He always hustled. He was a good fielder. He didn't cover as much ground as some, but he had a good arm and knew where to throw the ball.

Q. But in those two years you saw him break all existing home run records didn't you?

A. Yes. I am not quite sure of the figures, but I think he broke his 1919 record in 1920 and then his 1920 record in 1921. The day in 1921 that he tied his 1920 record we were in Philadelphia. He came to me and said, "Hey, kid, I think I'll save the tie-breaker until we get back home; it will give the fans something to cheer about." Of course, he didn't mean that. Every time he went up to the plate he wanted to bust one out of there. But no one can compare to Babe Ruth in the home run department. Even if Hank Aaron ties and goes on to break the Babe's all-time home run record, you still can't compare Aaron to Ruth.

Q. What about Carl Mays?

A. Carl? Fine fellow. I suppose you're bringing that up because he hit Ray Chapman? In my book, the ball that hit Chapman was almost a strike. Ray batted with his head hanging over the plate and he crouched down.

Q. You were in that game weren't you?

A. Yes, I was in the game and saw the pitch. Chappie must have frozen because he turned his head around. If he hadn't done that he might have gotten a broken nose or something like that, but it wouldn't have killed him. But he turned his head and the ball hit him right over the ear. And it hit him so solid that we weren't sure that it hadn't hit the bat. We couldn't tell. And it bounced right down to the third baseman, who was Frank "Home Run" Baker, fielded the ball and threw to first base. He was down but I didn't know whether it hit the bat or not. He had collapsed and a couple of the players picked him up and started walking him to the clubhouse, which in the Polo Grounds is in center field. They got him just about to second base where I was standing and then his legs just completely gave out.

Q. But he did walk part way then?

A. Well, with help. Actually, the players may have really been carrying him most of the way. He probably never regained consciousness. I've often thought that if he hadn't turned his head he would have a smashed nose and cheek bone, but the ball just "jellied" his brain, as they say. Carl Mays threw underhanded and he threw what they called a very "heavy" ball. It sinks and when you catch it feels heavy enough to almost go through the glove. So when you get hit by something like that you don't have much chance.

Q. Would a batting helmet have saved him?

A. Oh, sure. It would have protected him right over and behind the ear, which is the worst place you can get hit.

Q. I wonder why they never adopted batting helmets earlier. Even the killing of Chapman on a pitch where a batting helmet would have saved him, did not lead to the adoption of batting helmets. I don't think anyone even suggested the idea after Chapman was killed.

A. Well, I don't know why. And after all, he was the only fatality... Carl? Oh, he was a real nice fellow. He died here not too many years ago.

Q. How did he feel about this?

A. Oh, naturally, he felt very badly. He absolutely was not throwing at Chappie. It was purely an accident. If it had been anyone but Chapman, the ball would not have hit the batter. He just leaned over too far, his head hanging right over the plate.

Q. I think I read that Mays pitched a shutout on his next outing, so he was able to concentrate on that, which must not have been easy to do. You must have batted against him when he was with Boston? Was he pretty tough to hit against?

A. Well, if he kept his pitch low. If it came in around the knees and then dropped, he was tough to hit. If he got it up higher it was like most other pitches. He was really tough to hit most of the time. He threw every ball underhand and would often scrape his knuckles on the ground.

Q. Well, what about the trade that took you from New York to Washington?

A. That one hurt a little bit because it wasn't my fault. Here's a little bit of history that isn't too well known. The only guy Babe Ruth didn't get along with, as far as I knew, was Miller Huggins. They just didn't get along. The Babe was openly knocking Huggins down as manager and boosting me to be manager of the club. He made no bones about it. During the winter they got rid of me... No, they didn't tell me this, but I knew what the score was. I had a beautiful year in 1921 and I had been with the club quite awhile. But this was creating quite a commotion and Babe was having a little trouble and they talked about fining him and things like that. But nobody compared with Ruth in drawing fans into the ballpark. We would go into St. Louis where they would normally draw 400-500 and they would have a policeman on horseback driving the crowd back into the outfield. And just one man was doing that. Nobody could [come] close to that. So they had to be very careful about suspending him. One night they put a detective on him and he came back with all the goods on the Babe. They were all set to fine him and suspend him after the next game. Then in that next game he hit two or three home runs and won the game [laughing]. Ruppert said, in disgust and admiration combined, "Oh, what can you do with a guy like that?"

*Roger Peckinpaugh, shortstop for the Washington Senators in the early 1920s. Peck had helped the New York Yankees win the American League pennant in 1921, but then, because of indirect pressure from Babe Ruth, was traded to Washington. He helped the Senators win pennants in 1924 and 1925. He was voted the American League's "Most Valuable Player" in 1925. The luster of this award was somewhat tarnished in the World Series, however, when Peck made eight errors, a "record" which still stands. (Photo from the author's collection.)*

They sure couldn't get rid of Ruth, but they could get rid of me. And I didn't get started very well in Washington for half a year or so. It kind of knocked me down that trade. I read about it in the newspapers.

Q. How did you get along with Ruppert and Huggins?

A. Oh, I got along fine with them. I got along with any manager. Managers didn't mean anything to me. I would do what they told me to do and go out and play ball.

Q. How about Ruppert?

A. He didn't interfere with the players too much. I was holding out one year and I went to see him down in the brewery. I went into that great big room. In those days you might be asking for $1,000. Today they practically give you that for meal money. So I walked in there and Ruppert started telling me what a great shortstop I was [chuckling]. Then when it came to asking for the $1,000, I wasn't such a good shortstop any longer. That was the only meeting with Ruppert. But then things got going pretty well in Washington and we won two pennants. So I didn't lose out too much, pennant-wise.

Q. You lost two pennants in New York [1922 and 1923] and picked up two in Washington [1924 and 1925].

A. Yes, that's right.

Q. Who was your manager when you went to Washington?

A. I'm a little confused on that. Donie Bush was manager and then Clyde Milan was a manager for awhile. When I went there in 1922 it seemed that both Donie Bush and Milan were managing. And then in 1924 when we won the pennant Bucky Harris was manager. [For the record, Milan managed in 1922, Bush in 1923, and Harris from 1924-1928.]

Q. Harris has always been labeled the "boy manager," although it now comes out that you were a younger "boy manager" than he was. Now he became manager of Washington in 1924 at the age of 27. I would have thought they might have picked someone with more experience. You obviously had managerial abilities and more experience than Harris. Do you know if you were considered for the job at that time?

A. I may have been considered, but I don't know if I was or not. That old foxy Griffith, you know... No, I wasn't looking for the job. I considered my job to be playing shortstop.

Q. Now Walter Johnson?

A. You're talking now about one of the greatest fellows I ever knew. Walter and I were very good friends. We became very close in Washington and our wives and children also became very close.

Q. Where did you live in Washington?

A. Oh, we lived in several places. Out in Chevy Chase once, and then another time we had an apartment out near Rock Creek Park. In the off-season we would come back to Cleveland where we had our permanent home. Walter and his wife would usually have a suite of rooms in the same apartment we were in. Walter was a wonderful fellow. If you would boot one behind him, he'd say, "look, don't get killed back there. He never should have hit the ball so hard." Things like that; he'd take the blame for everything.

Q. Was he the fastest pitcher ever, would you say?

A. I think so. And he was a very shy person. I remember one time in New York, he and his wife and me and my wife went down town to see Will Rogers in one of the Follies shows. Somebody must have tipped off Will Rogers that Walter was in the audience because during the show, he came down off the stage swinging his lasso. And when he got to where we were he lassoed Walter and dragged him up to the stage. Walter blushed, oh, how he blushed. When he got back from the stage, he said, "C'mon, let's get out of here." Everyone was looking at him. That shows you the kind of fellow he was. He'd much rather be out in the woods. He liked his dogs and to go out in the woods hunting.

Q. He doesn't sound to me like the type of man you would want to manage your club.

A. No, he was not. It was a mistake to make him manager. He was close friends with one of the big stockholders of the Cleveland club so that's how he became manager of Cleveland in 1933 [succeeding Peckinpaugh, incidentally]. He didn't know how to be tough with his players and when he tried to be tough he got sarcastic. Sarcasm doesn't go with ballplayers. Call them anything you like, but don't get sarcastic with them.

Q. Rather odd that he should succeed you, too?

A. Yes, it was, but we never talked about it... But unless you have a super ballclub you're going to have problems.

Q. It takes a certain temperament to be successful at managing, doesn't it?

A. Yes. The big thing in my book is getting the best you can out of your ballplayers. Most of them know their business, or are supposed to. Of course today there has been so much expansion that, in my opinion, you have a lot of minor leaguers playing in the major leagues. Some of them even have to be taught the fundamentals. In those days you didn't have to worry about that when you were managing a big league ballclub. The idea was to get to know the players and know how to deal with them. You had to know when to kick a player around to get the best out of him, or in another case, when to pat a man on the back to get the best out of him.

Q. You had to be a master in applied psychology, it sounds like?

A. Well, yes. That was what it was about. We had a man here when I was managing the second time, Jeff Heath, who could have been one of the greatest players. He had the ability to do about anything. He could run, he could throw, and he could hit. But he just had no hustle, no nothing. If a ball went by him, he might just walk after it. Or if he was on third base and a ball was hit to the infield on which he should have scored, his mind would be on something else and he'd still be standing on third.

Q. How would you try to deal with him?

A. You had to explain patiently what he should be doing and encourage him all the way; tell him he could become a great ballplayer, boost him up. For if you went the other way, he became like a mule and wouldn't do anything. He wouldn't do anything if you bawled him out too much.

Q. How did you happen to become manager of Cleveland in 1928?

A. Well, that was the year that Alva Bradley and his associates bought the club and hired Billy Evans as general manager. Billy and I were old friends. I had known him for a long time and he liked me. He went out and got me from the Chicago club. The new ownership wanted an all-local arrangement, with the general manager and the manager both being Clevelanders. And we got along pretty good as a team. We were just shy of having a real good team. We needed a shortstop who could hit.

Q. What about Jonah Goldman?

A. Well, there you are. He was a great fielder, but he couldn't hit a lick. And then there was Eddie Montague, another good field no hit. We had a good outfield with Vosmik, Averill, and Porter.

Q. One of my boyhood heroes was Eddie Morgan, who hit all those home runs for Elgin watches. Why did he have such a short career?

A. Well, Eddie was just one of those playboys. That was his main trouble.

Q. I could never figure out why he didn't last longer. He hit twenty-six home runs one year, a Cleveland record to that time, and I think he batted over .350 in 1930, but then after a couple of years he was gone and in came Harley Boss who couldn't do anything. So that was it then -- a playboy?

A. Yes, that would be my opinion about it... Oh, no, he was not a difficult player to manage. Just the opposite. No trouble with him at all... Johnny Hodapp was another fine boy. He was a pretty good hitter, although he didn't cover the ground the way some could do. He was a solid ballplayer... Wes Ferrell? He was a fine pitcher, but he had a terrible temper. He never wanted to be taken out of a game. He would be mad, not at anybody else, but mad at himself. Because he didn't think anybody could get a base hit off of him and when they did he would get mad. Of course, his temper was the same on the golf course. I played with him a couple of times and if he made a bad shot he would break the club right in two or jam it into the ground. He wasn't mad at the manager for taking him out of a game, but at himself. But he was a good boy and a fine hitter. He helped himself in many a game with his bat... Charlie Jamieson and I were good friends; he was a nice fellow. I think he died recently and we used to get Christmas cards from him until recently. He was a guard at some plant in Jersey.

Q. I began going to games in 1929 and that was when Jamieson was about at the end of his career and Vosmik was coming up. I saw Jamieson play for awhile, but then Vosmik moved into left field.

A. Well, now that you mention it, we came up from spring training and were ready to start the season. Vosmik was with us. I put Jamieson in to open the season because we had an overflow crowd in old League Park, and I thought that Joe might get into trouble out there, being in his home town and with that overflow crowd. And I know what can happen if you get started on the wrong foot. On the next day when things calmed down I started Joe and he stayed in there. It might have been all right if I had put Joe in that first game, but I just didn't want to take the chance. I explained it to him and he seemed to take it all right. [This had to be the 1931 season. 1930 was Jamieson's last full year, and 1931 was Vosmik's first full year.]

Q. I always thought that Vosmik, after a fine start, more or less faded away, that his career kind of went down hill. In about six or seven years he was through. Earl Averill?

*Roger Peckinpaugh, manager of the Cleveland Indians, 1928-1933, batting the ball for infield practice. Peck had been "the youngest boy manager" in history in 1914, but that was just a temporary assignment. He managed the Indians in 1941, in addition to the late 1920s and early 1930s. Well-liked by the players, Peck was not a very successful manager. He led Cleveland to one third place, four fourth place, one fifth place, and one seventh place finish. (Photo from the author's collection.)*

A. Oh, he was a fine fellow... Yes, I would think he should be in the Hall of Fame... He was easy-going, but he played hard; he didn't loaf. He was a real good ballplayer... Yes, Dick Porter had a rather short career. He was here when I left. He stayed in the minor leagues longer than he should have. The scouts didn't think he could hit major league pitching, I guess, but he showed them he could. He had a style of his own and he was a good hitter.

Q. Now getting back to your career with Washington, you got into two World Series. In 1924, you had a great Series, but I guess you don't want to talk about 1925 [I chuckle; he doesn't]?

A. That 1925 Series was not as bad as it seems. I had a lot of errors, but the field was bad and wet. I never counted them, but I think about four of the errors were on low throws, with that soggy, muddy ball. Joe Judge, who would normally eat up those throws wasn't able to come up with them. Anyway, I wound up with getting credit for eight errors. I seriously doubted two of them. And whenever I see Max Carey down at the Hall of Fame game in Bradenton each spring we talk about that. He always says, "How could they give you an error on that 'fifth hit' of mine? They should have given me a hit, not you an error. Five hits off Walter Johnson could have meant thousands of dollars." He was convinced I should not have been given an error on the one he hit. But as I tell people, what the Pittsburgh scorers were trying to do in that Series was to let me break Honus Wagner's World Series record for errors. He was the finest shortstop of all time, but he held the record for shortstop errors in a World Series -- six. So they wanted me to break that record and they helped me along [chuckling]. So I got eight. I didn't know it then, that Wagner had the record with six errors. I don't know how many games that was in; mine was in seven games.

Q. Having all those errors charged against you, did that upset you very much?

A. At the time, oh, yes. It seems that everywhere I go, after my long career in baseball and all the things I have accomplished, the first thing that always comes up is those errors in the 1925 World Series. Nobody seems to know about or is interested in anything else.

Q. They don't ask about your .417 batting average in the 1924 Series, only the eight errors in the 1925 Series.

A. That's right.

Q. It must have been quite a thrill being on that 1924 pennant winner in Washington. I guess they had never won a pennant before.

A. Yes, that was a good team. We had a good infield with Ossie Bluege at third, Bucky Harris at second, Joe Judge at first, and myself at shortstop. A fine outfield with Sam Rice in right, Earl McNeely in center, and the Goose, Goslin, in left. Muddy Ruel was catching. And we had some pretty fair pitching with Walter Johnson. That year brought out the real value of relief pitching with Fred Marberry. I had never realized before how important that was. And he loved it. You could bring him in there with two balls and no strikes on the hitter and you just knew he wouldn't walk the batter. He saved game after game after game for us. He would go down to that bullpen every day and just loved to come in in a tough situation. And besides him we had some good left-handed pitchers in George Mogridge and -- oh, I've forgotten his name. He just died. I was looking over the list of players on that team recently, and my heavens, just about all of them are gone.

Q. How did that team compare with the 1921 Yankees?

A. The 1921 Yankees was probably a better team; it had more power. We had Frank Baker, who had a lot of power. Bob Meusel in left. A fellow named Elmer Miller played center field... Whitey Witt wasn't there then. Our catcher was Wally Schang.

Q. How did you happen to leave Washington and go to Chicago?

A. Eddie Collins, Boston's general manager, wanted me. After I was let out here in Cleveland in 1933, Eddie called me up -- he got me off the golf course -- and said he wanted me to come to Boston. Marty McManus was the manager and he wanted me to replace Marty. Marty balked at the idea, saying he thought he should have one more chance -- to take the club on the road one more time. So Eddie told me that since McManus was the third baseman as well as the manager, if I came in there and Marty wouldn't play very well for me, it might get awkward. So he told Marty to take the team on the road trip to Washington. Now the Boston club was a notoriously weak road team. Anyway I came back home and got my wife and we went up to Canada to fish at our cottage. I had bought a cottage up there after the 1921 World Series. [After that Series] I played some games with some people up there for the benefit of Canadian veterans of World War I. One of the men who promoted it was a lumberman from Marmoret, Canada. He invited us up to his place and I liked it so much that I built a cottage next to his place. We still have that place -- it has been over fifty years now. So I went up there and expected to hear from Eddie Collins. I followed the papers and saw that Boston kept winning and winning and winning, so I realized I wouldn't be hearing from Eddie Collins after all [chuckling]. Then over the winter I read that Tom Yawkey had bought the club and had signed Bucky Harris to manage it. That's how close I came to manage the Boston club.

Q. How did you happen to come back to Cleveland in 1941 after the Oscar Vitt saga?

A. Well, Alva Bradley just wanted me back... I didn't know whether it would be just a one-year appointment or not. I'm trying to think what happened. They sent me down to get Burt Shotton to manage the club and in the meanwhile Boudreau called on the owners and said he wanted the chance to manage. And I guess he convinced them. It happened when I was down in Florida looking for Burt Shotton to manage the ballclub. So, I talked him into coming up and helping Boudreau out.

Q. But you were the manager in 1941 so why didn't you stay on in 1942?

A. They wanted me up in the front office... I liked that very much until Bill Veeck came along in 1946. He ruined that for me. He cleaned out the entire front office and brought in his own people.

Q. What have you done after baseball?

A. Oh, I have been a salesman here ever since I've been out of baseball. I was a manufacturers rep with about half a dozen railroad accounts. Then I was with the Cleveland Oak Belding Company where I visited many shops around here. George Uhle was in the same business so we ran into each other quite a bit for lunch. We were "peddlers," as I call them. But I haven't seen Bill Wamby... Speaker was very nice; I've played a lot of golf with "Spoke."

Q. How about your biggest thrill in baseball?

A. Oh, I suppose it was being voted the "Most Valuable Player" in the American League in 1925. I heard later that the Philadelphia writer [Jimmy Isaminger] was on the fence between myself and somebody else. Then we were playing over in Philadelphia late in the season and I made a diving catch of a low line drive behind second base and saved the game, and that, I've been told, is what convinced this writer that I was the man.

Q. When did you first hear about the award?

A. Oh, I'm not sure. It was after the season ended, but before the Series began. They wrote in the paper that it jinxed me in the Series and that I made all those errors because I was jinxed by having gotten the award... Yes, its a good thing that they didn't decide on the award after the Series instead of before [chuckling].

Q. What did they give you?

A. I'll show you the plaque; it's hanging in the living room... I don't remember who made the presentation of the plaque, if anyone did.

Q. Do you recall any unusual events in your career?

A. Oh, I've often thought if I had only made a few notes after each game about little things that happened, things that didn't seem too important then, but would be very interesting now, if I had only done that, what a great wealth of material I would have now. It's too late now and I just don't remember much. The emery ball deal, when I first joined the Yankees, I remember that quite well. A fellow named Russ Ford discovered that emery ball down south. He was warming up down there in Atlanta with his batterymate Ed Sweeney -- they were both members of the Atlanta team, I think, and the ball got away and struck a concrete wall. On the next pitch Ford threw, the ball sailed wildly. They looked at it and noticed a big scuff mark where the ball had scraped the concrete. So he began experimenting with it and found that if he held the ball one way the ball sailed in a certain direction and if he held it another way the ball sailed in another direction. That was the way the emery ball was discovered and he became a great pitcher right away using that pitch.

Q. How did he do it?

A. He was very smart the way he did it. He had a ring made with emery paper on it and he had a whole in the glove. He was satisfied that he could sail the ball just a short distance with a small spot on it the size of dime. He got away with it for so long because he would go to his mouth every time as if he was throwing a spitter. Everyone thought he was throwing a spitter, but it wasn't at all. After he got out of the game, Ed Sweeney told some of the other pitchers what it was. Now they weren't satisfied with a little spot the size of dime, they wanted a bigger spot. They wound up scuffing about half the ball [we chuckle], so it wasn't long until the emery ball was outlawed.

Q. Umpires didn't check the ball very much in the old days, did they?

A. Oh, no, they stayed with the same ball for a long time. When I first came up we used the same ball until it went into the stands or over the fence. You might have one ball in there for two or three innings. Sometimes it would get pretty soft. I recall that if you were behind two or three runs and an old ball was in there, a leadoff man's duty was to get up there and try to foul the ball into the stands so they would have a new ball to hit against. Today they put a new ball in when there is nothing really wrong with the old ball.

Q. How was it to hit against the spitball?

A. It just had a good break to it, that's all. And there were some good spitball pitchers too. Ed Walsh, the best, I guess, then there was Coveleski, Jack Quinn, and Allan Russell. And there were some guys who weren't regular spitball pitchers who threw it once in awhile. This was tough on a hitter because such a pitcher could really surprise you with the spitball. The other guys threw it most of the time.

Q. Why did they ban the spitball?

A. The reason for the banning of the spitball was to get rid of all of those other pitches that were being developed, like the shine ball and emery ball. It was an excuse to get rid of all of these pitches where something was put on the ball or where something was done to the ball.

Q. Have you had any great hitting games?

A. Oh, I have hit a couple of home runs in a game once or twice, although I wasn't a home run hitter. And I have had a few 4-for-5 games. And I had a batting streak of twenty-eight or twenty-nine games in a row. That was with the Yankees. I remember the day that that string was broken. I went down to get the bat that I had been using throughout the streak. I couldn't find it. Finally, someone took me aside and told me that a pitcher had used my bat in batting practice and had broken it. Oh, was I burned up. A pitcher using my bat in batting practice! That was a no-no. And I didn't get a hit that day and the streak was broken [chuckling].

Q. When you first broke in with Cleveland were they playing in the present ballpark?

A. Yes, I think it had just been opened the year before.

Q. Where had they played before then?

A. Well, you've got me there. I can't remember if they had another park or if they just built the new one on the site of the old one. I don't know where else they might have played, however... Yes, the park was pretty much then the way it is now. Both the concrete and wooden bleachers were in place and it was double-decked all the way around.

Q. It was a great park -- to me. I saw my first game there in August 1929. The Yankees beat Cleveland and Ruth hit a homer. That was my big thrill. Tom Zachary pitched for New York.

A. Zachary! That's the left hander I was trying to think of who pitched for us with Washington when we won the pennant... Walter Miller was a good pitcher for us, as well as Willis Hudlin... My father was in the insurance business. He played some semi-pro ball down around Kent, Ohio. He always played in this old-timers league in Florida.

[The following is from an untaped interview with Roger Peckinpaugh at Cleveland Heights, Ohio, on October 28, 1974.]

Q. On Ray Chapman's beaning. Muddy Ruel has written that when the ball hit Chapman and bounced out into the infield, he was catching and he ran out and fielded the ball and threw it to first, rather than Frank Baker.

A. I'm almost sure it was Baker because it bounced so far out that it would have been too far for the catcher to field. [He demonstrated Chapman's stance, indicating that his bat was cocked back over his head and might even have been sticking out in front from around the back of his head, so it looked like the ball might have struck the bat.] The Boston Red Sox, when Bill Carrigan was their manager [1913-1916], had a regular "knock down" pitch. That is, there was an actual signal which Carrigan flashed, calling for the knock down. Every time you played in Boston you could expect to be knocked down on at least one pitch on each time at bat. You didn't know which one, but you knew it was coming. And it gave you something to think about; it could make you a little nervous.

Q. Were you ever hit on the head?

A. Once in spring training. That was when they allowed the quick pitch. That is, the pitcher could throw as soon as he got the ball back from the catcher. He caught me off guard and hit me pretty good on the left side of the head. I really saw stars, even though I wasn't knocked out. I can't remember who the pitcher

*Cleveland manager Roger Peckinpaugh [second from left], discussing ground rules with Bucky Harris [right], the Detroit manager, and the umpires, prior to opening day in Cleveland in 1932. (Photo from the author's collection.)*

was, although I think it happened while I was with Cleveland in 1912-1914. They outlawed the quick pitch before that season began.

Q. Did they throw at you much?

A. Hah [chuckling]! Not me; I wasn't that good a hitter. I got hit a few times on the arm and side, but that quick pitch was the only one in the head... Those Red Sox had some good pitchers who threw that knock down pitch. Ernie Shore, Hugh Bedient, a little guy named Foster, Dutch Leonard.

Q. Do you remember Pinky Shoffner?

A. Oh, yes. I brought him in one day when he was just a kid, to face Ruth. I was just hoping he could get the ball over the plate. [Having just interviewed Shoffner about a month earlier, I had to remind Peck of the real drama of that situation. It was a big Sunday crowd, it was Shoffner's first appearance in a major league game, and he struck out Ruth. Peck marveled that he had forgotten the drama of it all.] Another time in Chicago I had this big pitcher, Walter Brown, who could throw hard, but was a little wild. It was a bases loaded situation in the last inning with the score tied. All I wanted him to do was to get the ball over the plate. But he did just what I had hoped he would not do. He walked the guy and the winning run scored.

Q. I am going to interview Walter Miller tomorrow. Are there any good questions I should ask him?

A. Ask him how he liked to pitch to Goose Goslin. He could always handle Goose. That was one case where a left-hand pitcher against a left-hand hitter really worked well. Goslin had trouble with some left handers. Walter always seemed to outguess Goose. When we played Cleveland and Walter was warming up, we'd call to Goose and say, "Look who's pitching."

Q. Shoffner complained that he was not given enough opportunities to start?

A. Well, we had some pretty good pitchers -- Hudlin, Ferrell, Harder. It was not easy to break into that starting rotation.

# Waite Hoyt



*"Player-Philosopher"*

To my mind Waite Hoyt is the "player-philosopher" of baseball. Besides being a Hall of Fame pitcher and a fairly good broadcaster, he was able to place the game in an historic and cultural perspective that most players did not think much about. While occasionally becoming entangled in his own diction, Hoyt discussed baseball with a special knowledge, perception, and understanding. Two points, in particular, struck me. First, he was totally disenchanted with writers who wrote pontifically with inadequate information. They just did not know what they were talking about most of the time. When they wrote of Babe Ruth's "spindly legs," for example, they were all wet. Ruth had strong, muscular legs. In many cases, he continued, writers were biased, did not do their homework, and distorted facts. Hoyt also criticized the role the Veterans' Committee of the Hall of Fame was expected to play. He served on the committee for many years and was still wondering how committee members were supposed to evaluate players of a much earlier era, players they had never seen and knew little about. At the time of the interview I was a strong supporter of the election of Sam Thompson to the Hall. [He later made it.]  The issue aroused Hoyt, who warmly responded by inquiring how he was expected to vote intelligently on Thompson?  He had never heard of the guy. He was honest and forthright, admitting the weaknesses of the selection process. I spent a stimulating and illuminating evening with the player-philosopher of baseball.

Q.  I have something from an article in *The Sporting News* in March 1938 by Taylor Spink that your father was with a minstrel group. Could you --

A.  I would rather not have that projected.

Q.  O.K. How about your parents' background; where they lived and what they did?

A.  My father's family, from the genealogical books I have, came over from England and Holland, mostly England. I don't know what year. That is in the books. Around 1640 or something like that. They were quite American and patriotic and all because of the Revolution. In fact I am qualified to be and am, a Son of an Officer of the American Revolution. And I was a Son of the

American Revolution here in Cincinnati until some nitwit wrote me a letter that I was delinquent in my dues. It got lost in all the papers and I hadn't realized that I hadn't paid them. I wrote back something to the effect that I was sorry I hadn't paid the dues, but that I didn't like the tone of his letter so I was resigning from the organization... One of my ancestors, according to my father -- you see you get these old fathers, my grandfather and father, and perhaps your father -- you have there some of the biggest liars in the world. [We chuckle.]

Q.  Like old ballplayers.

A.  Just as bad. My father told me about these things, but as a boy I was not interested in those matters. He pointed out some fellow who was in the honor guard who escorted Lafayette when he came over here, but I don't know the details. You get all these stories and... One thing I do know, I was in the Hoyt mansion in Manchester in 1950 or 1960. My cousin Russell was one of the trustees of Columbia University and his two sisters, Grace and Frances, never married and were society entertainers. They entertained playing the harp and harpsichord and they were with Elsie Janis in the first World War, when she made that tour over there. They also made the Chautauqua circuit a lot with William Jennings Bryan. They were quite famous and lived in the Dakota Apartment House on West 72nd, Central Park West. You may have heard of the Dakota, that's a famous apartment. Russell was quite prominent, too, and he never married either. He was an inveterate baseball fan and a fine fellow. He used to appear at the ticket gate in New York once in awhile without my knowing it. But for some reason all those cousins kept their distance from us. I never quite knew why. Except for one time when one of the sisters, Frances, invited Mrs. Hoyt and myself up to their place in the Dakota for dinner. We were quite entranced by it all, the antiques and such. And they still kept the house in --, they kept that until Russell died. I can't remember the name of the chap [to whom the house was sold], and that aggravates me very much. His family puts on the biggest national dog show over there in New Jersey. He is a Rockefeller associate. He was Russell's executor and administrator of the estate. Then Russell became violently ill and was incapacitated for years and that sort of stripped that end of the family. Then they had to sell the place in Vermont. Mrs. Hoyt and I always hoped we would get some fabulous antique. Because they were so patriotic. Every year instead of a typical Christmas card, you'd get a picture of the house, or a picture of the interior which showed these antiques and things worth thousands of dollars. We were always hoping we would get something like that, a relic of the Hoyt family. Nothing ever developed like that, except that one day, we had a house here in Cincinnati and the mailman delivered a packet. This was after Russell's death. I opened the packet [laughing] and out dropped a rose petal. Actually it was the flag that covered Russell's casket. So this was my inheritance from all the antiques they had [laughing again]. But their story was a very fascinating one and I always thought a lot of them.

Q.  How did your father get into the Swift Company?

A.  Through my uncle. My uncle was my father's sister's husband. My father originally was with an outfit called Mason-Hanson, who were sort of tailors, who provided cloth for suits to companies like Brooks Brothers. He left there to go to L. Heller and Sons, who were among the first, if not the first, importers of pearls. They were not synthetic, but deliberately bred or made pearls. But my father left there because there were so many [Heller] sons in the organization that there was no future for him. Once he reached a certain point, the "sons" took over. But my father was a great ball fan who had played semi-pro ball in Brooklyn.  He helped build one of the original ballfields there, Hawthorn Field in Flatbush. The Hawthorns played all-star teams and after the season was over they would play big league all-star aggregations. They were pretty good, I understand.

Q.  Did he live in Chicago when he worked for Swifts?

A.  Oh, no, no, no. We lived in Brooklyn all our lives. They are all buried in Brooklyn, in Greenwood cemetery.

Q.  It has here [I am using the Taylor Spink article as a sort of guide], you thought about your high school career and your becoming a pitcher. It mentions a number of leagues which existed then.

A.  Well, the newspapers used to have leagues. There was the Brooklyn Times League, the Brooklyn Eagle League, and another one which I forget the name of. They had twenty diamonds in Prospect Park. Most of the fellows who played in the Brooklyn Times and Eagle leagues were members of the high school teams around town. We won the city championship. At off-times they played under the name of this other team, the Wyandots, a pretty good team.

Q.  Were you pitching at this time?

A.  I started as a second baseman -- well, that's kind of a joke story. This other team was being formed and in those days we didn't have organized leagues and things, so to play with a team that had uniforms was rather unique. This new team was going to have uniforms so I heard that they needed a pitcher so I asked about it. The chap said they needed a pitcher and I said "Well, I'm a pitcher," though I had never pitched a game in my life. I could throw the ball well and so I became a pitcher because they were going to have uniforms.

Q.  I would have thought you would have been a pitcher from the start, throwing as hard as you did. Weren't the kids who threw the hardest always the pitchers?

A.  Well, my father was an infielder, a third baseman, and he wanted me to be an infielder. Those were different days. It has become a trite utterance to say that those were different days. Of course, they were different. You see, in Brooklyn where I lived, in Flatbush, there were no paved roads. My home on Olive Street wasn't paved for a long, long time. My father would take me out to the middle of the road and throw the ball on the ground to me. I had to learn to stop it in all the ruts and things. You learned to field that way.

Q.  It says here that you were contacted by the Brooklyn Feds. How did that come about?

A.  Yes. That is a bit of a mystery. I can't remember who the person was who first -- oh, now I know. If I'm not mistaken, and I could look it up, I think it was Fred Jacklitsch, who had once played in the Federal League. He used to work out on that big parade ground at Prospect Park. He had some connection with the Brooklyn Feds and got me to go down and work out with them one day. And Grover Land was the fellow who caught me in the tryouts. He was probably one of the most profane men who ever played baseball and he recommended that the Brooklyn Feds sign me. Now the Federal League clubs didn't have any minor leagues, except the Colonial League. They wanted me to go to New Haven in the Colonial League. But I was only fourteen years old and the family wouldn't let me go. They were quite right in that.

Q.  You and your dad must have been quite thrilled that the Brooklyn team had showed an interest in you?

A.  Oh, yes. Sure, that was a big deal.

Q.  Was your mother interested in your baseball career?

A.  Oh, yes, but she didn't want me to go away. She was very despondent when I did finally go away to play ball. You see, I went away when I was sixteen years old.

Q.  You were the youngest National Leaguer until Joe Nuxhall?

A.  That point should be cleared up. I was the youngest boy to ever sign a contract up until that time. And that brought a lot of publicity. But the first contract I signed was not a play-for-pay contract; it was an option contract. If I decided to play professional ball I would be the property of the New York Giants... No, signing that optional contract did not make me a professional because I had not received any money for signing. No money changed hands. But that didn't last long. I signed in August of 1915 and I was sixteen in September. Then in the next spring the Giants wanted to know if I wanted to go away to play for money. But getting back to Nuxhall. He was fifteen when he signed and I am not sure if he was younger than me. He might have been and I guess he was. On the other hand, he was the youngest to ever play in the big leagues. You see, I didn't play in a big league game until I was eighteen... Now here is Jacklitsch [he had been checking through the Encyclopedia]. He was with the Philadelphia Nationals, the Brooklyn Nationals, and in 1914 he was with the Baltimore Feds. That's how he recommended me to the Brooklyn Feds. [I ask why Jacklitsch didn't recommend him to the Baltimore Feds, with whom he played again in 1915, but he can't explain that.]  Anyway, I didn't go to the Colonial League. There was a family meeting which decided that I couldn't go... No, I really wasn't too disappointed, which shows my lack of awareness of what it was all about. But you see, that same year of 1915, I was pitching batting practice for the Brooklyn Dodgers. The Giants came over to Brooklyn and my father asked Red Dooin, who knew my father and was a Giant coach at the time, to look me over. Dooin looked me over and McGraw asked me if I would like to come over and pitch batting practice to the Giants in the Polo Grounds. It sounds easy, but it required two or three changes of trolley cars, a couple of elevated train rides, and it took me two hours to get from my home in Brooklyn and two more hours to get back home again. I was doing this all summer and I wasn't playing any ball in my own classification and I was getting tired out. So one day I went into McGraw and explained to him that I couldn't do that any more. He called in John B. Foster, the Giant secretary, and they asked me if I could come down with my father to the Giants' offices on 23d Street at 11 o'clock the next morning. So we met them down there the next day and that's when we signed the optional contract.

Q. Did you have the opportunity in batting practice to really show some of your stuff?  You must have if McGraw wanted to sign you.

A.  Oh, yes... I really liked McGraw. He was beyond belief. He really knew baseball. Of course, he was very profane, very tough in his talk, but with it all, a gentleman. Mrs. McGraw was a perfect lady.

Q.   Mathewson and McGraw were very close personal friends, yet their life-styles and personalities seemed quite different.

A.   I didn't like Mathewson. He never said five words to me in the year and a half I was associated with the Giants. He did ask me if I was going to go to college and when I said no, he seemed to lose interest in me. I never had a great deal of respect for Mathewson, as a man. He may have been the finest person in the world. How can a fifteen-year-old kid pass judgment on a person so much older? But that was my impression then.

Q.   He asked if you were going to go to college and I wanted to ask if you had the opportunity to go to college?

A.   The best opportunity I had to go to college was when Harry Hempstead, the owner of the Giants and chairman of the board at either Lafayette or Lehigh, I can't remember which, offered to pay my way all the way through if I would go to his college, whichever one it was. I hadn't started my junior year in high school yet. I hated Latin and I hated mathematics and I would have to pass the regents in two years and do a lot of catching up. The big story there is the fact that I was somewhat efficient in writing and in the classic end of the thing. Miss Scoville, my English teacher, didn't want me to go away to play ball. She offered to tutor me through the school of journalism if I would agree to become a journalist and give up the idea of playing ball. If I would become a writer. That never developed, but that was the other road I might have taken. I have always wondered, even today, I have wondered what might have occurred if I had taken the other road.

Q.   Well, having listened to you broadcast for so many years, you have always struck me as a well-read person and one who expresses himself well. It is almost as if you have had some graduate work in journalism.

A.   Well, I have always read a lot, but it kind of aggravates me that, in some recent books about baseball, where I have collaborated, they haven't gotten their facts straight: writers like Bob Creamer and Bob Smith, who is a very good friend of mine. Smith and I may still do a book together on kid baseball. A guy named Mosedale who wrote about the 1927 Yankees and didn't do a very good job. And there's the fellow up at Notre Dame.

Q.   Yes, Marshall Smelser. I know him, he is a fellow historian.

A.   Why should he write a book about Babe Ruth?  What does he know about Ruth?  I told Bob Creamer -- I like Bob Creamer -- he writes me letters. In one of them he said that "You told me in Palm Beach that I couldn't write this [a book about Ruth] and you were right." He said "I've written this book and I don't know if I am right or wrong." I told him, nicely, that "You couldn't, nobody could write a book about Babe Ruth unless you lived with him and smelled him." But so many people write untruths about Ruth; more untruths have been written about Ruth than any man I know of. They persist in their false delineations of this fellow -- his "spindly legs," for example. I'll show you pictures of me and Ruth -- they called him "fat." He wasn't fat at all unless in his last couple of years. He wasn't fat in his prime. I don't want to get into all that; that's too --

Q. The trouble with all of that is that in the future, it will be that image of Ruth which will survive, because it is in print. Wrong as it may be.

A. I was going to write a contrary opinion, but you get into that thing with Aaron and Ruth and the differences. Nobody attacks it from the truthful angle because they don't know; they're writing about things they don't know. Some things they do know, but they are not aware of. For instance, they write pieces about Ruth and the right-field pavilion. What they don't know is that the right field pavilion wasn't there when Ruth was playing.

Q. They speak of the Polo Grounds, you mean?

A. No [impatiently], Yankee Stadium. No, the right field pavilion wasn't there, where Maris hit his sixty-first home run. That wasn't added on until Ruth was away from there. That gets utterly ridiculous to hear people talk about it... And then a man [Aaron] may go to bat 3,500 more times and hit more home runs than he [Ruth] did, that's not a record. Not to take any credit away from Aaron for all the great things he did; he is entitled to that credit. Nevertheless, if Ruth had gone to bat 3,500 more times, he would have hit 250 more home runs. I have a letter here; this is from New Jersey. "I'm putting together a series of yearbooks of the great teams of baseball. The expense is entirely mine. One of the teams is the 1927 Yankees of which you were an integral member. Could you take a few minutes of your time" -- this would take three hours to write -- "to give me some of your remembrances to include in the yearbook. For instance, I am particularly interested in the 1927 Yankees pitching staff and your thoughts on that, a staff which I think was greatly underrated and overshadowed by the awesome hitters that made the team famous. What was it like to pitch for a team that was likely to give you all the hitting support you would ever need? Was the pitching staff underrated? Did you or the other pitchers ever feel overlooked or unappreciated because of all the attention being heaped on Ruth, Gehrig, and so forth... " [He reads more of the letter.] In other words, I should sit down and write... Now if he would take the book, you see, and he'd look at 1927, he would see that we pitched the most complete games of any team in the league, 87. No, we didn't do that. Chicago did; they had 85 and we had 82. We allowed the least number of bases on balls, 409, we didn't strike out the most, but we had the most shutouts, 11. We had the lowest earned run average in the league, 3.20. If he had looked these things up, he would have known how we performed, and how could we be overshadowed?

Q.  Remember those "rain delay" commentaries you made during the Reds games? Well, they put some of them on a record, which I have. I understand you made two records, but I could never get a copy of the second one.

A.  I don't think there are any copies of the second one; I have one and that may be the only one left. The first one was taken off the air and it kind of stutters through as people talk extemporaneously. The second one was made in the studio out in Hollywood.

Q.  There were some great stories there and I remember in particular your sale by New Orleans and Heinemann. But I am especially interested in the Baltimore Drydocks. Could you tell me something about them?

A.  That was just after World War I and there is a little bit of a misconception about that, too. Interesting, though. During World War I many of the leagues broke up. There weren't enough players and patronage was down. I was in the Southern League in 1918 and it broke up and we went to Newark in the International League and that was switched up to Hamilton, Ontario. At the end of 1918 that league closed down. The war didn't end until November. Of course, a lot of the steel factories and shipyards had leagues of their own and a lot of pro ballplayers went into those leagues to avoid the draft. [The "Work or Fight" order, of May 1918, compelled players to go into essential war work or be exposed to the draft; many went into shipyards and steel factories.]  After the war, things had gone so well in those leagues that they continued them. In 1919 the shipyard leagues were still going. The Baltimore Drydocks, and the teams in the shipyards around Philadelphia and Brooklyn, continued. Well, I had quite an argument with Newark at the time, and McGraw, and Arthur Irwin, who was probably the most disgusting man I ever knew. I never wished any person ill luck, but I hated that guy and he fell off the boat on the Fall River Line and was drowned. He was the manager of the Newark club. He didn't like me and I didn't like him. Well, I had a Montreal shirt and another team's pair of pants, and some other cap. At the end of that 1918 year my three years was up. In other words, a team could send you out for three years and after that either had to keep you or trade you. So they traded me to Rochester for a fellow named Al

Nixon. Since I had never won in the minors and had enough of the minor leagues, I decided I wouldn't go to Rochester. A rubber company from Chickopee Falls, Massachusetts, came down and asked me to come up and pitch --

Q. Not to work; just to pitch?

A. No, no; I was supposed to work and pitch. They were going to teach me the rubber industry [chuckling]. I thought it over and decided not to go with them. It didn't pay that much money anyway. Then I got this offer to come down to Baltimore and go to work for the Baltimore Drydocks and pitch for them, which I did.

Q. Did you work on the ships?

A. Well, we made a pass at it. We had to do something. We had to report at work every morning at eight o'clock. We played Saturdays and Sundays and once during the week. We worked out every day though. We had a pretty good ballclub. We had "Lefty" Russell, whom you wouldn't recognize, a pitcher who played first base for us. They were all pro ballplayers. Norman McNeil who went to the Red Sox. So I wound up pitching for them.

Q. This is the begining of the 1919 season.

A. Yes. This is where it gets involved; a little hard to explain. The big leagues and the minor leagues had a big fight. The big leagues did not recognize the reserve clause in the minor league contracts. If you hadn't signed a minor league contract, the minor leagues had no claim to you; it was the same as if you were a free agent. I played and pitched for the Drydocks that year and we beat damn near everybody, including the Cincinnati Reds. I shut them out 1-0, and remember that was the year they won the pennant. They came down there and I shut them out. Tom Swope the sportswriter went back and told Pat Moran that there was a pretty good-looking kid for the Drydocks and he should look at him. But Moran said something to the effect that he didn't want to fool around with young kids. At any rate, this Norman McNeil, who was our catcher, went to the Red Sox and told the Red Sox manager, Ed Barrow, about me. When the Red Sox made their next trip to Washington, Barrow asked me, through Norman McNeil, to come over and pitch batting practice for them. I did this and about three weeks later I got a wire from Barrow asking me to come to Boston and perhaps sign a contract. I went to Boston and I told them I would sign a contract if they put in a clause there that I would start a game within four days of the time I arrived in Boston. I wasn't going to sit around on any more benches or be farmed out.

Q. Wasn't that a rather unusual demand for a newcomer?

A.  Yes. Barrow said I was "a fresh kid." I said I was sorry, but that's the way it is. It was either that or I would quit the game. He never heard of anything like that. At any rate, he started me and I beat Detroit, 2-1.

Q.  So you pitched against Cobb in your first game?

A.  Yes. That was funny, too, because... You see, in those days, two or three batters were allowed to stand up, waiting for their turns to bat. There wasn't any batting circle then and they stood where they wanted to. The guy ahead of him, I think it was Bobby Veach, called me every dirty name he could think of. Then when it was Cobb's turn to bat, he stepped in the center of the home plate and turned his back on me. It seemed like five minutes that he stood that way, although it wasn't. Moriarty, the second base umpire, used to play for Detroit and hated Cobb. He came in and told Cobb to turn around and get going. The umpire didn't do anything and Moriarty took the matter in his own hands. So when Cobb finally got into place, I stepped off the rubber for about five minutes. I got this profanity all over again. He tripled in the eighth inning and tied the score, 1-1, but we beat them 2-1 in twelve innings. We won it peculiarly, which seemed to be indicative of my entire career. Everett Scott [for Boston] got on second base with one out and they put in Mike McNally, who could run pretty fast, to run for Scott. The next batter hit a ball to the shortstop and McNally tried to score all the way from second base on the infield out, which you don't see much of today. He was run down between third and home and catcher Eddie Ainsmith for Detroit didn't have the ball, but he bumped into McNally and knocked him aside. That was interference so McNally was awarded home plate with the winning run.

Q.  So a twelve-inning complete game to start off with. How did you like Ed Barrow?

A.  Oh, very much. He later brought me over to the Yankees... Harry Frazee? Oh, he was an affable man. I'll tell you an interesting story. This has to do with Ruth. If you were writing a book on Ruth, or if I was, there's so much to Ruth that has to do with the entire world. Ruth wasn't confined to a home run atmosphere and isolated in that category. Things happened to that guy. He was a man of the entire world, like the Japs shouting his name in World War II. He was a world figure in a way. Ruth was sold to New York for over $100,000 because of part of a loan that Ruppert had made to Frazee. Frazee paid back part of the loan -- which was about $300,000, and Ruppert took Ruth as the balance of the loan payment. This is the truth, although I may not have the facts exactly right. At any rate, Ruth came to the Yankees for the money. In 1920 Ruth was with the Yankees and that year the Red Sox played the Giants on the way up from spring training and the Red Sox played a series with the Giants in the Polo Grounds. Frazee put a notice up on the bulletin board that he had a show going on down on Broadway and that the members of the Red Sox were invited to come to the show. All they had to do was identify themselves at the box office and there would be tickets waiting for them. Now I'm not quite certain of the name of the show, but I think it was "I'll Say She Is." It was a straight comedy produced by Harry Frazee. Now it was actually produced by money that Frazee got for Ruth, or part of the loan. Four years later the show was produced again and what is the show? "No, No, Nanette." It was "I'll Say She Is" set to music. So what happened. Ruth is indirectly responsible for one of the greatest shows ever produced on Broadway; is that right? [We chuckle.]  So Ruth's influence ran in all directions.

Q.  Fred Lieb told me that Frazee had so many flops on Broadway that he had to sell all of you star Boston players to the Yankees to recoup his losses. What do you know about that?

A.  I don't know anything about that. That could be true. No doubt that happened if Lieb told you that.

Q.  I guess Frazee's New York office was just down the street from Ruppert's and he spent a lot of time in Ruppert's office.

A.  Everybody was. What people don't understand today from the public relations angle. You see there were about fourteen newspapers in New York in those days and the Giants and the Yankees had hospitality rooms in their downtown offices. And if you went up to these rooms in the wintertime why the place would be crowded with baseball people. So a lot of stories grew out of those occasions. There was always an open bar during Prohibition and they were very much of an attraction in those places.

Q.  Was Frazee very popular with the Boston people, in view of the fact that he was an absentee owner?  Or didn't they think about things like that?

A.  Oh, no, we sold ourselves... When Ruth was sold? No, we didn't feel like he was breaking up the team. Mays was the first to go.  Have you seen the Mays book by McGarigle?

Q. No, I haven't. I was thinking of getting it. How do you rate it?

A. It's not very good; not very well-written. There are a couple of big lies in there about me. I have the book if you want it. [He ended up giving me the book, which I still have.] The last chapter has Huggins saying this and that about me, which Huggins never said at all. Huggins was a good friend of mine and I always thought the world of him. But Mays was the first to go and then Ruth was next. Then, as far as the trade was concerned, it was four-for-four and that's where I think Lieb was a little off.

Q. You mean the trade involving yourself?

A. Yes, there was Harry Harper, myself, Wally Schang, and Mike McNally traded for Herb Thormahlen, Muddy Ruel, Sam Vick, and Del Pratt [December 15, 1920].

Q. I had one more question about the Mays business. You came up in mid-year 1919. Now were you there when Mays walked off the field?

A. No. He was already gone when I got there. [Short break while he gets something to read to me. It may be McGarigle's book. We should find out.] This is the most malicious thing I have ever read. I don't know if I owe it to him or not; he must be disgusted with me.

Q. You mean about Mays, or what?

A. Oh, I'm not interested in Mays. I know more about Mays than this guy does. Mays used to lie up in the bed, on the other bed and talk about knocking guys down, and don't let them get too close to the plate because they're taking the bread-and-butter out of your hand, and that kind of stuff... Oh, sure, he threw at hitters. But the strange thing is I don't think he threw at Chapman. He told me and I'll swear to God that he hit Chapman with a curveball and you don't throw at guys with a curveball. What people don't realize is that Fewster and Chapman stood at the plate with their heads over the outside corner. Nobody throws at... This is what I have against baseball books and baseball writers. They don't know these things; they conclude. If you want to write, be objective and write on both sides of the question. That's my opinion, don't you think so? It says in here: "Carl says, 'Rube Marquard was a great pitcher and I'm glad he's in the Hall of Fame. But my record was so much superior to his that it makes me wonder. I guess the answer is that they don't like me.'" I've got to say, although I wouldn't want to be quoted on this, nobody has ever mentioned Carl Mays in that respect. As a matter of fact his name came up for qualification this year in the Hall of Fame. [Hoyt was a member of the Veterans Committee of the Hall of Fame at this time.] Nobody said anything about the hitting of Chapman. There has never been an ill-word said about Carl with respect to keeping him out of the Hall of Fame, or anything of that nature. There is no doubt that the fellow is an excellent pitcher, one of the better ones, but he did some things which... One of the sad things was and I feel sorry for him -- I have kind of a sentimental streak, I guess -- was we were playing the Athletics one day. I don't know what his record against them was, but the Athletics hadn't beaten him in years. He had gotten in bad with Miller Huggins and he beat the Athletics in Philadelphia, 3-2. And he didn't pitch again in two weeks. I'm not sure what year that was, but I don't think he finished the season with us. He was sent here to Cincinnati. It was 1923, I think. We got in trouble; the Yanks got in trouble. Miller said to George Pipgras, who was just a kid on the club then, "go down to the bullpen and get ready." Then Carl said "What's the matter with me, Hug?" You see, there was a discipline on the Yankee bench, which was nothing like any other team in the history of the game. It was like the third grade in school. You sat there and paid attention. You didn't kid around. You paid attention to what was going on. Hug turned around and said to Carl, "Carl, I've forgotten you were even on the club." And this guy had won twenty-seven games for him one time. These are the kinds of things that are not known. Over in 1921 we were playing the Athletics in Philadelphia in the next to last series of the season. We were heading for the Yankees first pennant and were only a game and a half ahead of Cleveland. We needed these games as we were in trouble. And Carl had been so good against the Athletics that -- he had pitched with one day's rest. That was the year he won twenty-seven games. Hug asked him to go down to the bullpen because our pitcher was in trouble. Carl said, "No, I've done enough pitching for the year." And here were the Yankees about to win the pennant and he wouldn't go down to the bullpen. Huggins hated him from then on. Then there was something about some gambling; I don't know about that.

Q. Well you must have gotten along quite well with Mays. You roomed with him for awhile.

A. Well, he made a lot of trouble. He was trying to isolate me from the rest. Carl was a trouble-maker. Now here it is. In 1921 Carl led the league in wins with twenty-seven. Now here is the worst thing I've ever seen in print about myself and it's absolutely... It says "Waite Hoyt and Cobb." [I have to dig the McGarigle book out at this time because he has made so many references to it. The chapter 28 heading is "Waite Hoyt and Cobb." But I got reading the preceding chapter and spent about twenty minutes totally absorbed in it. It was Mays' version of Huggins' reasons for letting him go. Fascinating. Waite reads a couple of paragraphs from the chapter "Waite Hoyt and Cobb," which deprecates Huggins' behavior on the bench and shows him as a weak man for whom the players had no respect.]  Well, this is all spite stuff. I don't remember any of this at all. Huggins had what we called "traveling palsy" or neuritis, or something like that. He couldn't keep his legs still. His legs would go like this. It was an affliction, really. [Hoyt reads another passage from this chapter in which Ruth repeatedly called Huggins "little boy" and yet another where Huggins supposedly called Hoyt "gutless" before the whole team when he had a bad stretch.]  I never heard of Ruth calling Huggins "little boy"; I never heard of that. [With respect to the "gutless" charge] Huggins never did anything of the sort. Huggins and I were good friends; I felt that Huggins was sort of a father to me in this business. [Another long story read from the McGarigle book about a time Hoyt was shelled from the mound and after the game Huggins ordered him not to go into the clubhouse until the other players had gone in. At this moment Mays spoke up in defense of Hoyt and said that this was shabby treatment and that he [Mays] was going to room with Hoyt. Huggins said he'd fine Mays $250 if he did that, but he did it anyhow. Back in their room Mays locked the door and stuck the key in his pocket to keep Hoyt, who had a date with a girl that night, from getting out.]  That is the goddamnedest story I ever heard!

Q.  Did Mays tell this story, do you suppose?

A.  He must have told it. [More quotes from this passage.]  Mays must have made these things up.

Q.  Well, what was he like to room with?  Was he pleasant at all?

A.  He could be a perfect gentleman. Perfectly mannered. [Another passage where against Detroit -- "he says I let my little finger stick out when I threw the knuckler"  -- Mays told Hoyt to leave the little finger sticking out as he pitched to Cobb, but not throw the knuckler. He was to throw the ball as hard as he could at Cobb's forehead. He decked him once and then did it again. After the second time, Cobb sat at the plate puzzled and finally looked out at Hoyt. "You must be rooming with Mays," he said.] That's a good story, but every damn word in it is a lie. Nothing like that ever took place. Where he gets those ideas from I don't know. But he was a great pitcher, there's no doubt about it. More happened to Carl, it strikes me that when a fellow becomes beset -- no, that's the wrong way to start this thought. Certain fellows seem to have a career or a lifetime or a life of ill-luck or peculiar happenings, which they are not responsible for. Victims of some lifestyle that is unanswerable. There is a story in there about his wife's death. I know this -- how you can get in trouble. He never mentions that... His wife lived in Springfield, Ohio. Frederika. We were in Chicago and I had a fight with umpire "Brick" Owens. I was suspended for three days. We were in the outfield running down the ball before the game and Mays came up to me. He said "that sonofabitch." "Who are you talking about?" "Huggins." "What's the matter?" "Well, last night Frederika's baby was being born and got stuck on the way out." I don't know what you call that. "I asked Hug to let me go home and he wouldn't let me go. I don't know if Frederika's going to die or not. She's in a very serious condition." I told him to hold the fort a minute. I was suspended -- I'm getting ahead of myself. We had an exhibition game in Toronto the next day after Chicago. Hug was going to have Carl pitch the game -- Carl was in bad with Hug, you see. I went in and spoke to Hug and reminded him that Carl had this problem with the baby, and his wife might be dying, and that he just couldn't do this to him. I said that I would pitch the game in Toronto because I had nothing to do since I was suspended. As a result, he did let Carl come home. On the other hand, our ballclub in Toronto made a joke out of the game. I tried to pitch the game for three or four innings and -- we had Hinky Haines, not our regular shortstop, playing short and various players playing out of position, throwing the ball way over the first baseman's head. We committed something like seven errors. After some time I thought "the hell with this, they're not even trying." Joe Dugan limped to the little wall by the clubhouse and then leaped over the wall, and all this sort of thing. And by God, they held my pay up for a month, saying that I wasn't trying. All this because I volunteered to help a guy who was in trouble. Then it said in this book that Frederika died later on from some ear or throat infection. I'm not sure. You take that book with you.

Q. Well, thank you very much. I have quite a baseball library, but I don't have this one, although I have been meaning to get it. Mays was a pretty smart pitcher wasn't he?

A. Yes, he was. Carl was a very smart fellow. Carl dressed well, acted well, and was a perfect gentleman off the field. You would never believe, to talk to him, that he had these altercations on the field.

Q. He just seemed to have a quirk in his personality. I have an extensive collection of the *Baseball Magazine*, going back to 1920. [Actually, to 1911.] And, it must have been in the November or December issue of 1920, there is an article by Mays about the Ray Chapman episode. It is very well-written as he tries to explain his position on the matter. I almost became a Carl Mays fan reading that explanation. He understands that people don't like him and that he has caused trouble. He's sorry about all of that, but can't seem to do much about it. Then going on to this particular game, it was an accident and I would think

*Waite Hoyt, New York Yankee pitcher, 1921. Hoyt was a mainstay on New York's pitching staff in the 1920's, helping them win six pennants, 1921-1923 and 1926-1928. He had two 20-plus winning seasons and missed one other by a bad break. With a lifetime record of 237-182, this "player-philosopher" was elected to the Hall of Fame in 1969. (Photo from the author's collection.)*

that for a guy to be as much on the spot as he was, to write and think so clearly was quite a feat.

A.  He had a way of alienating people. Fellows he played with. He seemed to realize he was an object of dislike and he set himself apart from the other players.

Q.  Did he take good care of himself?

A.  Oh, yes. Carl was a not a rounder.

Q.  I have read so much about how the Yankees were so well-disciplined on the field, but then went on a tear off the field [chuckling.]  Is that exaggerated?

A.  Is that in my interview?  They were the best disciplined club on the ballfield that I've ever known.  Off the field, there was only a handful, but they were no better or worse than insurance salesmen or anybody else.  You see, what you must recognize is that they played during Prohibition.  That was the "Roaring Twenties" and they lived according to their times.

Q.  Did you go out in crowds after games?

A.  Oh, no, no.  They never went in crowds.  A few fellows might go together, but that was all.

Q.  Well, it sounds like it was a pretty well-disciplined team off the field, too.

A.  And another thing; I've got to say this.  Where you might read of Ruth patronizing some "houses" down in St. Louis and around, which more or less is the truth, but by and large, the team was a highly intelligent, well-educated team that traveled in the best of company.  The best of company.  They were fine people; fine people.  They didn't cat around.  Dan Nolan in Cleveland, the Wurlitzer agent there [he mentions some more leading businessmen and citizens in different towns that I can't pick up], all top bananas.  They were a real high-type ballclub.  The Babe had his moments, of course.

Q.  How about Wally Pipp?

A.  Well, Wally had a university degree, didn't he?  He came from a very well-to-do family.  His father was a wholesale butcher in Grand Rapids, Michigan.  Wally was very well off and well thought of.  And he was a good ballplayer.

Q.  Were you present when Whitey Witt got hit in the head with a pop bottle?  [We chuckle.]

A.  Yes, he got [it] in the head; he didn't step on it, as was reported.  The crowd was standing around the outfield and someone from the crowd threw it at him.  The ball was headed into the crowd and somebody skulled him with a bottle.  Charley O'Leary smeared blood all over his face to make it look like his head was cut off and then they carried him into the clubhouse on a stretcher.  That threw a pall over the entire crowd. The fellow who threw that bottle may have cost the Browns the pennant. The team seemed to be deflated right away. Then Whitey got the hit off Urb Shocker that beat them in the final game of the series.

Q. This was in 1922?

A. Yes. But there is so much that's true and so much that's untrue. And it is discouraging after awhile to read all that you read about... There's a great deal of truth about a great many things that have never been printed. Which is just as grievous as the printing of untrue things about events which really happened. My objection is to the people who don't know [who write about things as if they knew]. And here's another thing I told Bob Creamer when he was doing the book *Babe*. He said he was going to interview Joe Dugan and different people. I said, "Look, you're going to interview Dugan." Now Dugan likes his drinks. He's not an alcoholic, but he likes to drink a great deal. He can handle his liquor. But he is the kind of a guy who lives in that atmosphere. His favorite stories or his embellished anecdotes are about Ruth and his drinking, and he would think that's funny. But they would be all shallow recitations, no depth to them. Ruth had a certain depth that people didn't know, that's never been printed. The more I read Creamer's book, the less I liked it. He got finally into four-letter words that were ridiculous. Ruth was profane and he used four-letter words, but coming from Ruth you paid no attention to them. I don't know why, but some people are like that. You became tolerant of that. He had a "largesse," I guess that carried him so far above...; he was such a unique guy that you tolerated these things.

Q. Roger Peckinpaugh told me, in connection with his trade from the Yankees to Washington after the 1921 season, that Ruth was partly responsible. He said that Ruth didn't like Huggins and was quietly pushing Peck for Huggins' job. Since they couldn't get rid of Ruth in this "conspiracy," they had to get rid of Peck. Do you remember anything about that?

A. That could be. But there is one fallacy in that story. You see, Ruth's existence at that point, he was only then coming into his own. Everett Scott came to us in 1922 as shortstop and that was only the second year of Ruth's popularity and he wouldn't have had the initiative, gumption or audacity at that time to face the front office on behalf of anybody.

Q. So it was really too early for him in his career as a home run hitter to attempt anything like that?

A.  Yes. And furthermore, there was a definite split between the the colonels, Ruppert and Huston; they didn't get along at all. Huston was very anti-Huggins and Ruppert was pro-Huggins. Huston didn't like Hug. When I say that I don't mean he didn't like him as a man, but rather he didn't like his operation of the club.

Q.  As I understood it, Huston wanted [Wilbert] Robinson to manage the Yankees, and while Huston was away in France in the war, Ruppert went ahead and hired Huggins.

A.  That's right. Huston and that bunch used to go down to Dover Hall in Georgia in the fall for hunting.

Q.  Did George Stallings own Dover Hall?

A.  No. Robinson owned it. Ruth used to go down there. Quite a group used to go down there.

Q.  What was it like going into Ruppert's office in the brewery?  You mention something about that in one of your "rain" stories.

A.  Well, you had to go up four floors. His office was on the fourth floor. Of course, when you went into the place you entered a long hall, a long marble hallway. You didn't see much of the brewery because you went up in the elevator. All the woodwork was rosewood and paneled, and the brewery was immaculate. You could eat off the floor. You could not imagine it was a brewery. Of course, this was during Prohibition and the brewery wasn't operating at full strength.

Q.  How could it operate at all during Prohibition?

A.  Because they made near beer. And you have to make real beer before you can make near beer. You extract the alcohol or something. Ruppert's office was on the fourth floor and it was bigger than this whole apartment here. Well carpeted and well-rugged. A sumptuous place. He was a king. And Ruppert himself  was immaculate. One of the best dressed men of his time. He operated his Rolls Royce. His Rolls Royce always looked brand new when it was ten years old. He was that way about everything.

Q.  He had a heavy accent, didn't he?

A.  Yes, but the more excited he got the heavier the accent got... Yes, he spoke to some of us in plurals: "Hoyts" and "Ruths."  [I mention another Ruppert phrase that Hoyt had told about in one of his "rain" broadcasts.]  Yes, he said to somebody, "Vin da pennant und I gif you da brewery; I gif you da brewery." [Hoyt was excellent in imitating Ruppert's German accent.]

Q.  And in 1921 when you were winning your first twentieth game, they brought Ruth in in the late innings and he blew the lead and then won the game with a homer. [We chuckle.]

A.  Yeah, and he got the victory.

Q.  Well, what happened in 1925?

A.  We fell apart. We started bad. Still we had the best ballclub in the league. That club did wear out, however. Everett Scott wore out at shortstop and Aaron Ward wore out at second base. Whitey Witt was about through or was through. Hug was a genius at that kind of thing, though, knowing when his men were wearing out. In fact, I think without a question of a doubt. This is my personal opinion. You see, anything I may talk about or talk to you about, if you got five other players and interviewed them, you'd probably get five different opinions. I am conscious of the fact that what I tell you is just my opinion. The other fellows might be more correct than I am. How are any of us to know? Much like the government today; with all those brains, or supposed brains, at the top, and they are making mistakes all over the place. One man says one thing, another man says another thing and they are all smart men. I'm smart about my business, baseball. And there are other fellows as smart or smarter than I am. Now when I talk from the depths, when I'm sincere about what I say, which is all the time, I cannot be positive about the veracity of what I am saying as being absolutely true. But it is my positive belief that Huggins was the finest manager that ever lived. We are certainly influenced by publicity and public relations, and things of that kind. Like Stengel, with his colorful personality and then wins all those pennants, he becomes the greatest manager who ever lived. Joe McCarthy, for awhile, was considered one of the greatest who ever lived. So on and so forth. Now they talk about this guy and that guy. Now suppose Huggins had lived and not died and had inherited all those great guys Joe McCarthy had, how many pennants do you think Huggins would have won?  [Huggins died unexpectedly in 1929 at the age of 49 and at the peak of his managerial career.]  The man was a genius in his method of handling players and he had some of the toughest players in the business to handle, in my opinion.

Q.  How could a little guy like Huggins handle all those big guys?

A. He had the backing of Ruppert and was a good psychologist. There was one thing that was infallible. Ruth had to play to hit home runs and keep the club ahead. When you took Ruth out of the lineup, as when he was suspended, and he was having a bad season, he automatically lowered himself in the opinion of the fans and public. Consequently, it scarred his arguments for money. And if anybody needed money it was Ruth. But it more than team spirit. A team spirit is an arousal of an additional eagerness and desire for a short period of time. But a family, your family or my family, we take on a lifestyle or personality, and adopt a philosophy as a family that seems to follow on through. I'm talking about fairly successful families. They talk about breeding, mostly in speaking of animals, but also of human beings. They ask where certain qualities come from? Well, it's breeding, or it's bred into them. By the same token, the Yankees -- it may have started out as a team spirit, but it developed into a breeding characteristic. If you became a Yankee, you took on the qualities of breeding which the Yankees exemplified. You became a Yankee, and that answered a whole lot of questions. For some reason you were able to perform a little better. Like that letter I read you earlier where the fellow wanted to know about the pitching on the 1927 Yankees as being overshadowed. You'd think they scored ten runs in the first inning every day. Many of our games were won in the eighth and ninth innings and if you didn't start well, you weren't in there in the eighth or nineth inning. We used to call it, in fact, I coined the expression. "Five o'clock lightning," to describe our late inning victories. The games used to start at three o'clock and the eighth inning generally came at about a quarter to five. We used to win a lot of games around that time of day.

Q. Well, you won 110 games in 1927 and the closest team was nineteen games behind you. One would think that the team must have won many games in easy fashion. Yet you say many of them were close, won in the later stages.

A. Well, we won a lot late in the game. I would like to see, and I never have, a game-by-game summary of our games that season just to see how many were won late. It was Pat Harmon down here, the Cincinnati sportswriter, who looked it up and wrote a piece about pitchers and their records against different hitters He looked up my record against Cobb. Cobb hit .163 against me in his career. But don't let that fool you because there were guys like George Burns of Cleveland and Johnny Bassler of Detroit, and a few others who must have hit .500 against me. All these things are open to conjecture, they're open to qualification and ramification. What I am constantly trying to suggest and plead that they do -- there is so much -- that whenever a person writes a piece, he should qualify it, or say "as I understand it," or "I was given to understand." Everything is open to [debate]. My God, some of the things that I read... [I suggest some of the problems I have had with historical interpretations when there is conflicting evidence or insufficient evidence. We talk of the difficulties of historical objectivity.] Just take for instance -- and please don't misunderstand me and I don't want anybody to ever misunderstand me -- take the question of Johnny Bench. Bob Hertsel, this writer for the *Enquirer* here, says off the top of his head, that "Johnny Bench is the greatest catcher that ever lived." How does he know? Johnny Bench is one of the most agile, clever, accomplished catchers in tagging a man, sliding into home plate, or blocking the plate, or any activity at the plate. As far as Johnny Bench receiving the ball from the pitcher is concerned, I can tell you ten catchers better than he. But he hits a home run at an opportune moment and he's a hero for the day, but he is not as good a hitter as some of these other catchers of earlier days. But this appraisal is supposed to be all-inclusive. Now whenever you talk about people like this, to arrive at the truth all these things must be taken into consideration. Hertsel never heard of... You remember Pavlova and Nizamova, the ballet dancers, or whatever style I can pick out from the arts, say Fred Astaire, or someone with ultimate grace and style, that's what I'm talking about. And when you get down to that as a receiving catcher, and a stylist, and a handler of pitches, there was none better than Ray Schalk. Cochrane is very close, as are Dickey and Schang and Muddy Ruel and Al Lopez. Probably one of the greatest receiving catchers who ever lived was Cy Perkins, who played second role to Mickey Cochrane because he couldn't hit. Now these modern writers just don't know about these older players. If they saw them play, saw their grace and the handling of these older catchers [they wouldn't write some of the things they do].

Q. It is this infernal "present-mindedness" of writers and fans. They don't seem to understand that many things of significance happened before they were born, yet they always claim that the "greatest this ever" and the "greatest that ever," were things that happened in the past few years in their own experience.

A. This all becomes very ridiculous. I am very strong in my recommendation, but who am I; they wouldn't listen to me. But I am very strong in my recommendation for a line of demarcation between the old players and the new. They ought to take World War II, say 1942, and break it off there. Everything before that should be "old-time baseball."

Q. Speaking of that, I wanted to ask you as a member of the Veterans Committee, has Joe Jackson's name ever come up before you?

A. No. He was a Black Sox... No, there's no written rule against those guys; they just don't come up. Half that ballclub would be in the Hall of Fame if they ever lowered the bars. That Hall of Fame thing is highly misunderstood. I get it every day. Here's a *Sporting News* right here, giving us hell about Ernie

Lombardi. The average fan can't get it through his head that there must be fifty players, well let's say thirty, who really have qualified for the Hall of Fame. But we're only allowed to elect two. That would take fifteen years to get those thirty in. Meanwhile, there are additional names coming out of limbo that are being added to the eligibles for the Hall of Fame. What are we going to do about it? We run into this situation like this Lindstrom thing. The fellow writing in the *Sporting News* says "The election of Freddy Lindstrom is utterly ridiculous." This fellow doesn't know what he's talking about. He doesn't know balance, he doesn't know style, he doesn't know shift, he doesn't know anything. And he's saying we don't know anything. As Frankie Frisch used to say, "Doesn't defense count for anything?" Defense is one of the best things about the game. This isn't one of the things I am talking so much about. I went in in 1969; I forget who went in in 1968. Nevertheless, there have been about four Yankees who have gone in starting with me. Myself, Earle Combs, Whitey Ford, Mickey Mantle -- four in about five years. Now there's been almost an equal number of Cardinals, with Chick Hafey, Jess Haines, Musial -- he went in with me. Before Lindstrom there was Dave Bancroft -- so New York seemed to have a corner on the market. So people were beginning to resent it and you can't blame them. On the other hand -- and I wouldn't ever want to be quoted on this -- you take Ernie Lombardi. I live around here now where Ernie Lombardi is a big number. He did lead the league twice, compiled a .310 average, and Bucky Walters says he was a great catcher. A couple of other people said he was a great catcher. Now among people in baseball the general opinion was that he was a lousy catcher. Any guy who would reach out and catch the ball with his bare hand, and can't shift -- and they don't know what they're talking about. They say that "if Ernie Lombardi was a faster man he'd have hit .350." They don't realize when they say that a man is slow, that that is a defect that kept him from being something else.

Q. Has Joey Sewell come up much? [Sewell was elected to the Hall of Fame a year after this interview took place.]

A. I proposed Joey Sewell for one and Riggs Stephenson for another. In fact, Joey Sewell has been on the ballot. You see, what they do is to send you a form sheet around the first of December, or perhaps earlier. It will have all the list of the eligible players on it. A list of about fifty or sixty who have been nominated before. You select ten of that group and send their names in. That doesn't mean that there won't be others or that changes can't be made in your list when you get to the meeting. You can cross some of your names out if you want to. But that is only a guide. They boil the list down to those who have received the highest number of mentions. Then at the meeting they will name some additions who have been proposed and comments are invited. A few names may be added.

Then they pass the ballots around and you vote for five on this list... No, not in the order of preference; you just vote for five. If somebody gets a quorum then he is elected. If nobody gets a quorum, they read off what each one got and they have a second ballot. The bottom ones are eliminated after the second ballot. Then they go around a third time. The one difficulty, between you and I, is if it ends in a tie; then you have to hold them over for a year. That's happened, too. Before this year you could not vote for a manager, an umpire, or a league official unless two players had already been elected. But with the selection of only two players you don't have much choice. There are plenty of guys who got plenty of votes, like Lombardi. I've voted for Lombardi, to tell you the truth, for some years, although I didn't vote for him this year because I thought it was useless.

Q. Do you have to be at the meeting for your votes to count?

A. Yes... No, no mail ballots are allowed... Yes, Fred Lieb still comes. This last time Dan Daniel was sick and Bill Terry didn't make it for some reason. Ford Frick is no longer on the committee and in fact, I have also resigned as of this year. I resigned because of my heart. I have a very bad heart and I damn near went to the hospital up there last year. In fact, I'm not supposed to do much public speaking or anything of that sort.

Q. Several years ago I made a detailed study of the top sluggers of the pre-1900 era and found that a number of the top people, leaders in seven different categories, were not in the Hall of Fame. Sam Thompson was one of these and Roger Connor was another and I am happy to see that they are both now in the Hall.

A. Well, let's be honest. We don't know -- Lieb would know something, Dan Daniel would know something, but actually, Musial, myself, Terry, Charlie Gehringer, we don't know anything about Sam Thompson. Really, this is stupid. Fellows like Vic Willis, these guys -- there should be a meeting of the Hall of Fame governors or whoever, and they should go over that old-time list, and whoever they think should be qualified should be brought into the Hall of Fame in a group. Or recognized in such a way that they are in the Hall of Fame, whether they are... It's pretty difficult to take a fellow and put him in the Hall of Fame when the rules were different -- when the catcher stood way behind the batter and they bounced the ball up. My belief is that organized baseball started in 1900 or 1901; there should be a line of demarcation there, too. Back before then they should be classified as "old timers" and there should be special standards applied to them. There's an awful lot of difference between what takes place today and what took place in our day. I refuse to make comparisons between the two different ages because you can't compare them. They make a big deal out of strikeouts today. Strikeouts didn't mean anything to us. Ridiculous.

Q. There are a couple of things in your own career I wanted to check on. You came in just about the time the spitball was outlawed. Did you throw the spitball before it was outlawed?

A. No, I never threw it. I didn't think about it and neither did anybody else. If you're writing about it, make a point of that. We didn't think much about the fact that some could continue throwing it while others could never use it. We didn't think about that at all. We didn't think the spitball was any better than the curve. It wasn't that effective. Mainly, the spitball pitchers were effective, but there were a lot of spitball pitchers who weren't very effective too. We didn't think the spitball was very unusual. We thought our stuff was as good as that.

Q. What about the use of other foreign substances?  The emery ball, etc.?

A. The emery ball was barred when I was pitching. Dave Danforth and those guys, they...

Q. What did Dave Danforth do with the ball?  I know he always seemed to be in hot water with Ban Johnson over the use of foreign substances?

A. I don't know what he did with it. He had some kind of a rough finger nail, or something with which he roughed up one side of the ball. Billy Evans saved thirteen balls against us one time when we were in St. Louis [Danforth was pitching for the St. Louis Browns from 1922-1925] and sent them in to Ban Johnson. That's what cost Danforth his job.

Q. Billy Evans saved all those balls Danforth was throwing to show how scarred they were for Ban Johnson to see?

A. Well, now you've gone overboard. I don't know whether they were scarred or "shined," or what. Urban Shocker, a spitball pitcher, used to suck the seams [he demonstrates], wet them, then get tobacco or dirt on them and press them. He was able to raise the seams a little bit this way. All you had to do was raise the seam a little bit and you could make the ball "sail" like hell. A lot of these fellows have little tricks they can pull once in awhile, if you don't catch them at it. Danforth was supposed to pitch an exhibition game against Walter Johnson after the season was over one day in Baltimore. There were two all-star teams. George Sisler played first base, Eddie Collins played second base, and so on.

Two teams of that nature playing for some charity and Johnson was going to pitch against Danforth. Before the game started, Johnson went over to the other team's bench and said something like, "You fellows had better be pretty loose up there in case any pitches sail."

Q.  Any of Johnson's pitches?

A.  No, not Johnson's pitches. Well, yes, Johnson's pitches, but he might be throwing a ball which had been scuffed up by Danforth the previous inning. The balls carried over to the next inning. His point was if he hit anybody it wasn't going to be his fault.

Q.  Johnson, I guess, bent over backwards not to hit anyone. Did you ever bat against him?

A.  Oh, yes... How did I like batting against him?  Well, you didn't do much batting; you just stood there. I would hit the ball off him, but I never got any hits, as I recall. He was wicked, the way he could pitch sidearm. I'd like to see him pitching today. Wow.

Q.  Was he the fastest pitcher you ever saw?

A.  Oh, yes. These fellows today don't know what a fastball is... Take a fellow like -- now this is a boast. People who ever hear this, can make little of it if they want to. I'm boasting, but I'm not being a smart aleck when I say this. But I was fast myself and I believe I was as fast as [Tom] Seaver -- easily. I never struck out many, three a game perhaps. But that was neither here nor there. We had on the 1923 staff Bush, Shawkey, and Mays -- Pennock wasn't fast -- but we had these guys, all of them who could throw as fast as I could. They talk today about Nolan Ryan and Seaver and Bob Gibson being so fast. Hell, we had three or four guys on one club who were that fast. In those days it was a different type of pitching. It was fastballs, curveballs, they did throw knuckleballs and they did throw forkballs. Joe Bush threw the forkball. It always makes me laugh when you hear Williams and DiMaggio and these fellows say that the pitchers only had fastballs and curves. Hell, we had more stuff and different kinds of stuff than these fellows have today. On our club alone, I threw the palmball -- I'll show you a picture of it -- three-quarters speedball, the fastball, and the curveball, although the curveball wasn't too good. But Joe Bush threw the forkball, Sam Jones threw the fadeaway and a curveball, Shawkey threw two curves and his fastball and a change of pace, Pennock had the overhand curve, the sidearm curve, and one of the best screwballs in the business. Shocker trew the spitball. When you get right down to it what are they talking about, saying all we had was the fastball and the curveball. I threw the slider towards the end of my career. The slider is nothing new. In fact, George Uhle invented the slider in Cleveland and if you ask these fellows today who George Uhle was none of them know.

Q. I had a good interview with George Uhle. He seemed to have arm trouble every other year. Did you ever have arm trouble?

A. Not from throwing in a game. I had some trouble from throwing ten cent balls at milk bottles in a carnival. One night in Philadelphia -- when Bob Carpenter, owner of the Phillies, was just a little boy -- Pennock took Babe, myself, and Dugan out to this street fair out in Kennett Square where Pennock lived. The Carpenters lived near there too. We threw balls at these papier mache milk bottles and hurt my arm. It swelled way out and I was out for five or six weeks. That was in 1926 and I might have won some more games.

Q. What had happened?  Was it an unnatural delivery?

A. Well, it was a ten cent ball; light.

Q. What did Huggins say about that?

A. Oh, he didn't know. He thought I hurt it in a game. I didn't care to enlighten him about it... No, my arm never tired from throwing the fastball unless I twisted it. A fastball should be thrown where it is released away from you, out from your body. The ball is released as far away from you almost as much as your step is long. On the curveball your elbow is brought in toward the side; you pull the elbow down toward your side and snap the ball as you release it... Yes, fastball pitchers are much less likely to have arm trouble than a curveball or screwball pitcher. It amazes me -- and I say these things not to, please don't misunderstand me, I say them not for personal aggrandizement in the image sense, but... In 1936 when I was nearly through, I was in Montclair, New Jersey, which was my home at the time. I was with Pittsburgh and Pittsburgh happened to be playing in Brooklyn. I was taken with appendicitis and carted off to the hospital on a stretcher. And within four weeks I finished a game in Chicago and three days after finishing that game I pitched a fifteen-inning game against Freddie Fitzsimmons and he beat me, 2-1, in Pittsburgh. We had the bases loaded in the ninth inning with no one out and we didn't score. And we lost, 2-1, in the fifteenth inning. Now these guys today find it hard to pitch five or six innings. Why?  I don't know. Don't look to me for the answers. These are the reasons why I refuse to make comparisons. I don't know why these things are taking place today. Whether they're not trained to pitch fifteen innings, or their philosophy is different, or they're following the philosophy of the young people in the world today, or they're following the philosophy of labor in doing specialization jobs with time limits and being paid a form of piece work. Whatever it is, it is not the philosophy used by the players of my day, nor the work philosophies of your father or my father, who put in a full day, come struggling home, and get up and go back the next day. A lot of fellows today in the factories, they get up, go to work, do the same thing, come home and they do whatever they do, and they go back to work in the factory again. But they're getting so many fringe benefits and time off and their work conditions are entirely different. So comparisons are a little bit stupid, I think.

Q.  When you came up with the Red Sox and even later with the Yankees, did any of the older pitchers or players or coaches give you any help or advice?

A.  No. we were on our own. The only fellow who ever helped me was Herb Pennock. And that was just a matter of personal friendship. And that's why I laugh at this Carl Mays thing. The only [one] who helped me was Pennock. We had a long conversation on the train one night. He explained what he thought I was doing wrong. It was a matter of pitching routine and it led to my developing almost a catechism by the next season. It worked. He was corrective in his judgment. There was another thing. We talked about pitching and playing. Now I am about to make a statement that can't be verified because I don't know. I don't travel with these fellows, I'm not around them, I'm not in their conversations. But it's an impression of mine that they don't talk about pitching or playing the way we talked about it. Joe Morgan [the then Cincinnati second baseman] does and Pete Rose does. I broadcasted for the Reds for twenty-five years and I have yet to have any baseball player, pitcher or otherwise, ask me one single question on how to do anything in the game. That's a truism.

Q.  Did the older players look on you as someone who might take their jobs away and not want to help you for that reason?

A.  No, no. That's a fallacy. When I came to the Giants in 1916, the regular players -- but that was the general disposition of the league then; it has changed. There wasn't any particular way to make it tough for me except during batting practice when I was pitching, they tried to hit me with the ball. No, they weren't mean to me. They were very nice in a way. Larry Doyle, for example. There were some rugged guys, Benny Kauff, Art Fletcher, and Buck Herzog. Of course, Herzog and Heinie Zimmermann didn't talk to each other. There were a different set of men. The men changed during the years.

Q.  How did you get on with umpires?  What happened with Brick Owens that day?

A.  Well, Brick Owens is still wrong and I'm still right. He couldn't be right because he was behind the plate to begin with. I think it was the last inning in Chicago and somebody singled to score the tying run. There was a runner on second base who tried to score, too. No, there was somebody on first base who went to third and the throw in from the outfield went by Wally Schang the catcher. I was behind the plate backing up and I ran to the plate and, God be my witness, I flopped on the plate with my whole body covering the plate. Schang threw me the ball and this guy, I think it was Barrett, slid into the plate. He slid around the plate and then tried to reach back under me and tag the plate. But I grabbed his wrist and put the ball on his hand which is a good six inches away from the plate. That couldn't be missed in any shape or form. But Owens said he was safe. So I jumped up and took a punch at Owens -- he could have whipped me without anything on -- I took this punch at him with his mask, chest protector, and everything else on.

Q.  You really swung at him?

A.  Yes. That shows you how stupid I was. That's when I was suspended for awhile. But I got along well with umpires. Dick Nallin, Bill Dinneen, and Jocko Conlan is one of my best friends.

Q.  Most people I have talked to say that Bill McGowan was a very good umpire.

A.  Yes, he was a good umpire... Billy Evans was the best.

Q.  Did you ever know an umpire named Ollie Chill?

A.  Yes. He's the guy who missed the third strike for me which cost us the 1921 World Series. And the ball was right through the center of the plate.

Q.  Why didn't you take a punch at him [chuckling]?

A.  I jumped about three feet in the air. That was the fourth ball to Frankie Frisch -- no, no, it might have been Ross Youngs. That put Frisch on second. Then they hit the ball to Peckinpaugh. It went through his legs about five feet onto the outfield grass. He couldn't find the ball at first and then got turned around and Frisch scored all the way from second.

Q.  I think Ban Johnson fired Ollie Chill twice, the latest time in 1917. Then to find him reinstated and working a World Series game, no less, I have trouble with that. I think he was indicted for murder in Cleveland once.

A.  Well, they used to -- and I didn't know the meaning of it; I was just a kid then and didn't know what it meant -- but the older players used to yell out, "What time is it by your [somebody's name] watch?", intimating that Chill stole a watch from that person. I don't know whether that's true or not.

Q.  But you feel that, generally, umpires are a pretty dedicated bunch?

A.  Yes. That's a tough job and they do very good. I'm very sad that to believe, know, to realize that their names are not included in the box scores anymore. That they are not mentioned and that they don't get enough publicity. You know that old "kill the umpire" thing and "the ballplayer versus the umpire" thing, was a source of entertainment in the old days. And the fans have been deprived of that. Maybe the umpires don't want it. But I think the lack of recognition of these fellows is deplorable.

Q.  Did you ever pitch when there was just one umpire?

A.  No, there were always at least two when I came along.

Q.  Well, back in the early days there was just one who would stand behind the plate with no one on base and behind the pitcher when there were baserunners. Of course, he couldn't see everything and baserunners made an art out of cutting bases when the umpire was looking after something else. That's what caused so much criticism and actual physical abuse of umpires in those times. He was asked to do the impossible and then condemned because he couldn't do it.

A.  No, there were always two and they do a good job. You know it is a little ridiculous to ask people something like, "What do you think of the play at the home plate in the World Series?"  How do I know. I saw the play [no doubt the Ed Armbrister-Carlton Fisk matter in the 1975 World Series] on television and I watched the replay and I still don't know what happened. I don't know whether he shoved whats-his-name or not.

Q.  I think I read somewhere here where your leaving the Yankees hurt you?

A.  Yes, it did. Huggins had died and Shawkey was now manager. It wasn't that a teammate was now manager; it was mainly my fault. I was going through some domestic trouble after the 1929 season. Shawkey and I didn't get along in spring training in 1930; we had some problems. Although I don't think Shawkey had that much to do with it. He may have, but I think Ed Barrow caused more problems. I think that if Huggins had not died, I would not have been away from the Yankees. It hurt me when I went to other ballclubs. They weren't run the same; they were more like corner-lot teams. It's my belief that I am in an enviable position, not of my own doing, being able to say that I was with and played with an organization whose philosophy and practices in its approach to the actual playing of the game, was so far superior to anything that these players know today. To describe it to these fellows, they couldn't believe it, they wouldn't believe it to begin with, and they'd think that you were boasting, or lying. I get a little tired of people telling me that as you get old, time colors your imagination. When I say that it was run like a primary school class, that you sat on the bench and weren't allowed to talk about anything but baseball and yell at the other club, that's the way it was. It was discipline at its highest. When I got away from there I found out why we beat those other clubs. It's the same with some of the loose organizations I have seen. And I would say to some of the fellows on these teams that "that's why we beat you. Because you're not devoted to purpose." It isn't a matter of dedication; it's a matter of realization. A dedicated man or player, that's an inborn desire. It's a natural motivation. The other, which is what I am talking about, is sort of a manufactured thing, where you become innoculated or revved up because of something.

Q. Who was responsible for this "devotion to purpose?"

A. Huggins and [after a moment] Barrow. And the players; they got to believing in themselves. And I think Ruth was a great factor.

Q. The most undisciplined of them all seemed to inspire this discipline?

A. Oh, the undiscipline had nothing to do with it at all. You're off the track, you see. Ruth was more disciplined than people believed. That's where the mistakes come in. Ruth was very conscious of the world about him. Ruth was very conscious, was taught to be very conscious of fandom. Ruth was very warm with the public and very conscious of the public, and a perfectionist on the ball field.

Q. He was a leader then?

A. He wasn't a leader in the common meaning. But he was a guy whose baseball performance was so good that the other fellows tried to be good along with him. You know, I've heard a lot of comments about Frank McCormick. They said that if he had Chick Hafey with him on the ballclub and had somebody on the club who could outhit him by ten or fifteen points, that Frank would have hit ten points higher himself. Frank was too satisfied with what he was doing.

Q.  There's a story here somewhere -- maybe at the time Huggins died, when Joe Hauser hit a home run off of you and you were taken out?

A.  Yes. He [Huggins, I presume] said you couldn't do after thirty what you did before. And he was correct. That's why he was what he was. He was a great student of individual psychology. He was the first man I ever heard say that -- I've heard it said a lot since --. You see, up until a certain period of time, there was a sort of general sports philosophy that you worked for the team; teamwork, teamwork, the team is the thing. "So-and-so doesn't fit in."  Well, Huggins felt the same way about some of the fellows on the team. On the other hand, I'll take nine Ty Cobbs in preference to all the teamwork in the world. [We chuckle. Actually, we have done a lot more chuckling than this transcript indicates.]  The point being, that Huggins was the first I heard say that you couldn't manage twenty-five men all the same way. You just couldn't bind twenty-five men to the same rules. You could try it, but don't expect it to work to perfection. You had to manage each guy differently, which he did. I don't know how he did it, but he did. Bob Meusel was fined many times in his life by the league for some altercation with an umpire or something, but he'd never pay a fine. The fine had to be paid before he was allowed on the field again and the fine had to paid by a personal check. Meusel wouldn't put on his uniform; he just said he wouldn't submit to a fine. He'd lay low for a couple of days and Huggins would call him into the office and -- he was very quiet, Meusel; he hardly spoke a word, you know. He'd come back out of the office and sit on a chair and not say a word to anybody. But it was fixed up. I don't know what they did, but they fixed it up. That's an example of how Huggins had to manage him. There were a number of [such] instances on the team. It was a pleasure to play for them, I'll tell you that. They had supreme confidence in themselves. I think Joe McCarthy was a tremendous manager; I think he was almost the equivalent of Huggins. In his little specialties and so forth I think he was good. I never played for him...

Q.  For whom did you play after leaving the Yankees?

A.  I went to Detroit then I went to the A's. The funny thing over there in Philadelphia, I won ten and lost three for them, but I was fat and out of shape. And you know Connie Mack sent me a contract containing a $2,500 cut in pay for the next season. After I had won ten and lost three, although I wasn't in shape when I went there. During the winter I got in shape, trimming down from 206 pounds to 170, and I went down to spring training. When I went to see him in Fort Myers, he said, "I'll restore the money," and he gave me the original amount. I told him that I had already talked to Brooklyn and I would have to see what they wanted to do. They offered me this bonus so I went with Brooklyn, but I wasn't successful there. I was still having troubles. I kind of loused up my career around that time. My wife and --

Q.  You went over to the Pirates in 1933. Was Jewel Ens the manager?

A.  No, George Gibson.

Q.  You had a good year there in 1934 [he was 15-6].

A.  Well, that was after they let Gibson go. I didn't start any games until the fourth of July and I think I won twelve of those games from the fourth of July on. Traynor was managing then. There are many things I can't answer for you. And there were no reasons for them. I was just married in 1933. Then in 1935 I pitched against Cincinnati here in the opening game. We went from here to Chicago, and gee, I'll never forget that day. I pitched in Chicago and we were leading, 8-2. Then a fight broke out between Guy Bush, who had been traded to Pittsburgh, and, was it Charlie Grimm?  Well, somebody on the Cubs and they held the game up forty minutes. It must have been 34 or 40 degrees; it was cold. And I sat on the bench there for all that time without throwing the ball. I went out there the next inning and got the first guy out. The next guy singled and the next guy hit to Tommy Thevenow at second base and he booted the ball and I think I walked the next guy. Pardon me, let's backtrack. We won the opening game in Cincinnati and then we went back to Pittsburgh to open the season there and I beat St. Louis, 3-2. Then we went to Chicago. I'm getting mixed up here. At any rate they put in a guy named Jack Salveson and Traynor left him in there while he walked six straight men. And dammit, if the Cubs didn't score nine or ten runs in the inning and beat us, although I didn't lose the game. I didn't start again for I don't know how long. I don't understand why even to this day. I think the cold weather had something to do with what happened to me that inning. It didn't do me any good and, of course, I was no youngster either. Then things started to go haywire. I was through. You know what happens to you, when you're fifteen years old, or sixteen, it isn't a question of being tired physically, you become sated with the game and you kind of wish you'd had a change.

Q.  How did you get into broadcasting?

A.  Well, I started on a show called "Bandstand and Grandstand," a show sponsored by Wheaties. It was a guest show, but it had a thirty-five-piece band. It was a three-hour show and I used to do three different bits in the show. It was at WMCA in New York in the afternoon. They had all kinds of celebrities on that program, football players, actors, actresses, everyone you could imagine. I was a regular on the show like the actress Mae Murray, or people coming off the boats. Ely Culbertson and bridge players. It was quite a show.

Q.  Did you plan to go into broadcasting or did it just happen?

A.  No, I knew a fellow in show business. He thought it was good for me to get into radio. But it was a struggle for me for quite awhile. It was a struggle for me when I came out here in January 1942... That wasn't a good time because that was the first year of the war and not much attention was paid to baseball.

Q.  Why was it a struggle?

A.  Well, they didn't give me an audition in New York. They said ballplayers didn't have any vocabulary, so they wouldn't let me audition.

Q.  Were you the first ballplayer-turned-announcer?

A.  No, I think Gabby Street was the first, then there was Jack Graney in Cleveland and Harry Heilmann in Detroit.

Q.  How about your off-season life?  Where did you make your home?

A.  Oh, we traveled a great deal; we went to Florida a lot -- Miami... No, I never worked in the off-season. We went to Honolulu some winter. That was the first five years I was married to this girl. From 1933 on.

Q.  Was your present wife the one you tell about who was up in the grandstand when you were in a tough spot and you looked up to her for moral support and --

A.  Yes, that was this wife. She had her feet up on the seat in front of her reading the newspaper, paying no attention to the game. [We chuckle]... No, she wasn't nervous for me; she just didn't know anything about baseball... Say, I'm going to do something for you, if you like it, and agree to return it. [What he gets for me is a tape of his talk at his induction into the Hall of Fame in 1969. I took it with me, taped it when I got back home and then returned it to him. He also dug out some of his scrapbooks and pictures, which I started going through. He autographs a pile of pictures for me; he was kind and generous in this, as in all other aspects of the interview. In glancing through a scrapbook I spot a story in an article and ask him about it.]

Q. It says here in an article from the *Sporting News* that Will Wedge, baseball writer for the *New York Sun*, pinned on you the label, "The Aristocrat of Baseball."

A. Well, that's a very nice label. I've been called almost everything, but that's the nicest... That was Will Wedge was it? There's another writer for the *New York Times* who just died. What was his name?... Yes, Arthur Daley. He was a good friend of mine. You've got to be good friends with these guys if you want to get labels like that.

Q. I guess you had good relations with the press during your career?

A. Yes, very good. Frankie Graham was one of my finest friends.

Q. He's the one who wrote the history of the Yankees, isn't he?

A. Yes. I wrote part of that history. Yes. In fact, I finished my part of the book the night before we came out here to broadcast in 1942. It's verbatim in there from the time I joined the Yankees until 1930. To tell you the truth, Frankie Graham was such a lovely fellow that he didn't owe me ten cents. And, you know, he saw that they sent me commissions for five years afer the book came out. I knew Frankie Graham since I was a kid. I knew all those fellows, Tom Meany, Tommy Holmes, John Drebinger, Dan Daniel, Gary Schumacher -- oh, I knew them all and I had good relations with them all. And I want to tell you something while I am speaking of the press of those days. This was during Prohibition. It wasn't unusual for after a practice or after a game to have someone call up there and ask, "Have you got something to drink up there?" It would be one of the newspapermen. We'd say, "C'mon up." And we'd sit around there and talk and you know that never, never, was a confidence violated. You can't do that today. I remember one -- I'm not going to mention any names -- it was one of our most prominent writers in New York. I was on the plane with him going from New York to Detroit. I was in an intimate conversation with him. We had a very nice time together -- that is until I read his syndicated column in the paper. He had distorted every thing that I said. He is one of my favorite hates today. I can't understand those kinds of fellows. And then there are these fellows always criticizing the Old-Timers Committee of the Hall of Fame and want to know why so-and-so was elected. After we elected George Kelly they rushed in and wanted to know why we elected him. Well, George Kelly was not the greatest home run hitter in the world, among a number of other things, and -- it seems today that everybody is guided by the home run. I happened to say that he was a remarkable ballplayer and that McGraw used him for things that you don't see nowadays. He was the one who went into the outfield behind second base to catch the throw and relay it to home plate, which you don't see in the present day. They wrote the story and the story appeared in the paper that I said he was elected because he took the throws from the outfield and threw to home plate. George Kelly was an instrument of defense second to none. They just leave out that part. There have been so many of those things between the writers and old-time players on the committee.

Q.  Do you see a difference in writers of today and those of the past?  What I mean is do today's writers know the game, have knowledge of the game the way the older writers did?

A.  No, they don't.

Q.  I understand some of them arrive in the fifth inning and are gone by the seventh. And if you want to find out what actually happened during the game, you're out of luck. You find out all kinds of things in the locker room after the game with the interviews, but very little comes through about the game. Game accounts were always exciting stories to me.

A.  Well, I tell you; let's be fair. There are so many other sports today that have jumped into prominence and elevated themselves to the same plateau as baseball. They are asked to cover all these sports. And don't you think that today everybody, including writers, resorts to trickery -- well not trickery, I don't know what it is. But just get the job done as quickly as possible [without too much concern over the quality of the job]. Some ballplayers are the same way. But humanity is all the same and perhaps you and I are just as guilty about some things as the people we are criticizng are about other things. But I always did like the men of the press. They were always good with me.

Q.  Here's a question that you are probably sick and tired of hearing, but it is kind of a routine question for me to wind up interviews with. Does anything stand out in your career as your greatest thrill?

A.  There were four great thrills for me. This is what I write to people who ask about that. The first one was, of course, signing when I was fifteen years old. Because you must understand that in those days kids were seen and not heard. Consequently, when I signed when I was fifteen years old that became something of a national sensation. The second was that first game against Detroit and beating them 2-1 in twelve innings. That incident with Cobb and so on. And you must remember, too, that I didn't have enough money to telephone my father or write a telegram to him. I was walking on air and the poor man at home, he has seen that I had started the game, but he didn't know what had happened.

Q.  When did he find out?

A.  He had to call the *New York Journal* later that evening. The third one was the 1921 World Series and the election to the Hall of Fame was the fourth one. I can't make up my mind which was the more exciting moment -- the actual induction or the moment I was notified. I was notified while coming off the 18th green at the Bellaire Country Club down there. The caddy master said I was wanted on the long distance telephone from Dayton, Ohio. It was Ritter Collett of the Dayton paper congratulating me for being elected to the Hall. [He describes his reaction, he was all broken up, started to cry and was overcome by emotion.]  After I hung up I went back into the lounge -- one of the pros at the club had already told the people there what had happened -- and as I walked in they all stood up and gave me a standing ovation. It's pretty hard to beat a moment like that. The actual induction, a once-in-a-lifetime experience, is pretty moving in itself, so when people ask me which moved me more I have trouble telling them which.

Q. Tell me about the article Stanley Frank wrote in the *Saturday Evening Post.*

A. He came to me in Montclair with the finished article. I told him, "Stanley, that cannot go in the magazine the way it is. The last 600-800 words you'll have to revise. You're knocking the National League and I'm playing in the National League."  It was the day I was heading for spring training with the Brooklyn Dodgers. I said, "You cannot print it this way. I'm very bitter about this thing; it was one of the bitterest things in my baseball history."  He said he'd change it and I suggested that he had to sweeten it because I didn't believe in the way he had written it at all. By George, he never changed a word of it, not a word! Now Tom Meany had written a piece called, "The New Minor League: the National."  That appeared the week before mine. Mine was called "Why the American League Wins." I was trying to talk to him about the difference between the system of the National and American Leagues. The National League pitched low, for example, because they wanted you to hit the ball on the ground. I remember the article or piece I wrote somewhere where I said that you pitch low to Ruth and Gehrig and they hit home runs off you. That's nuts. Sid Keener, or somebody, wrote a book or something, devoted almost entirely to me I guess, telling what a clown I was to talk like that, that I was just offering some stupid suggestion. It ridiculed me all through the book. And Stanley Frank let the thing go and had me saying -- I never said those things that he wrote. I did say we would qualify what he wrote, which would give it all a different connotation than he implied when the article came out. How do I wind up?  When I went to pitch in St. Louis, a piece appeared in one of the St. Louis papers, which said, "Waite Hoyt, the guy who called the National League the Minor League" -- that was the title of Meany's article -- "will pitch today." That left me bitter; very, very bitter. And by the way, one item here from the scrapbook briefly. It says, "Hoyt picks his all-star team." This was in the Taylor Spink piece back in 1942. I would no longer pick an all-star team. There are too many great players. There are too many players with marginal differences to pick any all-star team. Anybody who tries to pick an all-time team is crazy. There is only one ballplayer, in my estimation, who was the greatest of them all, and that was Ruth. I don't hold with that over there [pointing to some current correspondence on his desk] with that fellow who wants me to pick an all-star team. That is ridiculous.

Q. While the tape was off I talked a little about Cy Marshall, who was with you on the Memphis team in the Southern Association in 1917. Could you say a little bit about the manager of that team, "Turkey Mike" Donlin?

A. I don't know too much about Mike Donlin. I know that he was married to Mabel Hite, who was one of the great actresses of the day.

Q. Mike went on the stage with her, too, didn't he?

A. Yes, and after that he did very well in motion pictures. What actually happened down there, Mike was a tough guy married to a very lovely girl [he was now divorced from Mabel Hite]. I don't remember her name. He was McGraw's bodyguard in one way.

Q. He was a pretty good ballplayer, wasn't he?

A. Damn right he was. He hit .368 and...

Q. Hall of Fame material?

A. No. I don't think he played long enough in the big leagues. But he was one heck of a ballplayer. But it came one Sunday in Memphis and it was raining. He had his best pitcher pitching; I forget who it was. The umpires wouldn't call the game. I can't remember if we were ahead or the other team was ahead. But the umpires insisted on playing, so Mike called his pitcher out of there. And to show up the umpires, he went in and pitched. Of course, the other team scored about fourteen runs off of him. The stands were very close and Mike was a very profane guy and he had a profane argument with one of the umpires and he was let go the next day -- me along with him. But I pitched well down there. I lost 3-2 and 2-0 and scores like that. Dazzy Vance shut me out three times. I had Dazzy Vance beaten one time in the ninth inning and the last man struck out, but

Smitty allowed the third strike to get through him to the grandstand, which let the tying run score from third base and they eventually beat us.

# Ed Wells

*Montgomery, Alabama, August 6, 1977*

"Bethany's Best"

Ed Wells was the only player I interviewed who played professional baseball while still attending college. No, he did not cheat, although in those pre-Walter Byers days it would have been easy to do. While he gave up sports at Bethany College in West Virginia, he did not give up his studies and graduated with his class. Since he was born in Ohio and went to school in West Virginia, I developed a particular affinity for the "Slugger." I was born in Ohio and have lived most of my life in West Virginia. Moreover, he almost went to Wooster College, which I attended. In addition, he was a hero-worshipper, like me. But while he worshipped Ty Cobb, I worshipped Hal Trosky. I had always thought that Wells pitched the first big league game I ever saw, when the Yankees were in Cleveland, August 10, 1929. It proved, however, that Tom Zachary and Wilcy Moore did the dirty work, as the Indians lost, 4-2. Wells struck me as a rangy, good-looking chap as he welcomed me into his Montgomery home; he hardly seemed the seventy-six years revealed by the record book. As a young player, he had been told by his manager, Ty Cobb, to "keep your mouth shut." Now, as a retired salesman, he did not mind talking and had plenty to say. I spent a pleasant two hours with "Slugger" Ed Wells.

Q. Tell me about growing up in Ashland, Ohio.

A. Now that's a long story. What do you want?

Q. Well, first your school days and then going on to Bethany College.

A. Are you going to interrupt me?

Q. Maybe, maybe not. You go right ahead. I want to hear everything you have to say.

A. As I said, it's a long story. I was born on a farm, three miles out of Ashland. When I was six years old, my dad bought me a uniform. Shoes, cap, pads, socks, shirt, and everything. He used to play ball himself when he was a kid. He called himself "Coonskin." He wore a coonskin cap. Anyway, he did that when I was six and from then on I always seemed to have a ball in my hands. As I grew up in that old red brick schoolhouse out there, I had a teacher named Fox, and he was interested in baseball. I was only about twelve years old then and he got to talking about the Cleveland ballclub and the big leagues. I didn't even know what he meant then. So I started reading the Cleveland papers, all about the Indians who played over at Dunn Field on East 66th Street. As I grew older, I was fourteen now, still going to that old country school. I got to playing ball on the weekends, back in the cow pasture. I just happened to have a fastball. I was left-handed. I am all left-handed; I think left-handed, I write left-handed; I do everything left-handed. Well, as time went by, in the town of Ashland they had some semi-pro baseball teams. They must have heard about me and asked me to come down one day. I was only fourteen then. I went to the YMCA field in Ashland. For some reason, I was very fortunate because I was never real wild. I got to playing with those fellows on those teams. I must have had a whale of a fastball then, although I was only fourteen. I didn't know what a curveball was. I was six feet tall even though I was only fourteen. Later that year I was cutting wheat one day in the field -- I don't know where my brother was -- but a fellow drove down there in a car. He came over there and introduced himself; he was a scout for the Cleveland Indians. I don't know how he heard about me. He asked me how old I was and I told him I was only fourteen, he said, "Forget it, you're too young." Well, as I got along into Ashland High School, I was just dying to get into that high school so I could play on the high school team. When the time came along to take that examination which you had to take at the end of grade school, and which I took, I was just ready to get into Ashland High School and play on the team. That fall I entered high school and played football, which I didn't care a lot about, and basketball too, then came baseball. The science teacher was the coach of that baseball team. We had two pitchers by the names of Ikey Gumm and a fellow named Baylor. Great big fellows, as big as I was; they were the pitchers. When we started practicing I didn't have a chance -- at least, for awhile. Finally he gave me a chance to pitch and I did all right. They got a couple of hits, but never came close to a run. While in high school I got to pitching for some of these fast semi-pro teams. We were playing Elyria, Lorain, and some of those Cleveland teams. I was doing the pitching. When I got ready to leave high school, I got to thinking. I was crazy about baseball. That was all I thought about. But anyhow I decided I was going to college somewhere. So I started looking around. Now I think your coach down at Wooster College was Coach Boles.

Q. Yes, L. C. Boles, I remember him well.

A. So I thought I would go over and talk to Coach Boles. [Wooster is about 30 miles from Ashland.] I found him out on the golf course. I introduced myself and told him about me. He said, "You get your records and credentials in here and I'll look them over. If everything is all right, I'll see if I can arrange for some work for you here which will make it so you won't have to pay so much to go to the college." He was courteous enough, but he had his mind on the golf course that day. [In 1939 Boles instructed my freshman class in golf.] Anyway, I don't know how many colleges I wrote to, and they all gave me the same story. "We'll give you a try, if your credentials are good enough to get into the school." I thought it over and over and decided to call old Coffman down at Ohio State, who was from Shelby, Ohio, over here. He said, "Sure," come on down and we'll give you a job waiting on tables or something to help with your expenses." That's about what I was going to do, but here's what happened. We went to Shelby one Sunday to play a team from Cleveland. We had a good game and I pitched well. Not meaning to brag about myself, but I was good. They didn't come close to getting a run; they might have gotten a couple of hits. Well, a fellow named "Bullet" Smith was playing first base for them. He was with the General Electric Company in Cleveland. He was a good friend of Billy Evans, the old umpire. We were going to play them again the next Sunday. So after that game was over this Bullet Smith came up to me and said, "How do you stand in school?" I said I was going somewhere to college that fall and that I was figuring on Ohio State. "Wells," he said, "how about considering Bethany College?" "Where's that? I never heard of it." "Oh, it's down there in the hills of West Virginia, about 18 miles out of Wheeling. If you go there it won't cost you anything. We'll have a baseball scholarship. We can get you board and you won't have to pay for anything. We have an athletic deal down there." "Who do you play?" I asked. "Oh, we play Georgetown, Penn State, Navy, Pittsburgh, Carnegie Tech, and West Virginia." "In baseball?" "Yes. We've got a good ballteam." He went on to say, this was after that first game, "When we come over here to play you next Sunday, would you consider letting me bring along the athletic director at Bethany, a man named Miller, to talk to you?" "Sure, that's all right. The idea of going to school for nothing appeals to me." [We chuckle.] The next week we went over there and shut them out again. Miller was there and he gave me the story. All about the school, all about the team, who they played, the facilities they had, and who the coach was, and everything about the place. I said I'd let him know. Well, I talked to my dad, and my dad was a man who would never give me advice. He'd always say, "Use your own judgment; use your own judgment." He'd never dictate to me. Well, I decided I'd go down there. I decided I'd rather be a big stone in a little creek than a piece of sand on the [unclear]. So I go to Bethany College. So we come along and they've got a fellow named Randolph who's a pitcher and a star. He's been winning all the ballgames. I went out for football and played that and I went out for basketball and played that and then we come to baseball. Buhlen's the coach and we have a heavy schedule. They had two pitchers besides myself. I forget who the other one was beside Randolph. Well, we played two ballgames and I didn't get into either of them. I was the newcomer and they didn't know anything about me. Now we come to play Marietta College in Bethany. Buhlen the coach came to me and said, "I'm going to start you in this game. You'll probably need some help, but I'm going to start you." "Fine." I just thought to myself, "I'll show them something." I think I struck out twenty-one of those fellows. I got established by that.

Q. What year would this have been?

A. Well, I entered in the fall of 1920, so this would be the spring of 1921. I graduated in the spring of 1924. Anyway, that established me. And I had a dag-gone good year. Then some of these coal mining towns came along and wanted me to pitch on Sundays. So I pitched on Sundays, too, for $100 a game. That was a time when the colleges weren't very strict about getting paid for playing. The rules were very lax. So I got to pitching up and down that valley -- Collingsvile, Uniontown -- all over in there, pitching these ballgames on Sunday, making some money too. So I got well-established. Now here's what happened. Now I'm young and going into my second year with Bethany in the spring of 1922. And here comes Billy Doyle, a Detroit scout. Well, now the year before that when I had a good year, here comes Mr. Veeck of the Cubs, Bill Veeck's dad, calls me long distance from Chicago. He said he wanted to meet me in Wellsburg, West Virginia, to talk to me. So I met him at the hotel in Wellsburg. We talked and talked. He wanted me to sign a contract right then. I said, "No, I'm not signing any contract now." I was a hero-worshiper of Ty Cobb. I kept up with him all the time. I had that in the back of my mind. Veeck finally asked, "Will you sign an agreement that you won't sign with anybody else for one year?" "Yes, I'll sign an agreement; that doesn't mean anything." He said, "That's right, it just means you won't sign with anyone for a year. This summer," he added, "come out to Chicago and work out with us." I said I would think about that. Anyway, I signed the agreement and forgot about it. Now in February 1922, I was in a chemistry class, when I got a phone call. It was Billy Doyle from Detroit. He was in Pittsburgh and said he wanted to talk to me. So he came down and we talked and talked. Now I was on a scholarship to Bethany and no one had ever given me any instructions about that thing and no one had ever said anything about it. Being a kid, I wasn't thinking. But I was never criticized for any of what happened whatsoever. The athletic director and coaches, none of them ever criticized me. But this is what happened. When he said he'd give me $1,000 for signing a contract, I said, "Good gosh!" I told him to wait until tomorrow; I had to call my dad. I called him that night and he said, "I can't tell you what to do. Use your own judgment." Anyway, I signed that contract. In about a week here came a $1,000 check. I liked to faint. That was a lot of money back then. Now we go into the 1922 season.

Q. They didn't know you had signed?

A. Oh, no. They knew the scout was in town. Harry Randolph was doing his best to have the scout sign him, but he wouldn't do it. Sure, they knew he was in town, but nobody ever said a word to me about being on a scholarship and [the problems this might create if he signed a professional contract. This is what he is talking about although he doesn't say it this way.]  I told Billy Doyle I was on a scholarship, but of course, he was looking out for his side. I spent the summer of 1922 with Ludington [Michigan] in the Michigan-Ontario League. I did pretty well there.

Q. Yes you did; 13-10 and an ERA of 1.93.

A. Yes. Now I go back to Bethany in the fall of 1922 for my junior year and the spring of 1923 when the baseball practice begins, nobody knew I had played pro ball. And I didn't tell anybody. Nobody around school would ever think of that and I kept my mouth shut. The season started and we got off to a great start. We go into the fourth game, and I think we were playing West Virginia. Here comes "Rat" Rodgers, that former All-American, with a clipping out of a Ludington paper. [We chuckle.]  I told Buhlen then, "That's it."  He agreed, "That's it." He said it was all right, he understood. The athletic director said it was all right, but that I would have to pay my own expenses from then on. They were very nice about it. So I played no more college ball. That spring when school was out, Detroit was playing in Boston. So I went to Boston. Like a kid from the farm who didn't know any better, I arrive there at 6:30 in the morning and head for the New Brunswick Hotel. The first thing I do is call Cobb up. He was sound asleep, but when he heard my story he said "Come on up."  So I went up there and we talked while he ate and dressed until about 10 o'clock. I went to the ballpark with him. I struck up a good friendship with Cobb right from the beginning.

Q. That must have been a big thrill, being with your boyhood hero just like that?

A. So we go to the ballpark and he introduces me to all the players. Gosh almighty, it's going into the eighth inning, I think, and he sends me to the bullpen. And I pitched that eighth inning in Boston. We was behind. The first man I faced was Ira Flagstead. He hit a line drive right back at me and I caught it, and then I got the last two men out. That was my first drink of water. That night we leave for New York and the Yankee Stadium had just opened up that previous

April. We get into New York and go to the hotel. Now we go out to the Stadium. It was on a Sunday. It was packed and the Babe was at his peak. It comes into the fifth inning. What happened was -- this happened a long time ago and George Dauss was one of our pitchers. On the train to New York Cobb told George that when he reached New York, "You leave the beer alone because you're pitching tomorrow." Well, when George hit the Stadium the next day he was as red as a beet in the face. Cobb went over and said, "George, you're pitching." "I am?" "You're red in the face, but you're pitching." He went out there and they got seven runs off of him in the first inning. Cobb was going to make him pitch. Anyway, we get way behind and he sent me to the bullpen. I pitched the sixth, seventh, and eighth innings. I got warmed up and went in there. Any player who tells you that when he goes in there in the big leagues for the first time that he's not nervous, he's crazy. Well, I walk in there and the first bozo I faced was the Babe. And about 50,000 watching. The catcher walked out and said, "Eddie, what do you want to throw him?" I said, "Nuthin'." Well, he walked back behind the plate. The first one I threw up there was a ball. The next one was a strike and he took it. The next one was over and he took a swing at it and missed it. The next one was a ball. The next pitch was a slowball and he took a cut at it and struck out. I never threw him a fastball then or after and he never hit a home run off of me in six years. That was my initiation into the big leagues. They didn't get a run off of me in three innings. I was satisfied with that. So on the train back to Detroit, the secretary of the club says, "Ed, you're going to be with us the rest of the season now and I want to tell you our schedule, hotels, how we eat, and so forth." Well, along about the 25th of July Cobb edges up to me on the bench and says, "Ed, how would you like to go to Birmingham, Alabama, and finish the season there?" I said that was all right, since I hadn't been doing much pitching. So off I go to Birmingham and I really enjoyed it down there.

Q. His idea of sending you to Birmingham was to give you more work?

A. Oh, yes. To give me more work, especially in holding men on base and in fielding my position. And he said when he sent me down there that I should send him newspaper clippings of every game that I pitched. So that's what I did; I sent him every one, whether I lost or won. So in the fall I went back to Bethany for my last year. I don't play any sports that year. That spring, when school is out, I go to Detroit. When I get there, Ty says to me, "Ed, I want you to come out and spend the night with me. Mr. Briggs and his family are in Europe and I'm staying in his house. That's Briggs Body now. You come out there. I've got my butler with me from my home in Georgia." So I spent the night with Ty. We talked about this and that and he said, "Ed, you're going to pitch tomorrow." We were playing Cleveland. Well, I hardly slept all night long; you know how it is. So the next day I pitched against a young kid by the name of Luther Roy. The Lord was with me. I just threw that ball; I never will forget it. We went into the ninth inning, men on first and second, and George Burns was up. Cobb had told me never to throw George Burns a fastball; he was too good a hitter. He held the record for two-base hits for awhile. So he dribbled the ball down to Fred Haney at third who stepped on the base for the final out and we win 3-2. After the game Cobb called me over and said he wanted to talk to me. He said, "That's how easy it is; there's nothing to it." Well, I found out different. I went along that year; I didn't do much. I averaged four runs a game, I guess, but I had potential -- they thought.

Q. Did he start you a lot that year?

A. I was in thirty-five ballgames in 1924, and won six and lost eight. I did some relief pitching, too. The next year, 1925, I go moseying along there, but I never got my feet on the ground. I don't know why. I had an awful year. Do you see that 6.19 ERA? Awful. The first two years we trained at Augusta, Georgia. Now we go to San Antone by train. I come back up there with the club and, my gosh, I think I won ten or eleven ballgames early in the season. I thought I was just going to tear things up. This is not an alibi, but I had a lot of stuff. A lot of stuff. We played a game in Washington and won that game and I got on that Pullman with the doggone window open. I was wearing a wool shirt. Passing through the Allegheny Mountains that night I woke up and was about to freeze to death. My arm was as stiff as a board. And, you know, I lost my fastball. I couldn't get anybody out. That's what happened there in 1926. I finished up 12 and 10. The sportswriters were saying after I won all those games in the beginning, "Ed you're going to win twenty way before the season is over." I thought that was a bit optimistic and it was. That's no alibi now, but that's what happened. Now the next spring, 1927, that's when Cobb's gone; he and Speaker went to Philadelphia. George Moriarty is the new manager. We're in San Antone again and the first day out, the first ball I threw, something hit me in my left arm like someone had stuck a needle in there; it hurt so. Well, I spent the whole spring training going to a chiropractor in San Antone, Texas. Well, that didn't help much -- hot pads at night and all that stuff. I had tendonitis. That's what Mark Fydrich has now. Well, I go with the ballclub, but I didn't do nothing; I couldn't do nothing. I was in eight games, but you know that Frank Navin kept me on the club until the 25th of July! I wasn't no good to that ballclub. I would go in there a few times, but I couldn't get anybody out, my arm was hurting. You know what happened? He called me in the office and said, "Ed, we've sold you to Washington and they're playing over in St. Louis. Their manager, Bucky Harris, thinks a lot of you." I said, "Mr. Navin, I can't help nobody. I've got a sore arm." "Well we've sold you to Washington, so you report to them in St.

Louis." Which I did. I go to St. Louis and Bucky Harris shows me the wire. He said, "Clark Griffith has optioned you to Birmingham." I told him that was O.K. because my arm was bad. I go to Birmingham and meet the team in Chattanooga, about the 26th or 27th of July.

Q. It looks here in the book like your arm came back then.

A. Johnny Dobbs was the manager; he knew me from 1923. "Ed," he said, "I want to start you in Memphis tomorrow." I told him about the bad arm and that we would have to wait and see. So we hit Memphis. I go into that ballgame, warm up, lose the game 3-1 and my arm hasn't hurt since. That's the heat, I think. It was hot. I think it hit 100 degrees in Memphis that day. So I go along there and win thirteen straight ballgames. Now what happens? Washington recalls me, to report to Tampa in the spring of 1928, and I have a whale of a spring training. I had that high hard one; I never had much of a hook. That's what they call a slider now. A "nickle curve" is what it is. Anyway, I have a great spring. Well, we play an exhibition game with Birmingham and I got the tar knocked out of me. I couldn't get them out. I couldn't figure out what had happened. Well, we hit Washington, the day before the season began. That night, here comes Billy Smith, secretary of the Washington ballclub. "Ed, we've sold you to Birmingham." That's all right. I had won thirteen games for them the last year, but Washington was shooting for the pennant that year. So I go to Birmingham. I got it through the grapevine that he was giving me a salary of $5,000. That's a whale of a salary for the Southern League in 1927. That was a whale of a salary for a ballplayer period. So I go down there and talk to Clark Smith, the owner. I forget what the offer was, but it wasn't $5,000. I said, "Wait a minute, Smith. I know you want to win the pennant and you saw what I did for you down here last year. I heard that you were going to give me $5,000. What are you going to do; back off of it?" He said, "We'll give you $5,000." So that ended that. Now we started out -- you know what I did that year?

Q. Yes. It says here 25 and 7.

A. That's what I did that year. So, when the season was just about over, here comes Billy Webb [or West], that was the secretary's name. "Eddie," he says, "we've sold you to the Yankees." "Fine." So we go ahead and have the playoff series with Memphis. We win that and then we play Houston and Bill Hallahan in the Dixie World Series. Well, we open up in Birmingham and I win that one, 1-0, on account of old Jimmy Johnston stole home. The old Brooklyn third baseman. We win two in Birmingham then we go to Houston, where we couldn't get them out. I started one game, went six innings and shut them out when the

*Ed Wells, pitcher for the New York Yankees, 1929-1932. Wells spent five years with Detroit before joining the Yankees. Although he never achieved the success expected of him, "Slugger" had a couple of good years and finished his 11-year career with a 68-69 won-lost record and an earned run average of 4.65. (Photo from the author's collection.)*

roof fell in. I couldn't get them out. That's the way that season ended up. Now, when I was with the Detroit ballclub, Babe came up to me one day and said, "Ed, I'm going to get you on the Yankees." I laughed at him. "I'm going to get you on the Yankees," he said again. I know what it was because he couldn't hit me. Anyhow, I report to the Yankees in the spring of 1929. When the Babe saw me he came over and said, "What did I tell you in Detroit? What'd I tell you?" "Yeah, you were right." "Well, we're going to win some ballgames with you." So Huggins called me into his office. He always interviewed players separately. He said, "Wells, you like hot weather to pitch in." "I sure do." He said, "I'm not going to pitch you until the latter part of May when it begins to get hot." So, along late in April an article appears in the paper which says I am going to St. Paul. I haven't been in a ballgame for the Yankees yet. So Chicago comes to town and Huggins says I'm the pitcher. Ted Lyons is pitching for Chicago. It is a nice bright, warm-cool day and that high hard one was jumpin. We win 1-0. I didn't hear any more about going to St. Paul. That was in the paper; nobody on the ballclub said anything about that. Anyway that's what I did that year. Hug said, "You're a spot pitcher. That's the way I'm going to use you." O.K. So I go through that season.

Q. Didn't Huggins die that year?

A. Well, here's what happened. In the first part of September we were playing Cleveland in a double-header in New York. Now Hug had a little pimple right there. I never will forget it. He was standing right on the steps of the dugout watching the ballgame and scratching this thing. It was getting red. Between games Doc Woods, the trainer, said, "Hug, you stay in here and let me put hot applications on that pimple; that thing is swelling." Hug said O.K. and when that game was over Hug was in the hospital. Three days later he was dead from blood poisoning. He was anemic. Hug was an anemic man. His head was twice its normal size in death. So we put the black bands on our arms and Fletcher took over the ballclub and finished. That year I had 13 and 9. Now in 1930 we have Bob Shawkey as manager. He said he wanted to use me as a spot pitcher like Hug had. That was O.K. So that year I finished 12 and 3. When that season began Ed Barrow had told me, "Ed, if you have a good year I'll give you a little bonus. "When the season was over I never heard from him. I wrote him a couple of letters and he finally sent me a check for $250. [He chuckles.] That's old Ed Barrow; he's a hot shot. So that's 1930, I was 12 and 3.

Q. I think I mentioned when I spoke to you on the phone that the first game I ever saw was on August 10, 1929, in Cleveland with the Yankees in town, I am sure you pitched that day as the Yankees won, 4-2. That day the Babe hit his 499th home run. The following day he hit his 500th. But nobody kept track of those kind of numbers then. How was Bob Shawkey as a manager?

A. He was all right, but I don't know, he just didn't have the respect of the ballplayers.

Q. He was a player himself not too long before. Was this a problem, being close to the players and then suddenly being put above them?

A. I think it was. He had been on the Yankees as a pitcher for some time and now he was manager. I think that was a reason for it.

Q. How did you like Cobb as a manager?

A. Oh, great. Cobb and I were very close friends. We went to the masonic lodge together a lot. Yes, we were very close friends. But listen, a lot of people hated Cobbs' guts. His hips were all full of holes where they spiked him, not him spiking somebody else. I saw him score on a bunt one day. He bunted the ball, reached first base and just kept on going. The ball was either behind him or if it was in front of him, they'd drop it. I saw that.

Q. I guess he made them nervous by his reputation and when they saw him coming at them they'd drop the ball.

A. That Cobb was a ballplayer. Of course, I didn't see him in his prime. I saw him in the fading years of his career. I think he thought a lot of me. I thought a lot of him. He only treated me like a gentleman, but some fellows didn't like him. He didn't like them either. We got along fine.

Q. How about Harry Heilmann?

A. Harry was a good outfielder and led the league several years in hitting. But there was competition there; publicity... Yes, there was a little tension between Cobb and Heilmann...

Q. Especially when Heilmann won all those alternate year batting titles, in 1921, 1923, 1925, and 1927, although Cobb was gone by 1927.

A. Yes, sir; there was a lot of feeling there... Bobby Veach? Well, I was only there for a cup of coffee in 1923, when Veach was there, but I don't think he and Ty got along worth a hoot, from the remarks that people made. That was a long time ago -- 1923; fifty-four years ago... I only knew Moriarty as an umpire and then as a manager.

Q. After Cobb was displaced as manager and forced to leave Detroit after the 1926 season, did this upset the team or mean much to the players?

A. There weren't any comments made... Our other pitchers with Detroit when I was there were George Dauss, Earl Whitehill, Bert Cole, Lil Stoner. They only had nine pitchers -- Smitty, Hoot Gibson, Ken Holloway -- that was about it. I think maybe they had only eight pitchers. Cobb used to say, "Get out there and give them all you've got and if you get in trouble I'll put somebody else in." We only had eight or nine pitchers, where they carry eleven or twelve today.

Q. Yes, the complete games totals have gone way down. Who was your first baseman?

A. Lu Blue. When I joined that ballclub, Bobby Jones was on third base, Cutshaw was on second before Charlie Gehringer, and I'm trying to think of who was the shortstop -- it wasn't Tavener. Rigney, Rigney. In the outfield you had Cobb, Veach, and Heilmann. That was when I was first up there. Then they had Red Wingo come in there and Bob Fothergill.

Q. "Fatty" Fothergill. He could really hit the ball, couldn't he?

A. He really could; a line drive hitter. Too fat, he had to fight his weight all the time. In spring training they had to slit a tire inner tube and put it around him so he'd sweat and lose weight. He couldn't lose weight, though. He was just plain heavy. As heavy as he was, he was a good fielder.

Q. Did Rigney ever make an unassisted triple play?

A. Johnny Neun did. I saw that. Here's what happened. There was nobody out with runners on first and second. Johnny Neun was playing first. A line drive was hit just to Johnny's left and when he caught the ball he was just a step from first base. He stepped on the base while the guy from second was all the way to third. So Johnny ran down to second and touched the bag there for the triple play. Old Ty was yelling, "A triple-play unassisted, a triple-play unassisted." You could hear him all over the ballpark.

Q. That was quick thinking by Neun, I would say. The tendency would be to throw to second and get the out there as quick as possible.

A. But the runner was way over towards third base; way over. That's what happened... No, I wasn't pitching that day. Oh, Moore was another pitcher on the Detroit team. He went to Texas and was in the state constabulary down there - the Texas police. He was picked up somehow by Boston and the Yankees too. Roy Moore, that was his name.

Q. Speaking of Neun's triple play, wasn't there another unassisted triple play in the league the very next day?

A. I'm trying to think. I know I remember that one very well. I think I witnessed another one somewhere, but I've forgotten where. Getting back to what we were talking about earlier, did Joe Sewell tell you about what he did in Chicago one day, about making hand prints in the ground? He didn't tell you that? Well, the Yankees were playing in Chicago. Joe was playing third base. The batter tops the ball down the third base line and Joe comes in to field it. The ball was in fair territory, but close to the foul line. Joe saw he couldn't throw the man out, so he began making little prints with his hand in the ground, a sort of groove right over into foul territory, and the ball followed the groove and wound up being a foulball. The next day the American League made a rule and you could not do that anymore. [We chuckle.] That ball would have stayed fair if he hadn't done that. I never will forget that. Have you got any more to ask about the Detroit club?

Q. All kinds of things. Who was your catcher?

A. Johnny Bassler and Larry Woodall. Johnny was a good catcher... I enjoyed pitching in Navin Field; it was fine, yes sir... In Cleveland that right field would give you fits. You'd try to pitch them outside and away, but when you're young up there, you're all over the place. You don't have control until you're older. Very few young ones have good control. You know that.

Q. Before your games in Detroit, would Cobb call for a team meeting?

A. Cobb didn't have team meetings before games very often as a team. You would just discuss things and he would tell us about pitching. A lot of times he would have the meetings with pitchers by themselves. He didn't have meetings often at all. He would always ask for suggestions. Now I want to tell you something else about Detroit there. In 1926 I had a streak of thirty-three consecutive scoreless innings. That was pretty good for me. Walter Johnson had the record then of fifty-six, and that was beaten by that fellow Koufax of Los Angeles. [And more recently by that other fellow of Los Angeles, Orel Hershiser.]

Q. How did you get this nickname "Slugger?"

A. "Slugger?" Well, Dizzy Dean was always popping off about his hitting. Now I have a lifetime batting average in the majors and minors of .250. So when I came down here in business, I was known as a ballplayer. I couldn't remember names, so I got to calling everybody "slugger." Since I called other people slugger, they started calling me slugger.

Q. Then it came after baseball?

A. Oh, yes. When I was playing I was "Ed." Then in Birmingham Dazzy Vance tacked the label "Satchel" on me, because I wear a 13B shoe. Not as big as Walter Johnson, though, he took a 15 size shoe. Walter was six-foot one inch tall and when he stood up the tips of his fingers reached to his knees. He had long arms, he did. I knew Walter very well. He was a gentleman... Yes, I batted against him and I couldn't get a foul off of him, mercy. He was too fast.

Q. Did he throw anything but fastballs?

A. That's all he ever threw. Now, listen, I get into controversies with people about pitching. I always tell them that Walter Johnson was up there for twenty-two years and he only threw a curveball in two of those years, his twenty-first and twenty-second years. For twenty years he threw nothing but a fastball. He was always worried about hitting somebody. That was Walter's biggest worry. He'd tell you so. Boy, he was fast!  That ball was just a buzzing.

Q. I've heard stories that when a rookie was up there facing Johnson and the game might have already been decided, Johnson might lob one in so the rookie could hit it well and be able to brag that he got a hit off of Walter Johnson. Paddy Livingston told me that's what happened in his case... Riggs Stephenson told me he was hit in the head by a Walter Johnson pitch. It was luckily a glancing blow. He says if it had been down here lower it would have killed him.

A. I'll never forget Stephenson playing second base in Cleveland. Tris, the manager -- he and I were pretty good friends -- he talked about him and called him "musclebound," and that he got it from football. He couldn't play second base, Tris thought, because he was musclebound. So he sold him to Indianapolis and they put him in the outfield and you saw what happened. And then the Cubs got him and played him in the outfield and you saw what happened. [Meaning he became a fine major leaguer.] Why didn't Tris think of that?  I don't know, maybe he didn't have room for him.

Q. Stephenson told me what happened. He hurt his knee running to first base. He tripped over the first baseman and twisted his knee so that he couldn't make the pivot at second base. They sent him down to Kansas City first to play the outfield and then they sold him to Indianapolis for Johnny Hodapp.

A. That's what happened?  Well, Tris told me that one day before that ever happened: "He's musclebound."... Tris was a great man; a gentleman. They had a lot of good men up there in those days. I think they did. Old Bill Carrigan of the Red Sox. He was great too. And then old Connie Mack... Yes, you had better call him "Mr. Mack."  Bucky Harris. You know Bucky is in a rest home in a chair. He can't even walk... I want to talk a little about McCarthy. Can I do that?

Q. Certainly; go right ahead.

A. When McCarthy arrived in 1931, Joe was a man who was always respected. In the clubhouse there was usually a lot of frivolity and fun. But when Joe walked in the door that was the end of it. They all respected Joe McCarthy... Yes, even the Babe; they all did. Everybody wore a hat, except the Babe who wore a cap. Joe said that everyone had to wear a hat or a cap. Joe was a quiet man; he never said much. Now here's what happened to me with Joe. In 1931 I had an average season and we had some good pitchers coming in. We had Gomez and Ruffing and Allen coming in and they were good pitchers. They were great. And you still had Pipgras and that old slugger, Pennock, who was my roommate on the Yankees for four years. Well I didn't get to pitch much. I won nine and lost five. Now we come into 1932 and now they've got a ballclub. I spent the entire year in the bullpen; I got into twenty-two games. I remember one distinct time that year with Joe in Cleveland. In the late innings, we had to get them out. It was the last of the ninth and Homer Summa was the first man up for Cleveland. We were one run ahead and Joe sent me in to pitch to Summa. I said to myself, "I've got to get that boy out."  They just wanted me to pitch to Summa a left-hand hitter. [The problem here is that Summa's last year with Cleveland was in 1928.]  I never will forget it. I give him a sidearm curveball and he pops it up to Joe Sewell at third and Joe lost it in the sun. But he caught it. Then another pitcher comes in, a right-hander by the name of Sherid. I never will forget that, but that's the way Joe would use me. I thought I was doing some pretty good relief pitching. Now we come into spring training in 1933. The papers had Zachary and me going to the Braves. I knew I was going somewhere. They had too many good pitchers and I was going down hill. I didn't have much of a fastball anymore. We got to New York before the opening day of the season and Joe called me into his office. No, I want to revert back to early August in the 1932 season. Art Fletcher, the coach, came to me one day and said, "Joe wants me to give you a message for him."  The message was, "You tell Wells that he's not pitching any, or very little, but he's going to be with us through the World Series" -- we had a fourteen-game lead -- "and I just didn't want him to be worried about us shipping him off for new players as we got close to the World Series."  That made me feel good, no kidding. That World Series check was worth $5,652. Joe did that. Now we come into the next year and he calls me into his office. "Ed," he says, "I have a letter here. Read it." It was a letter from Wilbert Robinson, who was then with the Atlanta club in the Southern League. He wanted to buy my contract for $20,000. Joe let me read it. I told him, "Joe, I appreciate everything you've done for me; you've been a gentleman. I'll never forget it." He started smiling and said, "You've got a friend over there in St. Louis named Bill Killefer, the manager. If I ship you over there I get $7,500. If we sell you to Atlanta we get $20,000 for you. I could call Wilbert on the phone and sell you to Atlanta. But I'm not going to do it. I'm going to ship you to St. Louis." You don't forget a man like that. Actually when they came to St. Louis, I'm the first guy to pitch against the Yanks. We win 5-1. After that game Joe comes up to me and congratulates me for beating his team. How about a man like that! He's in a hospital in Buffalo, New York, with a broken hip. I wrote him a letter just the other day.

Q. I interviewed him back in 1975.

A. You did? What kind of shape is he in?

Q. Well, he was getting around pretty well then. This was at his home. He got a little tired after awhile, so I didn't stay too long.

A. Well, I wrote him one of the nicest letters I could write to him and I sent him this picture to remind him of who I was. That was last week I did that... But I didn't have a bad manager in my professional career. Hornsby, Killefer, Huggins, McCarthy, Cobb...

Q. Where and when did you have Hornsby?

A. At St. Louis in 1934. Killefer was there in 1933 and they fired him near the end of the season. Sothoron took over to finish the year and then in 1934 old slugger Hornsby was there.

Q. Now how about Hornsby as a manager?

A. He was great, great. I'll tell you one thing about him, which doesn't happen today. Sammy West was playing center field and he sprained his ankle. It was all taped up. Well, the lineup for the next game is posted and Rog has West playing center field. Sammy saw that and went over to Rog and said, "Rog, I've got a sprained ankle, I can't play." Rog said, "Go out there and work it out; you can play." So he went out there and worked it out. Now I'll go back to something else in Detroit. Bob Fothergill had sprained his ankle. I'll never forget this. We needed a pinch-hitter in the late innings. This would never happen today. Cobbie says to Bob, "Can you wiggle to first base?" "I'll try." Old Bob Fothergill now. He usually pulled to left. Well, this time he hit one right over the first base bag down into the right field corner. He started wobbling to first base and about twenty feet from the bag he fell down. He crawled the rest of the way and got a single because they couldn't get the ball back in. [We chuckle.] Can you imagine ballplayers doing that today? They just don't do those things.

Q. They don't seem to have that kind of dedication today.

A. No, they don't... Well, I didn't do much in St. Louis. That was the time we was traveling in coaches; we didn't go Pullmans. Old Phil Ball, the ice man, owned the team. He was crazy about baseball, but he didn't have any money.

Q. You didn't travel by coach from St. Louis to Boston, did you?

A. Oh, no, just the short trips, like to Chicago or Detroit, where it wasn't overnight. The Yankees always traveled first class; Detroit traveled first class.

Q. What did you do on those long train rides?

A. I never did nothing, but Babe, Gehrig, Koenig, and Dickey played hearts. That's all they did. All I ever did was read, if I did anything. Every ballclub I've been on, there was never any gambling. I never saw any gambling to amount to a hoot. Very small limits when they did. But I've heard about the years before when there was quite a bit of it. It broke some of these players and their kids would go hungry. I'm talking about years ago when after the game they couldn't wait to get to the Brass Rail, the saloon across from the ballpark.

Q. You didn't see much drinking among players in your time?

A. Oh, no. The Babe would do the drinking. Beer... Oh, Gehrig was always in good shape. His parents were German. They were entirely different personalities, the Babe and Gehrig. Babe was a hale-fellow-well-met, while Gehrig was a reserved fellow. The kids would stampede Babe, but they wouldn't Gehrig... Yes, the Babe called everybody "Kid." He was a character. I loved that man... I never heard of any tension between Ruth and Gehrig. I never knew of any animosity there.

Q. Tony Lazzeri now. He had epilepsy, right?

A. Yes. Here's Tony. He had these epileptic fits. The funniest part about that was that he'd always have them in the morning. On these Pullman cars you were assigned a seat for the year. I had number six and I think Tony had number five across from me. He told me when I joined the Yanks and we went on our first road trip, he told me that if he had a fit, what I should do. He said they happened in the morning. He said, "When I feel it coming on, I'll wake you up and you get a wet towel and put it on my forehead. I'll foam at the mouth, but you take my tongue and hold it so I don't swallow it." Well, that's what I'd do. The fits lasted about four or five minutes.

Q. You actually did this?

A. Oh, yes; quite a few times. In 1946 we were at the Imperial Council session in San Francisco. Tony had a saloon there. We went down there to see Tony. His wife and little boy were living down by the river. Tony was living by himself. When we got home Tony was dead. He had fallen at the bottom of his steps and his skull was fractured. I think he had an epileptic fit and fell down the stairs.

Q. And he never outgrew this? It must have been a rather frightening experience to tend to one in this state?

A. No, you never outgrow those. Well, he said how he would do and that was just what would happen. I got kind of used to it. He said, "Hold my tongue, don't get excited about the foaming at the mouth, and put a cold towel on my forehead." That's what I did.

Q. I had a student in class once who was an epileptic and we were told that whenever she had a seizure, we were to put a thin stick or piece of wood in her mouth so she would bite that and not bite her tongue. She never had a seizure in class, however. Did Tony have these seizures very often?

A. No. It always happened in the morning... No Jake Powell wasn't in the league when I was there. I got out in 1934. Went to Hollywood, California. I was a mediocre pitcher up there, but I enjoyed it and the batters always respected me and, as I said before, I always had great managers. The owners were always very pleasant. And the umpires -- I'm telling you. An umpire misses very few strikes. And if they miss one they'll make up for it.

Q. Who was your favorite umpire behind the plate?

A. I had a lot of them. I was close to a lot of them. Old Bill Dinneen. Slugger Billy Evans. Slugger Morlarty when he was umpiring. Ormsby and Hildebrand. All them fellows. And the umpiring chief was Tommy Connolly. He was still umpiring when I first joined the Detroit club in 1923. He was there when I started that first game. I had a herky-jerky delivery. So Cobb took me in to see Tommy Connolly and said, "Ed, make that motion."  I did and Connolly said, "That's out."

Q. Did you have any trouble adjusting your delivery?

A. No. Here's what I did. [He demonstrates.]  To save all that time and energy I just shortened it all up.

Q. They all had that long elaborate wind-up and now they don't have any. I wonder why it took so long for them to decide not to have that windup?

A. I don't know, but I want to get to that bean ball. In Detroit, you know how Cobb was always in the dirt; he was living in the dirt. They was knocking him down all the time. So Cobb out there in center field would give you this sign [a twist of the wrist] and if you didn't knock that hitter down it was a $50 fine. In that day you expected to be knocked down.

Q. To keep the batter loose?

A. Yes, to prevent him from digging in and getting a toehold. That was a common thing for everyone, except Walter Johnson. You threw under the chin, or in back of the head so he'll go down. If you throw behind a man's head he's going to go down. The place a hitter don't like being thrown at is his feet. But you got to throw down there, carefully, or it will be a wild pitch with a man on base. But listen they used to hit the dirt -- aw, it was pitiful. They never threw at the Babe.

Q. Why not?  He of all people?

A. They respected him.

Q. Did the pitchers have any misgivings about having to throw at hitters?

A. I don't think they did... No, it never bothered me. It was all part of the game... Sure I hit some... Sure, in the head... I hit a man named Johnson, a utility man for the Yanks. Cobb gave me the dickens for that. We was way ahead in the Stadium one day and I thought he was getting too big a toehold up there so I decided to brush him back. I hit him right on the side of the head, right here. Down he went. He got up in about two minutes and walked to the base. After the game Cobb said, "Ed, you don't have no sense. As far ahead as we were, why pick on a dinky utility man and knock him down?  You don't have no sense." Oh, man, we used to brush them back; no kidding. You take Bucky Harris. He'd pull a little bit of his shirt out at the belly to get a nip of that ball as it came by. A lot of them did that.

Q. The umpire wouldn't give it to him would he?

A. Sure, he would. Just as long as he's standing in the batter's box.

Q. But if you don't make an effort to avoid a pitch --

A. But wait a minute. Kid Elberfeld used to be a shark at that. Sure, I knew him. He managed in the Southern League at Little Rock. I'm talking about fifty or sixty years ago... No, I never applied foreign substances to the ball. This, is all; that's all. And, you know, I never saw anybody cheating. The only fellow I ever saw cheating was Dave Danforth with New Orleans in the Southern League. You'd pick the ball up after his half inning on the mound and you'd spot that big wet spot on the ball. You'd show it to the umpire, but they would laugh at you; they wouldn't call it on him.

Q. He got into a lot of trouble in the big leagues. He did more than wet it; he scraped it, emery-balled it, and did other things too.

A. Boy, he knocked me down one time in Birmingham, I mean to tell you. He was a left-hander and I was hitting .300 in the Southern League, so he was loosening me up. The most vicious spitter I ever looked at was Ed Walsh. He had a spitter!

Q. When did you see him?

A. With the White Sox in 1923... Yes, he became an umpire for a short time, but he didn't like it. Now you take a fellow like Eddie Rommel. He had short fingers and he pitched that ball off the end of the fingers. Just like that. He never threw it hard, but it would spin, like that. He could do that all afternoon. He never went for speed. There was nothing to it. He'd tell you after the game that he didn't feel like he had worked any. Knuckleball like. I used to throw a knuckleball, but it's harder to throw. Listen, the trick to pitching is pulling the string on a fastball. It gets them off stride. You see, on a fastball, you grip it tight and give it everything you've got. The next pitch hold it a little looser, but make the same motion and throw it just as hard. Finally, you get down to where you are holding it very loosely and it is going up there at mediocre speed, but you are throwing with the same motion as hard as you can. You throw as hard as you can with your arm, but the ball is loose in your hand. They react to your motion. And then zip that fast one right by them. They don't know what's happening.

Q. How was Coveleski's spitball?

A. I was just breaking in then; I don't really remember. I remember George Uhle. He had the infernal screwball; he drove the Babe crazy.

Q. I talked to George Uhle and I asked him how he liked pitching to Ruth and he said, rather modestly, "Oh, the Babe never gave me much trouble."  [I chuckle thinking of all the pitchers that have told me that. I wonder how Ruth ever hit 714 home runs and had a lifetime average of .342 over twenty seasons.]

A. Uhle didn't. It was that screwball... Yes, old George could hit. And old Wes Ferrell he could hit. I pitched to his brother, Rick, in St. Louis.

Q. Who were some of the toughest hitters you have faced?

A. Now, listen, this sounds funny. You know, Eddie Collins, the Chicago second baseman. I could not get him out.

Q. Not many pitchers could.

A. But he's a left-handed hitter and I'm a left-handed pitcher. Eddie would stand up there and laugh at me. That's no kidding. I couldn't get him out for nothing. I'll tell you another tough one was Al Simmons. He could hit the devil out of me... No Lou Gehrig never gave me no trouble; the Babe never gave me no trouble.

Q. I suppose you preferred to pitch to left-handed hitters?

A. No, I preferred to pitch to right-handed hitters. I don't know why it was, except that it was just more natural. I'm trying to think of some of these good hitters. Hank Severeid of St. Louis used to hit me hard. The catcher. Earl Averill he hit me fair. But I remember Simmons and Collins, they were the worst... No, I never had to face Cobb or Heilmann. They were gone when I got to the Yankees. Harry Heilmann was with Cincinnati and I never will forget when he came up to me down in St. Petersburg in spring training, and he showed me his hands -- they were withering all up. He had something. Then he died a few years later. He was a broadcaster with Detroit and he died from cancer of the lungs.

Q. Did this withering of the hands have anything to do with ending his career?

A. He was about through anyways... Oh, I know who that shortstop was with the Yankees when I joined them, it was Durocher... Yes, Meusel -- I was only with him one year when they sold him to Cincinnati -- Meusel, Combs, and the Babe were in the outfield, Gehrig, Lazzeri, Durocher, and Lyn Lary in the infield. Bengough was the catcher and Dickey... No, Ben Chapman was still with St. Paul that year -- 1929. I never will forget when I was in the Central League with Ludington and we were playing Grand Rapids one day, and, what's the name of that old first baseman -- yes, Wally Pipp -- Grand Rapids, that was his home. He came down there and sat on the bench with us and said he had stomach trouble and I guess that was the end of it for him. But I never will forget Cobb. The first time we hit Yankee Stadium with Gehrig in the lineup. Cobb said [speaking of Gehrig], "He'll never make it; he'll never make it. He can't play first base." [We chuckle.]  You know what happened. Well, Gehrig never was an artistic first baseman.

Q. Perhaps his heavy body?

A. The most artistic first baseman I ever saw was Joe Judge of Washington.

Q. Did you ever see George Sisler?

A. Well, he was a little ahead of me. He was still around for two years while I was up there. He had eye trouble. Oh, yes, old slugger George. I forgot about him. Oh, you've got to put him way up there; oh, gosh yes... Yes, he was a fine pitcher at the University of Michigan. Came from Barberton, Ohio.

Q. Well, how did you pitch to Joey Sewell?  Did you ever strike him out?

A. Now, listen. Joe don't like this. I've got the clipping here. Did he tell you about that year he only struck out four times?  I had two of them. He don't like that, but I struck him out two of the four.

Q. He said that Pat Caraway of the White Sox struck him out twice in one game, the only pitcher to ever do that. He said that in that game, the center field bleachers were filled with white shirts and this made it hard for him to pick up the ball. But how did you strike him out those two times?

A. Fastball.

Q. Do you think the umpires gave him a break because they knew he had such a good batting eye?

A. Now, listen. With good hitters, umpires always bear down on those fellows. They give them corners all the time. Those umpires are fair. But if you get rough with them, they'll make it rough for you too. I'll never forget one day in Detroit with Bill Dinneen behind the plate. Ruffing was pitching and they got into it about some balls and strikes. And boy, Dinneen burned him;  everything was a ball. They finally had to take him out.

Q. I talked to Ruffing in Cleveland.

A. You did?  How is old Charlie getting along?  He was unhappy because he didn't get a baseball job; is that right?

Q. Well, he's had about three heart attacks and a couple of strokes, and he's in a wheel chair with his right arm strapped to his body. His mind is O.K., but he is so frustrated that he can't get up and around.

A. But old Charlie, when he got out of pro ball and wasn't active anymore, he resented it because he couldn't get a job in baseball. I read all about that. Jimmy Foxx got all messed up.

Q. And Ruth, too, he couldn't get a job. Nobody wanted him.

A. Well, you know, what happened about Babe?  Babe wanted to manage the Yanks. Old Ruppert -- Rupe called him "Baby," "Baby Ruth" -- said, "All right, you can manage the Yanks if you go over to Newark and manage one year." That made Ruth hot, so he went to Boston.

Q. Didn't they say that since he couldn't manage himself how could he expect to manage a team of twenty-five players?

A. I don't know if the players respected the Babe that way or not... Babe was a character; there was nobody like him.

Q. Do you have any Waite Hoyt stories?  I guess he was gone when you joined the Yankees.

A. No Waite and I were on the team together for one year. Now when I was with Detroit I pitched against Waite one day in New York and we won 8-5, but he got three hits and I got three hits... Yes, that was a pitchers' battle all right. He had the high hard one.

Q. How did you like it out on the West Coast?

A. Oh, I liked it all right. I was over the hill. Frank Shellenback was my manager at Hollywood and we played at Wrigley Field there... Yes, that was a nice little park. I enjoyed it. Old "Hard Rock" Lane owned the Hollywood ballclub and he got mad at Wrigley, so he pulled out of Los Angeles and moved to San Diego, where he built a new ballpark down along the coast. A wooden park close to the Navy Yard. So we moved down there in 1936 with Shellenback still manager. I was floundering around, so he sold me to Seattle for "Dutch" Reuther, the old Yankee pitcher. I went to Seattle and finished the season up there. I didn't do much there; I was through and I knew it. Anyhow, my good friend Larry Gilbert of New Orleans bought me during the winter. So here we come. I go to New Orleans and I can't get anybody out; I'd lost my fastball. So I go out there on May 6 -- I had pitched the night before -- and the first baseman for Atlanta hit me right on the kneecap with a line drive. [Paul] Richards, the next hitter up, hit me in the stomach with a line drive. Larry came out and I told him, "I'm done" and walked off. The next day was an off day. I go out to the ballpark to see Larry. "Larry," I said, "I'm done. Give me my outright release." "No, Ed," he said, "I'll tell you what you do. Let me call Donie Bush up at Minneapolis. He's managing up there; you go there this year."  "You mean I should pitch in that daggone old bandbox up there?  I can't get nobody out. They hit flyballs off me anyway. C'mon, Larry, let's quit kidding. I'm through and you know it." "O.K.," he said. "I'll give you your pink slip if you promise never to pitch another inning of pro ball." "That's a deal," I said. So that day, May 7, 1937, I got my pink slip and went back to Birmingham where my wife's people lived. I started looking for a job. I went down and talked to Joe Sewell -- I told you that last night. Joe told me not to be in a hurry. Anyway, I shopped around. That's the way I got to Montgomery and, good gosh, I've been here since 1937. It will be forty years the first of September this year.

Q. Did you ever get back to Ashland?

A. I went up there in 1941 to visit my brother. Then my brother died about eight years ago and I was back for that. Then my sister and her husband come down here and spend a week with me in May. I never go back up there.

Q. During your years with the Tigers how did you spend your winters then?

A. I stayed in Detroit selling radios... No, I never did much hunting in the off-season until I came to Birmingham and then I hunted. Haven't done much in the last two years. I played golf. That's my game... I married October 16, 1929. I met my wife [who has joined us by now] -- she's from Tennessee originally and her dad was foreman of the Alabama Gas Company in Birmingham. I met Ann in Birmingham in 1928. In January 1928.

Q. [Addressing Mrs. Wells] Were you a baseball enthusiast before you met him?

A. Not before I met him; I didn't know a thing about the game. [He picks up.] Now listen, Honey, when you started going to big league ballgames when I joined the Yanks, you women would sit behind the screen at home plate and talk about recipes. [We chuckle.]

Q. [To her] Did you go out to the ballpark much?

A. Oh, every day... Oh, I always got nervous when he pitched. But we didn't pay much attention to the game. [We laugh.]  All the wives sat together, except Claire Ruth, and she sat down in a box by herself. She really watched the game and kept a scorecard. And the rest of us sat up there and talked; exchanged recipes... No, Gehrig's wife didn't sit with us either. I guess she sat somewhere by herself, too.

Q. Who were some of the wives you sat with?

A. Oh, my. Tony Lazzeri's wife, Ben Chapman's wife, Earl Combs' wife, George Pipgras' wife, and -- I can't remember any more of them... Oh, yes there was a nice friendly spirit among the wives, but, no, we didn't pay too much attention to the game. When Ben Chapman's wife joined us as a new bride, and we stood up for the seventh inning stretch, she thought we stood up to sing "America." [We chuckle.]  She really did. She came from Birmingham and I came from Birmingham, too. She, May Lazzeri, and I would stay together when they went on the road... No we weren't allowed to go on road trips. [He]  The only one allowed on the road trips was Babe's wife.

Q. Special rules for Ruth's wife, too, just as there were for the Babe.

A. [She] and Lou Gehrig's wife didn't go either.

Q. [To him] What was Ben Chapman like as a teammate?

A. Ben was a very aggressive ballplayer; very aggressive. He was a fighter. I wish we had more up there like him. He played left field. And he had a temper. And it is unfortunate that he didn't get along with the fans in left field. They used to call him in on the carpet all the time. It was rough; a tough deal. So finally he went to Washington, and then he went to Boston. Then he started managing the Phillies under Carpenter.

Q. Did Dusty Cooke come up with Chapman?

A. Dusty Cooke came up with Chapman and here's what happened to Dusty Cooke. We was playing in Washington and the Babe was in right field. It was a terribly hot day. The Babe wanted to be relieved and Joe told Dusty to go out there and take Babe's place. Dusty went to make a diving catch of a line drive and broke his shoulder. That ended it; he never came back again. Now here's what happened to Chappie. In that same ballgame, something happened to one of the other two outfielders -- I don't remember what it was. Joe McCarthy looks up and down the bench. You see, Chappie was a third baseman. Finally he said, "Who can go out there in the outfield and play one inning?"  Ruffing got up. "All right," Joe said, "Charlie you go out there."  About that time Chappie got up. "Let me try it," he said. "All right, you go out there and try it."  And he stayed there in the outfield; that's how he became an outfielder.

Q. Wasn't Cooke touted as a much more promising prospect than Chapman?

A. Yes, sir, he was. That's correct.

Q. How about Jimmy Reese and Lyn Lary?  Were they before you or about the same time?

A. Jimmy Reese played second base and Lyn Lary played shortstop or third base. Now that was in 1929. Well, then [looking to his wife apparently] where was Tony?  [She] Jimmy Reese was up there then. [He] Yes, remember his wife stayed with you six weeks in Birmingham. [She] She sure did. That's two more, Jimmy Reese's wife and Herb Pennock's wife also sat with us.

Q. They paid a lot of money for Reese. He was another very promising prospect.

A. Yes, they did. He's still a coach on the West Coast right now.

Q. I think the Yankees paid a lot of money for both Lary and Reese and Reese didn't even stay around very long. Lary did, but he was only a journeyman infielder. Did Frankie Crosetti come up while you were there?

A. Yes. A good ballplayer. I'll tell you about Joe DiMaggio. I was in the Coast League when Joe was with San Francisco. Joe was a whale of a hitter. That year out there, it was something just to watch that Joe DiMaggio develop. Whenever we played them, you could just see him develop. He could hit.

Q. Did he have that long hitting streak while you were there?  I know he hit in fifty-six straight games for the Yankees in 1941, but he had a sixty-one-game hitting streak for the Seals in 1935, I think it was.

A. Yes, I believe you're right. It was 1935 and now I do remember it. Now here's what happened with Joe one night. They wanted to sell him bad, see. I was pitching against San Francisco and Joe topped a ball down the daggone first base line. I ain't alibing, but the grass was all wet. I picked it up and tossed it to first base and it went over his head. Joe ended up at third base. The boxscore the next day read: "Triple: Joe DiMaggio, 1."  They were trying to sell him, so they slightly exaggerated on that one. But he was a ballplayer, and he could go get them out there, too.

Q. He must have had all that grace and style right from the beginning.

A. Oh, yes, you could tell it. I want to tell you about Ted Williams. In 1936 at San Diego, we were out there practicing and here comes this long sixteen-year-old kid out of San Diego High School. Old "Hard Rock" Lane, owner of the ballclub, was sitting up there in the stands. Ted Williams goes up to the plate and right off the bat he practically loses the ball; I mean, he drilled it. Old "Hard Rock" said he was going to sign that boy at once. They put him in the outfield and he couldn't catch nothing. But Lane signed him anyhow. That's the first I saw of Ted Williams and that was the beginning of his pro career. He could drill the ball then and he was just a kid. What a hitter!  You're born a hitter and you're born a pitcher. You know that.

Q. Was Ad Liska out there then?  Sam Gibson? Who were some of the best hitters in the Coast League in your time there?

A. Well, I don't remember a lot of them. But Mike Hunt of Seattle could hit a ball a country mile, but he wasn't consistent enough; they never bought the fellow. I don't know why. He was six-feet six and could hit the ball a country mile, but he just wasn't consistent.

Q. Gene Lillard, that little third baseman with the Los Angeles Angels. Was he around while you were there?

A. Lillard?  Oh, that little fellow. I've forgotten a lot of these names until you mention them. I forget the little guys; they didn't seem to impress me like the big ones... I never will forget in Washington one day -- it shows you what happens, that the Lord takes care of you sometimes. It was that first year, or 1924, with Detroit. I start that ballgame in Washington and I walk the first three men. I fill the bases and Cobb out in center liked to have a fit. I stood out there and thought to myself that if I didn't do something, I was going back to the minors. Well, here's where the Lord was with me. I decided to give them everything I've got. I was going to rare back and just let her go. Darned if I don't strike out three men in a row. and we win the ballgame, 5-2. Now if they had gotten a hit off of me in that first inning I'd have been out of there.

Q. Now after you had been up for awhile and gotten over those "rookie jitters," and a tough situation would come up, did you get nervous?  Or don't experienced pitchers get nervous?

A. Oh, no. Now here's what happens; I'll tell you. When you first go up there you're nervous. I don't care who you are, how old you are, or how experienced you are. Actors and actresses will tell you the same thing. Before the show starts, you're nervous. Now you're pitching this day. Your team has its hitting practice and then you go back into the clubhouse while the other team has its hitting practice. Pitchers will do this. They'll lie down on a cot and go sound asleep. Then when you wake up and go out there to start warming up, you're nervous. You're nervous until the first pitch of the game and then it's all gone. I've had a lot of pitchers tell me that and that's the way it was with me. When you're first up there as a rookie, you're scared and anyone who tells you different, that's a lot of hooey. After you're established, then that's gone. Now Herb Pennock. I roomed with him for four years. He was a pitcher and a good one. He told me plenty about pitching, although I wasn't any kid by then. I was twenty-nine years old then. But his philosophy was great. How to take defeat and all that.

Q. Did anybody with Detroit help you much as far as pitching goes?

A. Now, listen; I'll tell you what happened. You see, I was known as "the pitcher without a curveball."  I had a nickel curve. But I had a whale of a fastball. And I had a whale of a slowball, that I could get over. It was a slow curve -- not like Rip Sewell -- but a slow curve, that I could get over. The more I started to curve it, it would slide up there just like that -- well, it was a slider.

Down in spring training one year, Cobb was still manager and Lefty Leifield was coach. He could stand out there and just flip the ball like that and the ball would break just like that, with no effort, right over the plate. I told Lefty that I wanted him to teach me to throw a curve. Well, he labored with me for hours, when it's all added up, and I never did master that curve. I have what you call a "stiff wrist." Now Herb Pennock when he threw a curve, you could hear his fingers snap clear into the bench. He knew how to do it, but I had a stiff wrist.

Q. So good curveball pitchers should have loose hands and wrists?

A. Oh, Bridges --. I think Tommy Bridges was the best curveball pitcher I ever saw. Man, it would come up there just like a jackrabbit and break off --. Earl Whitehill had a good breaking pitch.

Q. What did Lefty Gomez have?

A. He had a fast one. Lefty had something on the ball all the time. He could snap that ball.

Q. Have you any good Lefty Gomez stories?

A. I've heard a lot of them, but I can't think of any just now. One day we were winning and Joe McCarthy was sitting on the bench and everybody was loose. Joe would always chew gum. Joe took the gum out of his mouth and stuck it under the seat where he was sitting. Lefty asked him, "Joe, why do you chew so much gum?" "On account of you. You make me nervous the way you pitch." He works for Wilson Sporting Goods now. He's been out here to the house a few times. [I tell the old familiar story about when Lefty filled out the application form when he was going to work for Wilson. At the point in the application form where it says, "Why did you leave your previous job?" he wrote, "I couldn't get the last guy out." And we all laugh.] That's Lefty all right. I'll tell you. We were going to catch the train out of St. Louis one evening, Gomez had just broken in that year and was having a lot of success. We were older than he was and were giving him some advice. We said, "Don't let this go to your head; keep your feet on the ground." He said, "That's one thing I'm never going to let happen to me. I am going to keep my feet on the ground." And he did, too.

Q. Did he keep the team loose with his humor?

A. Oh, gosh, yes. You'd be surprised. I'm a left-hander like Gomez, but I was never popping off the way he was. I don't know what it is, but if you don't have a left-hander on your club there's something missing. That's the way a left-hander is. We don't have the same logic as you right-handers. Now Earl Whitehill was a left-hander and a good one. He didn't talk much, but he had good common sense. Poor fellow, he was from Cedar Rapids, Iowa, and he got in a car wreck which killed him. He's been down here and I've played golf with him.

Q. Well I've talked to a left-hander who wasn't very talkative -- Lefty Grove.

A. No, he wasn't. Well, I wasn't very talkative either and I'll tell you why; listen. Cobb told me when I joined the Detroit ballclub, he said, "You're a young man and I'm going to give you some advice: Keep your mouth shut!" And I did throughout my baseball career. So. When I was in Montgomery and the Yankees came through here, I went down to see Joe and Gomez and all my buddies. Later Gomez came out to the house for a visit. He said, "You know what Joe McCarthy told me today?" "What?" "He said you had talked more in half an hour today than in the two years you were with him." [We chuckle.] Well, when you get to be a salesman you've got to talk. I'll tell you another thing about Cobb. I had an old fellow in Steubenville, Ohio, he used to catch for the Cubs and while I was at Bethany he sold suits in a store in Steubenville. He said, "Ed, take your time out on that mound. Don't be hurrying about anything." Well, when I hit Detroit, I took my time. Now this is 1924 and we were playing in Boston and then we went on to New York. On the train Cobb came up and sat down beside me. "Ed," he said, "I want to ask you something. It's a suggestion I'd like to make. Don't be so doggoned "bull-whinish" out there. Smile sometimes." Well I don't know what "Bull-whinish" meant, but I was determined to find out. So we got to New York and I looked in the hotel dictionary and it said that "bull-whinish" means "clumsy, like a cow."

Q. How could Cobb manage from center field? Did you turn around for signals?

A. Oh, he did all right. He moved the players around. Pitchers didn't look much for signals except for that "duster" signal. But, boy, he rode some of his players hard. He took a humble guy like Ken Holloway from over here in Georgia and just give him an awful dressing down.

Q. Why would he do that?

A. I don't know.

Q. I would think Holloway would be the kind who needed encouragement and support?

A. I think so too. But he just gave Ken the devil. Nothing he did was right. I never will forget it. It was just too bad. But he really respected Johnny Bassler's logic... Merv Shea?  Yes, he was a catcher... Heinie Schuble?  He wasn't there. Heinie Manush was there. Cobb made him a hitter. He was from Tuscumbia, Alabama. Ty had a lot of confidence in him. He was a line drive hitter and a good one. I saw Ty try and teach Heinie. He had a lot of patience with Heinie and Heinie did what he was told. He made a whale of a hitter out of him. Of course, you had to have some natural talent to begin with -- you know what I'm talking about. He had a problem in the outfield in throwing to the wrong base and letting the baserunner get an extra base. Instead of throwing to second and stopping the runner at first, he would throw to third and the runner would go to second. Cobb tried to break him of that. Oh, I liked Heinie. Well, I didn't have trouble with anybody. And those umpires -- I liked everyone of them. I complimented them on their umpiring [he's about the only one I ever heard of who did that] and don't think it don't make a difference.

Q. Didn't you ever get thrown out of a game?

A. No, sir. Never close to it. One day Bill McGowan was umpiring behind the plate. A pitch came right down the middle when I was batting. I stepped out of the box, and said loudly, "Oh, gosh!"  Bill held up his hands and said, "What's the matter, Ed, what's the matter?"  I said, "That fool ball was right down the middle and I let it go by."  He thought I was complaining, but I was just mad at myself.

# Eddie Onslow

*Scio, Ohio, September 20, October 18, 1974*

"From Scio, Ohio"

Eddie Onslow, younger brother of one-time White Sox manager, Jack, lived most of his life in the tongue-titillating town of Scio, Ohio. It is a coal mining community in the east central part of the state. But baseball provided an outlet from the mines for both Jack and Eddie. Even though Eddie did not have much success in the big leagues, he had a distinguished career in the high minors, rubbing shoulders with many famous figures of the game, such as Babe Ruth, Ty Cobb, Sam Crawford, George Stallings, Bill Donovan, Jim Thorpe, and Hughie Jennings. Onslow lost his wife some years before I met him and he lived alone in a modest house in the center of town. It was sparsely furnished and a couple of worn throw rugs covered the bare floor. I visited him twice in the fall of 1974. The weather was cool each afternoon I was there and it was a little chilly in the living room. There was not much light either and as the late afternoon approached it became rather dark. None of that, however, dimmed the pleasure of those two wonderful interviews. Following the first interview, Eddie took me upstairs to a room where his mementos of the game were on display. His favorite, as noted in the interview, was Ty Cobb's last bat. He found Cobb a very congenial friend and companion. He also let me borrow a few pictures of himself and other players, which I took back with me to have copies made.

Q. Could you tell me a little bit about your family background?

A. My father was the superintendent of an oil company, The Home Oil Company, which drilled wells in western Pennsylvania. I was born in Meadville in 1893. I came here from Noblestown, Pennsylvania -- west of Pittsburgh -- in 1896-1897. Then in 1896-1897 I went over to Mount Peasant. My brother Jack was a catcher over there and worked in the coal fields. I was too young to play ball when I first got there, but later I played some around Wheeling.

Q. With whom was your first professional contract?

A. With Lansing in the Southern Michigan League. I was there a week and never played. I was disgusted, paying four dollars a week for my hotel room and running out of money. Finally the team paid me $37, which I was ready to use to go home. But I went out to the ballpark and the manager, Jack Morissey, said he was going to let me play a little. He didn't want me to play if a certain Indian was pitching, but I wanted to play so he put me in the lineup even against this Indian. We lost 3-2, but I got two hits and the Indian hit me in the back of the neck with one of his pitches. I started to play regularly after that and the team began to win. One Sunday we played Saginaw at Waverly Park, outside the city limits, since Sunday ball was not permitted in Lansing. We were losing 7-5 going into the eighth inning. We got two men on and the next guy walked to fill the bases with me coming up. They brought in a new pitcher, a leftie, and I hit a grand-slam home run. Going back to the hotel on the streetcar, Manager Morissey came up to me and told me to write my brother Jack, catching over in Fort Wayne, that I would be staying in Lansing all summer.

Q. I guess he thought they'd be sending you down, but the grand-slam changed all that. Tell me, how did you happen to sign with Lansing?

A. I was with Jack at Fort Wayne in the spring of 1911. They needed help in shagging flies in the outfield. That's what I was doing. Somebody told me that they wanted me to hit a few so I went in to see the manager, a man named Casey, and he told me to go up to the plate and hit a few pitches. I hit a couple of them very good. When I was finished the manager said, "I'm going to send you to Lansing." I said I didn't want to go. But Jack came over and urged me to accept the offer and go to Lansing, adding, "It sure beats working in the coal mines." I couldn't disagree with that so I went to Lansing. I can't remember now why I did not want to go there at first.

Q. So you spent the 1911 season with Lansing. How did things turn out for you that year?

A. Pretty good. [He hit .303 in 127 games, playing first base.] At the end of the year I was told St. Louis took an option on me, but I went back to Lansing in 1912. I was there for about six weeks when Del Gainor, the Detroit Tiger first baseman, broke his arm. We were playing at Jackson [Michigan] and Morissey told me that scouts from Detroit were coming over to watch me. I told him that I didn't think I could make it in the big time, but he said that I had as good a chance as anybody. Well, I had a pretty good game that day -- a double and a triple. One of the scouts, an old catcher, came down after the game and asked me a few questions. At supper that night I was told that I had been sold to Detroit and that I should return to Lansing, pack, and go to Detroit.

Q. What was it like your first time up there with Detroit?

A. It was a big thrill. The very first day I saw Walter Johnson. Outfielder Sam Crawford told me before the game that I would see the greatest pitcher I would ever see. During fielding practice I was at first base and Walter was warming up along the side lines right near me. It seemed that he threw so easy; no exertion. I said to myself that he wouldn't be too tough, just throwing it in there like that. Johnson hald already won fifteen of his sixteen straight games at that time and he was going for his sixteenth against us. We were scheduled to pitch some young rookie. Walter went over to our bench and asked Manager Hughie Jennings not to pitch that kid, but to save him for the next day. He did not want to win his sixteenth against an inexperienced young pitcher. So we pitched the veteran Jean Dubuc and Walter beat us 7-0. First time up I fouled out. Well, the next time I was up, Walter called from the pitcher's mound for me to get ready. He just laid it in there and I pulled it for a single to right. I got two of our four hits. That night in front of the hotel the players were talking about how fast Walter was. I broke in by saying, "As fast as he was, I still pulled him to right for two hits." For years after I would get a card from Sam Crawford with the note, "Are you still pulling them to right field?"

Q. I see they sent you to Providence in 1913.

A. Yes, they sent me down and recalled me a couple of times so I wouldn't be drafted by other clubs.

Q. Tell me a little about Ty Cobb and Hughie Jennings.

A. Cobb was wonderful to me. He gave me the last bat he used in baseball. I still have it here. [After the interview Onslow took me upstairs to a sort of trophy room and showed me Cobb's last bat. I took a picture of him holding it.] Ty was tough on the field, nice off the field. Johnson was the greatest pitcher, Cobb the greatest all-round player... Hughie Jennings was a wonderful manager. A nicer man you'd never meet anywhere. If you made a mistake he'd tell you about it in a way that you would learn something. One day when we were behind, they walked Red Corriden to get to me. Hughie called me over and said he was not going to take me out, but that he wanted me to go up there and pick out a good pitch to hit. If I hit a good ball and was out that was O.K., but that if I went after a bad ball that wouldn't be so good. Well I hit the ball over the fence for a home run. When I returned to the dugout Hughie said, "You picked a good pitch."... Cobb was helpful to me as was Crawford. Sam and Ty never spoke to one another, but they played well together.

Q. You had a good year with Providence in 1914.

A. Yes. We won the International League pennant that year. When our manager Bill Donovan went up to manage the New York Yankees he said not to be surprised if I were to go with him. I thought that was very good, but I was surprised because I didn't go with him. The next time I saw Donovan I asked him what had happened and he said that Detroit wouldn't let me go... Draper was the owner of the Providence club, a real estate man. Whenever he saw us in his office he talked big money -- make out that he was a big money man. He spoke with a lisp. One day we went in to see him and was told that he was not in. So I mocked his lisp and his big money talk. Well, he was in his office all right and he stormed out red-faced and cussing in a lisping way... I had an agreement with him once to get an extra $500 if I hit .300. I hit it and he wouldn't pay up. Jack Flynn, the old Pittsburgh first baseman, was a Providence lawyer. He told me to have that $500 part in my contract, but he still wouldn't pay it to me. I filed a claim, with Flynn helping out, so they finally paid me. Later Draper was forced to sell the club, but they couldn't find a buyer. So the International League took over the franchise and shifted it to Reading. I was sold to Toronto and the proceeds were used to help pay the club's debt.

Q. When was this?

A. At the close of the 1917 season. I was sold to Toronto, but was never sent a contract. Ernest Barnard, general manager of the Cleveland Indians [and later president of the American League, 1927-1931], learned about this and called me up and told me to come to Cleveland. I went there and signed a contract with Cleveland. However, the National Commission ruled against me and returned me to Toronto. I don't think I would have stuck with Cleveland because Barnard had a deal brewing with Milwaukee for a first baseman so I don't believe I would have stayed with them anyhow. I did get in a couple of games with them, however. In a game at Detroit the wind was blowing a gale. There was sickness on the club and Manager Lee Fohl said he was going to put me in left field. I said I couldn't play left field, but he said I was the only player he had left. We won the game, I remember that. Shortstop Ray Chapman, you remember the guy who was killed by a Carl Mays' pitch, he hit a homer in that game.

Q. What other teams did you play with?

A. In 1925 I went over to Rochester in the International League. I was there in 1927 when Joe Judge, the Washington first baseman, was injured, and Bucky Harris brought me over there to fill in for Judge. After the season was over I returned here to Scio when I got a call that I was being sent to Indianapolis. I

*Eddie Onslow, first baseman, Baltimore of the International League, in 1928. Onslow is an excellent example of a fine minor leaguer who failed to make it in the big leagues. In a 20-year minor league career [1911-1931], he played in 2326 games, drove out 2712 base hits, and batted .319. 1928 was one of his best years, with 114 runs-batted-in and a batting average of .346. (Photo from the author's collection.)*

didn't want to go to Indianapolis so one night I called up Jack Dunn, the Baltimore manager, who had always treated me right. I wanted to play for him. I told him what had happened and he said Rochester could not send me to Indianapolis without asking waivers and they hadn't done that. He told me to sit tight and he would get back to me. He called back the next day and said that I had been improperly sold to Indianapolis to help pay off some expenses at Rochester. Then he said, "You're not going to play for Indianapolis; you're going to play for me!" So I went to Baltimore and played two years -- 1928 and 1929 -- for Jack Dunn. Then he died and I quit as a player.

Q. What about some of the places you stayed in while playing ball?

A. In Detroit we lived in Somerset Hotel where all the players stayed -- my wife and I, that is. We were married in 1911; she was from Mt. Pleasant and stayed with me in Detroit. She went on the road with me quite often... At Providence we lived on Elmwood Avenue in an apartment house. The greatest place I ever saw. It was built by those people in Providence who made silverware. They didn't let just anyone in that place; they didn't want the wild ones. They investigated you before letting you rent there... We played at Melrose Park in Providence. It was a large ballpark and very nice. You couldn't hit the ball out of there very easily. There were nice clubhouse facilities -- down the left field line for us and down the right field line for the visitors. The outfield fence was painted neatly with advertising signs. They had a pretty big parking lot so some people must have had cars. The grandstand was single-decked from first base to third, covered, and then there were open bleachers down each foul line. The biggest crowds we had were when we played Brown University.

Q. How about your off-season activities?

A. Oh, I worked around here in the wintertime until I almost lost my thumb and then I quit. I worked at the coal mines and got my thumb caught in a car. It required several stitches to put it together again, but I quit that work. Then I came back to Scio to live and I bought a little store and pool room, which I ran for quite awhile. Some fellow ran it for me in the summertime when I was away playing ball. Then some other chap wanted to buy the pool room so I sold it to him... My brother Jack lived in Boston and he'd come here to go hunting with me occasionally.

Q. You managed briefly while you were at Toronto, did you not?

A. Yes. I managed the club there in 1924. I didn't like it so I quit. One problem was that the players wouldn't stay in shape. I had to make reports on them all the time. It was too much trouble...

Q. How did you fare as a hitter in your International League years?

A. Pretty well. I think I averaged out around .317. [He actually had a lifetime minor league average of .319 for two years in the Southern Michigan League and seventeen years in the International.] My greatest thrill? Well, we came into Buffalo one year for the last four games of the season. A fellow on our team, Joe Kelly, was hitting .336. The Ontario Diamond Company promised to give a $300 diamond to the player who won the league batting title. I was hitting about .332. Buffalo was a left-handed hitting club. A left-hander Weir was going to pitch for Buffalo. Before the game Kelly ran around the outfield and came up lame. Some players said he didn't want to face the left-hander. So he was on the bench and I played.

Q. How did you do?

A. The game went fourteen innings and I got five out of six. At supper the fellows were talking, saying I was now within one point of Kelly and telling Joe that he had better play. The next day a right-hander was pitching and Joe played. First time up, he flew out and I walked. Next time he went out and I got a hit. By Jacks, I got a couple of hits in three at-bats and he was one-for-four. Now I was at .335 and he was at .333. The boys told me to stay out of the game. Next day I got two hits and Joe didn't play. The last game -- Miller pitched against us -- he beat us and allowed only three hits; I got one of them while Joe didn't get any. So I won the batting title and got the diamond.

Q. Did the Federal Leaguers try to sign you up?

A. They came after me once while I was with Providence in 1914. I spoke to Manager Bill Donovan about it and he said that the Federal League might last for two or three years then it would fail and I would be out of baseball. I figured he knew more about the matter than I did so I didn't sign with the Feds. We'd go into Baltimore and the street divided the Federal League park from the International League park. They'd hit foulballs from their park into ours. The Feds had built a new ballpark there. That was the first time I ever saw Jack Dunn, the famous Baltimore Oriole manager. I was going into the park and I heard him scream at somebody, "If I had a gun I'd shoot you; get out of here." It was some Fed Leaguers coming in to try and get "Babe" Ruth. I went into the clubhouse and told the story and players said that was Jack Dunn. I hadn't known that's who it was. I spoke to "Dunnie" later about it and he said, "Yeah, If I'd had a gun I would have shot him. I'm glad I didn't because I would have killed him."

Q. What about Ruth?

A. I batted against him when he was with Baltimore. He could pitch, but I got a couple of hits. We were teammates at Providence. He never bothered anybody. They tell lies about him. That priest [Father Mathias] used to come and be with him at times. Babe would stand out in a crowd with his big cigar. If there was a crowd of men and a crowd of boys, Ruth would be with the boys.

Q. Cy Young?  [Cy lived in retirement not far from Onslow in nearby Paoli, Ohio.]

A. Cy was finished when I came up, but I used to go with him to old-timers affairs in New Philadelphia. The last time I was with him he wanted me to eat with him because he couldn't see the potatoes.

Q. You played for George Stallings?

A. Yes, I played for Stallings at Rochester. He always claimed that "the table was set" and that you couldn't "buck the game." He always claimed that there was no man in baseball big enough to "buck the game." By this he meant that with runners on first and second there was only one play -- the bunt -- to move the runners over to second and third. If you didn't bunt in those conditions you were "bucking the game." Something would go wrong, like a strike-out, a double-play, or something else. You bunt, or you "buck the game." [He gave an example of this in a game he heard the previous night, in which the St. Louis Cardinals blew a chance to win the game by not bunting in such a situation.] Stallings used to say that the bunt brought pressure on the pitcher and the whole team in the field. Any kind of sharply hit ball would score the man from third... Stallings' pitchers on the bench kept charts of bases on balls, hits, and errors. He said that bases on balls caused the scoring of more runs than hits and errors. He kept the bases on balls charted on a blackboard.

Q. Didn't Stallings have a sense of humor?

A. Oh, a little a bit. One day "Stinky" Haines [a football player from Penn State] went up to bat and struck out. The next time up he also struck out. When he came back to the bench he threw his bat down in disgust and said, "Hell, I don't have to play ball; I got a degree." Stallings said "Why don't you back to school and get a degree on how to hit a curveball?"... One day, going off the field at Newark -- it was the worst game of ball I ever was in. We went into the ninth inning ahead 14-4, and by Jacks, they tied us. We finally won in the sixteenth inning, 15-14. Walking off the field with George Burns I said, "What are you trying to do, kill our manager?" Stallings heard me. He said, "That's right; it almost killed me." He gave me the dickens. The next day we were 2-2 in the ninth. They had a man on first and Lew Fonseca hit a ball over second base which went right through the center fielder's legs. The man scored from first with the winning run. After the game some kid came up to Stallings and asked him for a ball. Stallings told the kid to "get smart." "Stand behind my center fielder and you can get a whole damn bagful of baseballs!"... Stallings was rough on his players; he'd just eat you alive, especially the pitchers. They said he had catarrh of the stomach and he would belch a lot. One day some young player was sitting next to him and the kid said, "My God, there must be a sewer around

*Eddie Onslow, first baseman, Newark of the International League, 1929. Near the end of his career, Onslow saw only part-time service in 1929. He split the season between Baltimore and Newark and batted .308. (Photo from the author's collection.)*

here somewhere!" "Young man," said Stallings, "that's my breath and by tomorrow morning you'll be so far away you'll have no chance to smell it." [We both chuckle loud and long. I've heard from a number of players about Stallings' strong breath.]

Q. That's a good one. Can you remember any more Stallings stories?

A. Oh, yes. He hated the color of yellow. [Herb] Thormahlen pitched for us. We went to the ballpark at 10 a.m. each morning and one day the sign painter came by. It was the spring of the year and he wanted to know what color he should paint the outfield fence for background. "Paint it yellow," said Thormahlen, "the old man likes yellow."  So the painter painted the fence yellow. Stallings came in and sat down on the bench. Eventually he looked up and saw the yellow fence. "Look at that painter," he screamed and raced across the outfield. He gave that painter the damnedest going over you ever heard. He got back to the bench and said, "Yellow, yellow, that's all I ever see. I get runners on base and look at the batter and see a yellow streak down his back."

Q. You said something about managing Newark?

A. I signed to manage Newark in 1925, but I didn't want to go there. Toronto had sold me there. Molin was the owner. I went over to see him, but he never showed up. So I went down South to train with the team and there were only eleven players on the Newark squad. I told the secretary to call Molin and tell him to send some players down. We were at Rocky Mount, North Carolina. The secretary said there would be players on hand the next day; they didn't come. One day the secretary came to me and said he had no money to pay the players. "I can't write any checks," he said. We were supposed to pay hotel checks weekly and the secretary said he couldn't pay the hotel bills. I spoke to the hotel manager and he said, no, the bills hadn't been paid... Well, one day a couple of players arrived so we now had thirteen. I asked one of these guys what position he played and he said he was a pitcher. He started to throw and "couldn't raise a lump on my arm."  I asked him if his arm was sore and he said no, that was as hard as he could throw. When we got back to Newark Molin had picked up a few players from Reading. We started the season, but weren't beating anybody. I spoke to Molin and asked him if he was satisfied with the team and he said yes, that if you didn't win the pennant you might as well finish last. I said to one of the players, "Frank, we are going to have a new manager and it might be you." "Not me," he said, "I'm going to quit." "So am I," I replied. We had a catcher, "Rowdy" Elliott, who was sued for non-support. Our other catcher had a bad finger. We really didn't have any catcher, although we got some semi-pro kid and beat Reading somehow that day. But this was all too much, trying to manage that collection. After the game I went into the office and told Molin I was finished. Later that day I went over to New York and into the hotel where Stallings' Rochester club was staying. I ran into Stallings and after I told him I had quit managing Newark he made a deal with Newark and in about four days I was with Rochester. That's the story of my brief managing experience with Newark and how I came to be with Rochester... You've heard of Earl "Oil" Smith?  He caught with Pittsburgh for awhile. Well, he's catching for Rochester one day in a real long game. I came to bat in the sixteenth inning. As I was in the batter's box Smith said he was tired and told me that he wished to God that I would break up the game so he could go home. By Jacks, I hit a home run and won the game and old Earl was able to go home.

Q. You knew Tris Speaker, I believe, the great center fielder for Boston and Cleveland?

A. Yes, he was managing Newark -- after his playing career was over -- when I was at Baltimore. We had a left-handed pitcher named Polson on the mound and I was playing first base. Speaker was coaching at first base. The score was tied in the seventh or eighth inning and Tris told me that if his team got a man on base he was going to pinch-hit. By God, they got a man in scoring position and Tris went in to pinch-hit and knocked the ball out of the ballpark to win the game. The next day Polson, who had a good curveball, told me, "I threw a real good curve at Speaker; I have no kicks, he hit a good one." When Speaker came on to the field I said to him, "You hit a good curve yesterday." "I knew it was coming," he answered. "You did?" "Yeah, he tips his pitches." Tris asked if Polson was a very nice fellow and I said that he was. So Tris said, "Well, then, here's what he does. Whenever he's going to throw the curve he looks at the ball; when he throws the fastball he never looks at the ball." After the game I asked Polson to show me how he delivered both his curve and his fastball and he did exactly as Speaker said he did. "My God," he said, "I never knew that." The next time we played Newark Polson was pitching and Speaker was again coaching first base. Tris called over to me, "I see someone has corrected his delivery."

Q. Do pitchers often tip their pitches?

A. Runners always steal off the pitchers. They always seem to do things that give their pitch away. One day I was watching a pitcher and noticed him lean over and roll the ball in his hand. His name was Jackson and he pitched for Buffalo. When I came to bat he rolled the ball in his hand and I let it go by. It was a fastball. He did not roll the ball in his hand before the next pitch, which was a curve. I couldn't hit his fastball so I waited for his curve. Miller, the Buffalo pitcher, did things like that, too.

Q. Were there many spitball pitchers in the International League?

A. One day George McConnell was pitching against us in Rochester and beating us. About the fourth inning I put some vaseline on the tongue of my shoe. Playing first base I put the last man out in the inning. After the out I rubbed some vaseline on the ball and rolled it over to the mound. The next inning McConnell gripped the ball, got the vaseline on his fingers, then wet his fingers and the vaseline burned his tongue and his mouth... No, I don't remember if that helped us win the game or not.

Q. Were you ever thrown out of a game?

A. I was down at Augusta, Georgia, in 1931 when I was managing the club at Columbia, South Carolina. Cy Morgan, the old Athletics pitcher, was umpiring. One of my pitchers kicked on some of the calls so Cy put him out of the game. I went up to him and said, "Cy, why did you put him out, you know we're short of pitchers? Why didn't you fine him and let it go at that?" "Ah, nobody's going to show me up!" I went back to coaching first base and it suddenly dawned on me that that morning I had seen Cy walking down the street wearing glasses. So I went back to him and said, "Cy, why do you need glasses when you're walking down the street and not need them when you come here to call balls and strikes?" Oh, did he blow up! [Chuckling.] "Outa the park! Outa the park!" Well, they had no dressing rooms at the park; we had to dress at the hotel. So I went outside the park and saw our bus. I went up and sat on the roof of the bus, from where I could see the game from over the fence. Along about the seventh inning we went ahead, 4-3. In the last of the seventh they got runners on first and third with one out. The guy on first stole second. The batter, a fellow named Smith, was leading the league in hitting. He ripped the first pitch down the first base line foul. So I yelled across the fence to our pitcher to put Smith on -- to walk him. Nobody said a word; Cy didn't say a word. The pitcher looked up at me and I repeated, "put the man on first base." So Smith was walked. The next batter hit into a 6-4-3 double play. The fans just about fell out of their seats, they were so mad at Morgan for allowing me to manage from outside the park and to tell the pitcher to walk Smith. Cy came over to the fence and pointed to me and said, "Don't you say another word and come down off of there." I said, "Go on and umpire; you don't have any jurisdiction outside of the park; I'm not moving." By jacks, the first thing you know, sirens are screaming and the police are right there at the ballpark. The police chief came over to the bus and called up to me, "Who's in charge here?" I answered, "I am." He said, "What's the matter, they can't take you off the roof if you're in charge." "I don't know what's the matter," I said. Well, the police went into the ballpark and talked to Morgan then came back out and said, "They can't do anything, you're in charge of the bus." We won 4-3. That was the only time I can remember getting tossed out of a game... Each club had its own bus down in that league.

Q. Were you with Detroit in 1912 at the time of the players' strike?

A. No, I came up later in the season after the strike had been settled. I do remember the players talking a lot about it... I do remember an exhibition game Detroit played that year at Syracuse. The club brought up a lot of minor leaguers to play in the game. The team went on to New York and the next morning held a meeting on how to split the money from the exhibition game. The minor leaguers barged into the meeting and started to tell the regulars how to split the money. I stayed outside. Soon the minor leaguers came storming out, angry that they had been cut out of the money. Later the regulars came out and [George] Moriarty asked me why I had not come to the meeting. I said I felt I was too new on the club and if they had wanted me in there they would have invited me in. They gave me a full share -- $87.

Q. What was George Moriarty like?

A. He was a big, nice man. He was nice off the field and on. If you struck out or made a mistake he'd come over to you and console you.

Q. Tell me about Ty Cobb.

A. I got along all right with Cobb. He had a bad knee from all that sliding. At Cleveland one day the knee was swollen and big. Jennings came into the dressing room and said, "You don't need to play today, Tyrus, with that bad knee." "Oh, I'm playing, all right today. [Joe] Jackson is getting close to me and if I don't play people will say that I'm trying to protect my batting average." Well, I was in the clubhouse and I watched them soak the knee in hot towels and bandage it. You had to go down about six steps into the tunnel from the clubhouse to the dugout. I walked through the tunnel behind Cobb and [Cobb] could hardly walk. He struggled up the steps beside the Cleveland dugout onto the field. The Cleveland players asked him how he felt and he said he was O.K., that he was playing. And he walked across the field to the Detroit dugout without a limp; no one would have known how bad his knee was. He played the whole game and got a couple of hits. Out there the next day he went through the same business. He played all three games in the series... Jennings always called him "Tyrus." If we were a run behind with Ty coming up Jennings would say, "Tyrus, get on there; the sky's the limit." So he'd get on and everyone was expecting him to go -- to steal. The people in the grandstands would come to their feet yelling, "He's going, he's going." "There he goes." He'd steal second, and maybe third. They might have him out by five feet or so, but he just took them right out of the play. He'd twist in the air. I never understood how a defensive man could stand there... Many years later I read in the paper that Ty was in a hospital from a heart attack out West. I wrote him and said I couldn't believe it because I didn't think Ty had a heart. [Meaning, I suppose, a compliment, in that Ty had no fear of anything.] I got a nice letter in reply.

Q. How did you get Ty's last bat?

A. We were down in Augusta training one year where Ty was living. It was after his retirement. When we arrived there by train I mentioned to someone if he knew whether Ty would be there at the ballpark. He didn't think so, but the next day we got all our gear out to the clubhouse, and by jacks, there was Cobb. We saw him at the ballpark and the hotel almost every day. He said he wanted to work out with the club. Some young kid was pitching and dusted Ty off. He said, "Young man, I'm going to teach you a lesson." So he drilled one to left field and then he drilled one to right field. Next he warned the pitcher "to be alert," and he whistled one by his ear... He said his clue to batting success was knowing where he was going to hit the ball when he came up to the plate, waiting for the right pitch, and then hitting it where he wanted to... Well, Ty had two bats with him during those days when he worked out with us in Augusta. He said he wouldn't be coming out to work out anymore and that he was through with baseball. A couple of guys wanted his bats and I said that anybody would be happy to have one of Ty's bats. He said he wasn't going to give "Old Betsy," his last bat to just anybody, but that he would give it to me. I told him how proud I'd be to have his last bat, so he gave it to me. I took it up to my room and packed it in my trunk; I wasn't going to risk anything happening to it. When I got back home I suddenly realized that no one would believe me if I told them that this was Ty Cobb's last bat. So I wrote him a letter and he sent me a note saying it was his last bat and I pasted that note on the bat... Every time I was in a town where Ty was, or he was in a town where I was, we'd look each other up. I was up at a game in Cleveland many years later and heard that Cobb was at the game. I looked around and found him down in a box seat. He saw me and insisted that I sit with him in the box.

Q. Did you know Stan Baumgartner, the old Phillies pitcher and later sportswriter?

A. Baumgartner was a big sissy. We were playing Baltimore and he was pitching a good game. They got a couple of hits in the last of the ninth. The next guy hit a high foul back to the screen and our catcher races back to the screen and makes a great catch and we win the game. Baumgartner raced over and hugged and squeezed the catcher. His wife always brought a book to the ballpark and when he was pitching she'd sit there and read the book. I remember that he was pretty self-confident. When someone would try to suggest to him how to pitch to a certain batter, Baumgartner would say that he could take care of the matter all by himself. By contrast, there was a pitcher named Jess Doyle, who would stop the game and ask the catcher how to pitch to the hitter. This was the difference between good pitchers and average pitchers. Baumgartner was a good pitcher, but he had a problem with the bottle. He was sold to Detroit and celebrated by getting drunk the day he reported. Cobb, then Detroit's manager, sent him down.

Q. How did you like Bill Donovan?

A. Good manager and a great guy. He couldn't be nicer. He knew baseball and had a great disposition. Whenever the going got tough he was at his best. One day we beat Jersey City, 24-4, and all the boys were celebrating and having a great time over this big victory. Donovan said, "Don't celebrate too much; this is a funny game; we may get clipped the same way in a couple of days."  Well, we went over to Newark and got rubbed, 26-8... I never heard him jump on anybody. If someone would make a mistake, he'd come into the bench and Donovan would talk to him nicely and say, "Now let that be a lesson to you" -- that was his favorite phrase. If you got an important hit and drove in some runs he was more happy than you were.

Q. You played under Hugh Duffy, the old outfielder, didn't you?

A. That was at Toronto. Hugh Duffy was the best manager I ever played for. Why?  First, he knew baseball and then he had a great disposition. He had an easy relationship with the players. Any problems he might have with a player remained just between the two of them. In Canada they celebrated Orange Man's Day. On that day the players got a lot of orange flowers, which they put around Duffy's locker -- he was an Irishman. He took them down and told the players not to do such things. He never swore. When he was upset he would say, "Gracious me!"  If someone would swear he would say, "That won't do you a bit of good."

Q. What was life like on the buses the players traveled in?

A. There were two kinds of buses: the ones you went from the hotel to the ballpark in and the other was when you traveled from town to town. They weren't different kind of buses, but they served different purposes. Once at Newark when the clubhouse burned down we dressed in the hotel and took a bus to the ballpark. Normally, though, we traveled by taxi from the hotel to the ballpark. You were allowed so much money for transportation and four or five of us would group together in one taxi. In the lower minors each club would own its own bus. Down South, in particular, we had team buses and the roads weren't too bad. We played nightball in the Sally [South Atlantic] League and we might play a game at Jacksonville and then ride the bus all night back to Columbia, South Carolina. We might arrive there at three or four o'clock in the morning. There wasn't much sleeping on the bus. We would sleep the next day and get up in the afternoon and prepare for the game that night. The lights were terrible.

Q. Who was "Snowball"?

A. He was a colored man at Harrisburg [Onslow managed Harrisburg in the late 1920s]. Every time there was a parade he would lead it on a white horse. And out at the ballpark he was always in centerfield in practice. When the crowd couldn't see him they started to crow like roosters and he would appear. So they also called him "Red Rooster." The people and the players used to tease him and have fun with him; they were always doing things to him... Bitter rivalry existed between Harrisburg and York. It was a disgrace to lose to York. When we played at York many Harrisburgers went over for the game. They would fight and everything. The Harrisburg people would come down to our dugout and tell us not to let those "pretzel heads" beat us. One day we were on the bus to York and about halfway over we learned that some of the players had smuggled Snowball on the bus. By jacks, we lost a double-header that day to York, 2-1 and 5-4. We were getting set to return to Harrisburg and had gotten on the bus when we noticed that Snowball was not aboard. He was standing near the door and the bus driver called to him, "C'mon, Red Rooster, get on the bus, we got to go." "No, suh," he called back. "I ain't a-riding with such no good ballplayers." So we had to leave him behind. But so many people were over to York that somebody picked him up and brought him back... We got $3.50 a day eating money on short trips like that over to York -- twenty-two miles.

Q. Was there much drinking by the players in your time?

A. It's a great game, baseball, but so many of the players become drunkards. I could never understand it. I remember the case of a young pitcher, who had a brother who caught in the big leagues -- I can't remember his name -- who Toronto brought up from the South one year. He was fine for awhile, but then started drinking and they had to let him go.

Q. Speaking of drinking, did you know Grover Cleveland Alexander?

A. The first time I ever saw "Old Pete" was when we were playing an exhibition game with the Cubs. The Cubs had a working agreement with Toronto so we played them once in awhile in exhibition games. I saw him then. The last time

I saw him was at Harrisburg when he came in with the House of David team. He just lay on the bench drunk. They were playing some local amateur team and I went out to the ballpark to see the game. He looked terrible laying there on the bench. I went home and wired Judge Landis about the situation, saying it was a disgrace to baseball. The next morning I got a call from a scout for the Philadelphia Athletics, who wanted to know where the House of David team was going to play next. I said Lancaster, so the scout went over there, got Alex and took him home. I just read in the paper that Hornsby was drunk half the time in his last few years. Most of the time when I saw Alex he was real nice. The only time I saw him drunk was at Harrisburg.

Q. Who were some of the other players you remember?

A. Well, there was Jim Delahanty, one of the five Delahanty brothers from Cleveland, who played in the majors. Of course, Ed was the most famous. But Jim was with Detroit. He and Hughie Jennings had a difference of opinion when I first went up to Detroit and he didn't play much. They didn't get on. As for his brother Ed, he told us that he believed somebody shoved him off that train over Niagara Falls in July 1903 to his death. He used to talk about how Ed could hit and he could hit!... Lena Blackburne was with Toronto with me. We were down at Savannah and he said to me one night "Let's go out and see Joe Jackson." Lena had been with Joe on the Chicago White Sox, I guess. Joe and his wife were now running some cleaning and pressing establishment there. Well, we went out to see Joe and I never felt so sorry for anyone in all my life. He claimed he got no money in the "fix," [the 1919 World Series] and that Chick Gandil got it all. Joe was bitter about it; he didn't know what they were doing. Cicotte and some of the others should have been thrown out but not himself. They implicated him without his really knowing what they were up to. Joe felt he should be in the Hall of Fame.

Q. Is bunting a lost art?

A. Yes. In the recent World Series where the need for the bunt came up they didn't do it and it cost them the game. I've heard Jennings, Duffy, Dunn, and Stallings all say many times that there was nobody good enough to hit away with two men on base. The only thing to do is bunt. It brings pressure on the other team. But they didn't bunt. The don't stress bunting much anymore and they don't know how to bunt. The game has changed; all they go for is the home run.

Q. I see you have a damaged finger there. Was that from baseball?

A. No that came from an oil well accident when I was fifteen years old. It happened to the right hand and I was left-handed. It didn't affect my play at all, except that I had to use a thick-handled bat. The thin ones would sting my hand. The accident occurred while I was pulling rods in an oil well.

Q. Talk some more about the old ballplayers you knew and played with.

A. Well, there was Davy Jones the Detroit outfielder. A wonderful fellow. He never got into any fights, had a good disposition, never bothered anyone. Catcher Oscar Stanage was the worst type of drunk. He was drunk about two-thirds of the time. Jennings would have a fit when he'd show up that way. Donie Bush was a fine, wonderful fellow. The Detroit lineup as I remember it consisted of Del Gainor at first base, Louden at second base, Moriarty at third base, Bush at shortstop, Bobby Veach in left field, Cobb in center, and  Crawford in right. Jones would alternate with Veach. Veach, my brother Jack, and somebody else would catch. Pitchers included Mullin, a deadbeat and a drunk, Dauss, a wonderful chap who lost his mind while he was still playing ball. He was from Indianapolis and he and Bush were close friends... Yes, my Dad did see Jack and I play together, but I never knew who my mother was.

Q. Have you any Jim Thorpe stories?

A. I was with Providence one year when Thorpe was at Jersey City. We were playing at Jersey City. Our manager Bill Donovan said he wanted to see Thorpe run, so he told the pitcher just to lay the ball in there. The game didn't mean anything. I never believed any human being could run like that. He hit the ball to left field and the fielder let it roll. When Thorpe rounded first base he was already flying. Never saw anyone run like that; didn't think they could. He was at third base in no time. In the same series he dropped a flyball, which cost Jersey City a game. After that game, on the way down to the subway -- there was a saloon along the way to the subway -- Thorpe and Reynolds, a Jersey City catcher, went into it for a beer. Some of the patrons began to heckle Thorpe for dropping the flyball, so they began to throw them out. All these bodies came flying out of the saloon just as I and some others passed by on the way to the subway. Next day we asked Thorpe what had happened. He said, "Oh, those Hunkies started razzing us, so we cleaned them out."

Q. What's this about a box in a Philadelphia hotel?

A. The team leaving the hotel would leave a message in the box in the lobby about how the previous series went, for the benefit of the incoming team. There would be a message about Waddell, for example; how many hits and how many foulballs they were able to get off of him. The old-timers said he was the greatest left-hander who ever pitched... "Bugs" Raymond?  You never knew if he was going to show up. He always went chasing after fire engines... Some others I knew: Jack Chesbro, Jess Tannehill, Wagner. Honus was always hunting a beer. McGraw was O.K.; he was flawless.

Q. Who owned the Detroit club?

A. William Yawkey, Tom's father, never really owned the club. He bought it and gave it to Frank Navin. He [Yawkey] had so much money. Charley Bennett, the one-time Detroit catcher and for whom the old Detroit field was named, owned the club but it was losing money. They were out at the ballpark one day talking about the situation. Yawkey asked Navin if he could run the club. Navin, a racehorse man, said sure, he could run the club. So Yawkey bought it and gave it to Navin. Later when Tom Yawkey  wanted to get into baseball, he wanted to buy the Detroit club, but Navin  wouldn't sell to him. After all Yawkey's father had done for Navin, he wouldn't sell to Tom. Tom wanted Detroit and only bought the Boston Red Sox after he couldn't get Detroit.

Q. You played with Carl Mays, didn't you?

A. Yes, with the 1914 Providence club. We were playing Baltimore one day. Cooper was pitching for us and Baltimore had a catcher named Fisher. The first time up he hit a double and the next time he tripled. Mays told Cooper to knock Fisher down. "Aw, I don't want to do that," said Fisher. "Go ahead and knock him down," said Mays. "He's taking the bread and butter away from you." So the next time Fisher came up Cooper decided to brush him back a bit. By jacks, he hit him on the temple and knocked him out. We lived on Elmwood Avenue a block from the hospital and the next morning I went to the hospital to see Fisher, but they wouldn't let me in. Back at the ballpark that day I talked to Cooper. He groaned and said he hadn't slept a wink all night. "That Mays," he said. "I never should have listened to him. I don't know why he talks that way; that's no way to play baseball. I didn't try to hit him; I just tried to brush him back and the pitch got away."  I went back to the hospital that night to see Fisher, but they still wouldn't let me in. He was in the hospital six or seven weeks and never played another game of professional baseball.

Q. Tell me about that sixteen-game winning streak Providence had in 1914.

A. We went on the road for sixteen games. Rochester was leading the league by two and one-half games. Donovan told us when we left that if we wanted to win the pennant we would have to do well on this trip. Well, we won four straight at Buffalo, four straight at Montreal, and four straight at Toronto. Twelve straight victories on the road!  And now we move into Rochester. They were still ahead of us by two full games so we hadn't picked up that much on them despite our winning streak. Their manager was John Ganzel. Babe Ruth, still one of our pitchers, shut them out in the first game. Then Mays beat them, 3-1. The next day when we came out on the field Donovan told Bailey that he was our pitcher for the game. Ruth said, "No, I'll pitch. Let him warm up in the bullpen so they'll they think he's pitching, then I'll surprise them and pitch."  Donovan went along with that and Ruth beat them in the third game. Then Mays beat them again in the fourth game. Those two won all four games. So we won sixteen straight on the road, moved into first place, and went on to win the pennant. Ruth hit a ball that day in Rochester that they marked high on the wall. That mark was still there many years later and no one else had ever come close to it.

Q. Did you know Dick Hoblitzell?  He was a neighbor of ours in Williamstown.

A. Yes, I knew him when I managed at Harrisburg. He was the manager at Reading. But I didn't know him that well and can't remember much about him. As for Del Gainor, he was a great guy. The last time I saw him he was a federal marshal in Wheeling. Yes, I don't think he ever recovered from that broken wrist back in 1912. It interfered with his batting. He would try to play, but the wrist would swell up and they'd take him out and put me in in his place.

Q. What's your opinion of Hal Chase?

A. The greatest first baseman I ever saw. He beat them all. Sam Crawford said to me one day to look at Chase and tell him what I thought. It didn't take me long to decide. The first play he had was on a bad throw from third base. He scooped it up cleanly, nonchalant-like, as if there was nothing to it. A few innings later there was a low line-drive like a rifle shot right at Chase. He scooped it up and fired to second base for the forceout. The throw back to first was a desperation toss. Chase hustled back to the base and back-handed the ball while running at full speed just as he crossed the bag for the double play. He was graceful and quick. Hughie Jennings would tell us to be careful about bunting when Chase was out there. He'd tell us not to bunt to Chase because he would probably get the ball to second base for a forceout. We should bunt down the third base line. Chase had a good arm, too... Later Chase spent some years with Cincinnati. Heinie Groh, the third baseman with the "bottle bat," was one of his teammates there. He told me that you could always tell by Chase's fielding how the money was being bet that day. If he would neatly field a bad throw you knew the money was on the Reds. If he missed such a throw the money was against the Reds.

Q. How did you get along with umpires?

A. I got along pretty well with all of the umpires except George Magerkurth. He was the lousiest I ever saw. "Steamboat" Johnson was a wonderful umpire in the Southern Association and I can't understand why he never made it to the major leagues. In the International League, Bob Hart was another good one who never made it to the top. I heard that some manager didn't like Hart and was able to keep him out of the majors. I don't know how Magerkurth stayed up there. When he was in the American Association he went into a hotel and beat up some player. He came over to the International League and he wasn't there long before he attacked Jack Sheehan, a little guy, and practically busted him all up. In a game in Baltimore one day, with the bases loaded the batter hit a pop fly behind second base which was dropped. The base umpire called it an infield fly and thus an automatic out, but Magerkurth overruled him. There was a big to-do about that and four or five players were thrown out of the game. After that the fans would yell down at Magerkurth, "What's an infield fly?"  He would steam... A little footnote on that Jack Sheehan incident. The players drew up a petition not to play in games Magerkurth was umpiring, but nothing came of it.

Q. How about Billy Evans?

A. Billy Evans was in a class by himself. One day Philadelphia was playing Detroit. Cobb was on first base and somebody got a hit to right. Cobb rounded second and was headed for third. The throw looked like it had him beaten by ten feet, but Frank Baker dropped the ball. Cobb saw the ball lying loose as he slid in, so he kicked it into the dugout, then got up and scored. Connie Mack came out to protest, but Billy Evans said, "Show me the rule in the rule book which says he can't do that and I'll rule on it."  Well, there wasn't any rule on that, but by jacks, they made one right away so that a baserunner could no longer kick a loose ball.

Q. What are some of the toughest fielding plays for a first baseman?

A. I had no signals with the pitchers for pickoff plays at first. You just had to watch the pitcher carefully and be ready for a throw. With two men on base you watched the catcher for a signal to throw behind the runner at first. The toughest play is going to second base on a groundball. The runner from first is right in your line of vision and you must learn to avoid hitting him with your throw. The bunt is an easy play. It is right in front of you. If you can't make the play at second you turn and throw to the second baseman covering first. I made a number of unassisted double plays and quite a few times I forced a runner at third on a bunt. I've been in a few triple plays. There were two men on base and a groundball was hit to the shortstop. He made the out at second, threw to me to double the batter at first, and then I threw home to triple the runner from second base trying to score.

# Edd Roush

*Oakland City, Indiana, November 2, 1974*

"The Pride of Oakland City"

Peg and I had a wild afternoon and evening on Saturday, November 2, 1974, at Edd Roush's home in Oakland City, Indiana. As I noted in *Baseball Players and Their Times*, "the good cheer flowed so freely that we lost all track of time." We barely returned to our base of operations in time "to avoid being locked out of the house by an unsympathetic sister-in-law." I sent a copy of *Baseball Players* to my brother, Howard, and his wife, Mabel, and received a lovely letter of acknowledgment in reply. It was signed "your admiring brother" and "your unsympathetic sister-in-law." I never thought she would have remembered, but we all had a good laugh over that. And we had many good laughs at the Roushes. Edd had suffered a mild stroke some months before which, he said, impaired his memory a little bit. But he was mentally sharp nonetheless; in fact, I thought his recall was quite good. Roush pulled no punches. He was blunt and uncompromising, with all of his good humor. For example, he detested spring training, did not think he needed it, refused to take it frequently, and proved his point as soon as the season began. I had developed the belief -- and still maintain it -- that players of this era played baseball because they loved the game. They would have liked more money, but playing the game was the thing. How many old timers told me that their biggest thrill in baseball was just putting on the uniform and going out on the field each day! Roush would not admit this. I am sure he loved to play the game, but he kept insisting it was only "a business" to him. If he did not get the money he wanted he would not play. And he meant it. Nevertheless he was a grand guy and gave me one of my most enjoyable interviews.

[As tape picks up Edd is discussing the inadequacies of modern players.] They're not ballplayers, they're clowns... Of course, they don't know the fundamentals of the game; who's going to teach them? And the managers and coaches today, were the same kind of players these guys are. They don't know anything about it. They put that lively ball in in 1920 and got along all right with it. Babe Ruth started hitting home runs. And before that, Cravath was the home run leader in the National League and "Home Run" Baker in the American League. They hit nine, ten, or eleven home runs and they were home run kings. The Yankees got Ruth and made an outfielder out of him. And the ball kept getting livelier all the time. [Eighty-three-year-old Mrs. Roush enters the room after cooking turnips and there is a slight delay. Edd himself, incidentally, was only eighty-one at this time.]... I had this damn stroke two and a half years ago and this side of my head is cold and this other side is warm. It's a damn nuisance, if you ask me. This side goes all right, but this other side goes in the wrong direction. But there's nothing you can do about it. I asked if you ever got any better again and they said, "Very seldom."  A young person might, but elderly people don't get any better. So I just keep on going along.

Q. You look fine.

A. Oh, I look all right, but this thing's a damn nusiance. I got out of the hospital and asked him what I should take. He said to take Bayer Aspirin and some other kind, but all the others ain't any good. I asked when I should take them and he said take one at night before going to bed. I said I'd never taken an aspirin in my life and why should I start now. He said I'd better take them or wind up with another stroke. So I said I'd take them. He said 90 percent of all strokes occur at night after you go to bed. You wake up with them. So you take an aspirin before you go to bed. I woke up at 5 o'clock one Thursday morning and they took me over to the hospital. But there were no doctors there; Thursday is their day off. Besides they only got one doctor anyway [chuckling].  The next day we went to Evansville [about fifty miles south] and I was in intensive care three days there. So he took me out of there and said, "There ain't a damn thing wrong with you, except that you had a stroke."  So he took me out of intensive care and put me in with another fellow. I found out later that the other fellow had a heart attack and they were afraid he might die. So they wanted someone in there with him. I was in there three days and the doctor came in and said I was going home, that there was nothing wrong with me. So I came home. I couldn't remember anything at first, but it finally came back to me. I had to go over to Petersburg one day for that fellow who managed the Mets -- what was his name?

Q. Gil Hodges.

A. Yes, they were honoring him and putting up a monument. So I went over there. But I didn't know it was Petersburg or where it was. [Petersburg is about twenty miles from Oakland City. Gil Hodges was born and raised there.]  But all that stuff is coming back to me now. Some of it won't come back, they said.

Q. Tell me how you got started in baseball.

A. Well, we had a dairy outside of town here, which my dad ran. Then he sold the dairy and we moved to town. He let the fellow who bought the dairy have the place for a year. When the year was up we went back out to the farm. Everybody kept calling up, wanting us to bring them milk. They didn't like the way the other guy handled it. So we decided to have my twin brother and I take the milk into town with us on our horse on our way to school. When we crossed the railroad tracks we turned the horse loose and he went back to the farm by himself. Then we delivered the milk and went to school.

Q. What was the name of your twin brother?

A. His name was Fred. He's still alive and lives here in town... No, there were no other children. We used to play ball with ourselves. In the summer time we'd work and then when the old horse got hot, we'd play ball awhile.

Q. Where did you play?  Did you have regular bats and balls?

A. Well, living on a farm we had plenty of room, but we didn't have any kind of a baseball field. And back in those days, you didn't have any bats or balls. You usually made them out of something. There was always something you could play with. And you could buy balls at the "Five and Ten Cent Store." They didn't last very long, but you could play catch with them. Of course, every town around here and every place else had a ballclub, back in those days. There wasn't anything else to do. So every Sunday they had a ballgame. Playing around like this in different places, well, that's what made ballplayers. When I was about sixteen years old, I guess, I started playing with the town team here. So I started playing with them in 1907 or 1908 and played with them in 1909, 1910 and 1911. About the middle of the 1912 season I went over to Evansville and started playing with them. I was with them a year or two until I went with the White Sox.

Q. You went to school here in Oakland City then?  Did you go to school all through high school?

A. I didn't go through high school. Back in those days -- ancient history?  What did I care about ancient history?  All the stuff you had to take wasn't worth a damn unless you were going to be a lawyer or a preacher or something like that. Ancient history?  Who the devil cares about ancient history?  It's all right later on, but when you're a kid you don't care anything about it. Algebra and stuff like that. Why, fizzle!  Arithmetic; I was pretty good in arithmetic; I could figure anything out. I went two years in high school and quit.

Q. Did they have a baseball team in high school?

A. I went over here to college [Oakland City College, a two-year school] to play basketball. I was there when I started playing ball in Evansville. We had a good basketball club. We could beat any of them around here. Well, I went there to play basketball and wasn't learning much. So one day he asked me if I came there to play basketball or to learn something. I said I was learning some things, but I came mostly to play basketball. "Well," he said, "if that's the way it is we don't want you here." I said, "O.K., I won't be back" [chuckling]. That was the extent of my going to college... No, they didn't have a baseball team at the college.

Q. When you started playing ball around here as a teenager, did you already stand out as one of the stars of the team?

A. Well, yes, I was always one of the stars. I could hit and I was fast. I could go get that ball, see. I was a good ballplayer.

Q. Were you thinking about a career in baseball at this time?

A. Well, you never really think about something like that then because it's too far away. They only had one scout back in those days -- each major league club had only one scout. I was with Evansville in 1912 in the Kitty League, which was Class D. In 1913 they went back to the Central League, which was Class B, two classes higher. They kept the pitcher, the catcher, and myself, and let all the rest of them go. In the first month of the season I was hitting .556. ... Punch Noll was the manager in 1913. Evansville was in the Central League through 1910, was out of baseball in 1911, came back in the Kitty League in 1912, and then the Central League in 1913.

Q. How did you happen to sign with Evansville in the first place?  Who signed you up?

A. Well, it was a fellow from over here -- oh, I can't remember his name. He came from just above Princeton and had seen me play. He was now the secretary of the Evansville club. He thought I was the best player from around here. We didn't have much of a ballclub there in 1913, but I was hitting .556 in the first month of the season and the scouts began to come to see me play. I went with the White Sox.

Q. Were you pretty excited about turning professional with Evansville, or didn't you think much about it?

A. I didn't think much about it... The first year there I got $80 a month. That was big money in those days. We lived on a farm; we didn't have any money. We came to town on Saturday with 10 or 15 cents... No, I don't remember who the Chicago scout was who signed me up. That was way back in 1913.

Q. How did the Evansville team travel around the league?

A. Oh, by bus or car, and sometimes, like going to Dayton, Ohio, by train. In the Central League you pretty much had to take the train around.

Q. Weren't you pretty excited about being a professional ballplayer?

A. Well, I like to play baseball. But sitting around of an evening and doing nothing, that was the part I didn't like. At home it was fine, but in the city there was nothing to do. After the game was over what were you going to do?

Q. Play poker. Go to the movies.

A. Well, I wasn't very good at cards and there weren't any movies back in those days. There just wasn't anything to do. The fellows would stay in an apartment house, maybe eight or ten of us, and we'd eat there and some of them would play cards. But that was too slow for me; fizzle on that... I'd get home maybe once a week while playing at Evansville.

Q. Who was managing the White Sox when you went up there in 1913?

A. Jimmy Callahan. No, I didn't play much there. I was only in ten games, pinch-hitting and that. It was toward the end of the season and since they were going on an eastern trip, they sent me to Lincoln, Nebraska. I left the White Sox in Cleveland while my stuff was still out at the clubhouse. They said they'd ship it to me, but I never saw it for ten weeks. I was out at Lincoln for about two weeks before I had anything to play with. They wanted to get rid of me and didn't want to take me on that eastern trip. I went with them to Cleveland, then St. Louis, and then back to Cleveland when they sent me away.

Q. You must have been a little excited about being up in the big time?

A. Oh, I don't know. I enjoyed it, but it was not necessarily a big thrill. Fellows talk about a big thrill here and a big thrill there, but to me it was a business. I

*Edd Roush, outstanding outfielder for Cincinnati, 1916-1926, and the New York Giants, 1915-1916 and 1927-1929, is shown here during his second tour with the Giants. Prior to joining New York in 1915, he enjoyed a distinguished career with Indianapolis and Newark in the Federal League. A lifetime .323 batter with 2,376 basehits in his 18 years in the majors, Roush was elected to the Hall of Fame in 1962. (Photo from the National Baseball Library, Cooperstown, New York.)*

was up there for business reasons... Sure, I knew I was going to make it to the big leagues. Most things I tried I usually made a go of it. Anything I really tried, I always made a go of it. I was fast and if I ever got either hand on a ball, I had it. I didn't drop them. I could hit and it didn't make any difference to me if it was a major or minor league; they still had to get that ball over the plate.

Q. You were still White Sox property when you went to Lincoln. Now about this jump to the Feds in 1914?

A. In 1914 I wrote to Mordecai Brown over in St. Louis, manager of the St. Louis Feds, I wrote Phillips who had the Indianapolis club, and I wrote Tinker over in Chicago. Brownie wrote back and said he had too many outfielders as it was, but if he heard of a club that needed one he'd tell them about me. I never did hear from Tinker. Phillips called me up and told me to come to Indianapolis; said he wanted to talk to me. I went up there and my dad went with me. I was only twenty years old. Dad asked me what I wanted. He said when we got up there I had better know what I wanted. I said that I thought $2,000 would be all right. O.K., he said, that's what we'll tell them when we get up there. If they don't want to pay it we'll go back home. So we got there and Phillips asked me what I wanted and I told him $2,000. He said he didn't think he could pay it. I said O.K. I'll go back home. I already had a job with the White Sox, see... No, they didn't know what I was doing. But Phillips kept talking and finally he said, "I'll give you that $2,000. I've already got five outfielders and a lot of ballplayers around here, but I don't know what I've really got. So I'll give it to you."  So the next spring I joined the Indianapolis club. We trained in Waxahachie, Texas. The wind blew all the time down there; it was blowing so hard you couldn't hardly do anything. You'd throw your glove up against the grandstand and it would just hang there. We went jackrabbit hunting most of the time. We opened the season in St. Louis and Phillips said to me, "You're our first baseman."  We had a first baseman coming to us but he hadn't joined us yet. He asked me if I had ever played first. I said I had in amateur ball, but not in professional ball. "Well, you're the first baseman anyway. He'd gotten a letter from the president of the Federal League who told him to go out and get some ballplayers. He had mostly minor league players, you see. You can't get along with minor league players and do any good. We opened the season and won three out of the four games in St. Louis. From there we went back to In-dianapolis and by that time the regular first baseman was there. So I lost that job. I wasn't the world's greatest first baseman anyhow [chuckling]. So we're going along, winning to beat the band. Right up there in first place. They played everybody in the outfield but me. I was one of the pinch-hitters. I went eleven straight times pinch hitting. Chappie Scheer was one of the other outfielders. So he put me in one day to pinch-hit for the pitcher and I got a base hit. No, Chappy hit for the catcher and I hit for the pitcher. He got a base hit and I got I two-base-hit. Two days after that he hit for the catcher and got a two-base-hit and I hit for the pitcher and got a three-base-hit. Maybe a week later, he put

Chappie in to hit for the catcher and I hit for the pitcher. He got a three-base-hit and I hit a home run. So Phillips said, "I've got to put you in the lineup; I've never seen such hitting in my life." So in about the middle of the season, July I think, he put me in left field and I played there the rest of the season. I wound up hitting .333.

Q. Why wasn't he playing you?

A. The other fellows were older and more experienced than I was. They had been playing in bigger leagues than I had. He kept me out so the more experienced players were in, but with that hitting he told me "You're my left fielder."

Q. Did the White Sox contact you that spring?

A. No, they already knew I had jumped to the Federal League. It was in the papers.

Q. Did it bother you that since the Federal League was an outlaw league you might have trouble getting back into Organized Baseball at a later time?

A. Oh, fizzle. I never thought a thing about it. They're always after good ballplayers. If you're good somebody will be after you. I wasn't worried. I was getting $2,000 over there and I had only been getting $125 a month before for only five and a half months, that's only about $600.

Q. Did you also feel that maybe you had a better chance to play than if you stayed with the White Sox?

A. Oh, I don't know... Yes, I met Comiskey, but he didn't mean anything to me, if you know what I mean. Back in those days, nobody meant anything to me. I was there to play baseball and to win.

Q. Who were some of your teammates on the Indianapolis team?

A. God, it's been so long ago; I can't remember those guys names... Yes, we had Benny Kauff in center field. He was a pretty good ballplayer. He was the greatest poker player, to hear him talk... Sure, he knew baseball. That's all we had to talk about. Kauff was O.K.; I never paid much attention to him really. Fizzle on him [chuckling]. I played alongside of him in the last half of 1914 and then in 1915 he went to Brooklyn and Newark bought our ballclub. Brooklyn took an option on Kauff and a pitcher. We got the pitcher back, but he kept Kauff. So I was the center fielder in 1915.

Q. What kind of a ballpark did you have there in Indianapolis?  Did they build a new one?

A. Yes, it was a new one. It had been a cemetery. They took the people that were in there out, took them to another cemetery and built a ballpark there. It was right in the main part of town... We drew pretty good crowds, but back in those days nobody drew very big crowds. Thunder!  Take the major leagues. If you had 25,000-30,000 people, you had a heck of a crowd. Take over in Cincinnati. We played many a game over there on Monday, Tuesday, or Wednesday before 800 people. They would come out more on Friday, Saturday, and Sunday. It ain't like it is today when they have more money than they know what to do with. They go out to the ballpark and half of them don't even watch the game. They're eating and drinking beer.

Q. And watching scoreboards explode. Did they have any Sunday ball in the Federal League?

A. Oh, yes. Pittsburgh didn't allow Sunday ball and neither did Boston, and one other club... Yes, Philadelphia. We and the Cincinnati club used to go over to Canada sometimes on Sunday and play an exhibition game. When we were in the East. I played in all kinds of places in Canada, every year.

Q. Who was your manager at Newark; Phillips still?

A. Phillips was there until July and I think they made McKechnie manager then and let Bill go. He had been our third baseman at Indianapolis and at Newark.

Q. Who were some of your pitchers?

A. Well, that's where that dang stroke comes in. I have more trouble remembering names and who we played, and things like that. I know them, but I just can't remember the names. One of them came from Cleveland. He had been a star over there... A couple of our pitchers became stars in the majors. The rest of them played in the top minor leagues.

Q. How would you compare the level of play between the Federal and the American and National leagues?  Were they pretty equal?

A. Well, they were to some extent because they took a lot of the players away from the American and National leagues. Now in 1914 we won the pennant over there in Indianapolis. Most of us were kids. Benny Kauff in center field had played in the minor leagues and the fellow in right field had come from Brooklyn. He lived in Pittsburgh and had been playing in the majors. Our catcher was Bill Rariden and he had been with the Boston Braves. Our second baseman had been with Cleveland... I don't think Cozy Dolan was in the Feds. I knew him in the majors.

Q. Well, what happened when the Federal League folded after the 1915 season?

A. When they folded up, Bill Rariden, a pitcher, myself -- there were five of us from the Newark ballclub, we were bought by McGraw of the Giants. I was over there with the Giants until the middle of the 1916 season, when Christy Mathewson, McKechnie, and I went over to Cincinnati for Buck Herzog and Wade Killefer. They didn't want Killefer and sent him to the Coast League. They really wanted Herzog to play second base. It was the 20th of July when we left them in Chicago and the three of us sat in the observation car that night going back to Cincinnati. McKechnie and I were glad to get away from McGraw. He'd call you every kind of a so-and-so he could think of. He didn't say anything to me because I wasn't playing regular. Matty came back and joined us in the observation car. He sat beside me and didn't say anything so McKechnie and I kept talking. Finally I turned to him and said, "Matty, aren't you glad you're getting away from McGraw, with all that cussing and stuff?" He said, "Well, I'll tell you Roush. I've been with that fellow since 1900, sixteen years, and that's home to me. I realize I'm through as a pitcher and there's a chance for me to manage a ballclub. McGraw arranged the deal for me to come over here to manage Cincinnati. And I'll tell you another thing. He told me to put you in center field and you'd make me a great ballplayer." Well, now I thought I had heard everything. Because I didn't like McGraw. But Matty said I was to be his center fielder.

Q. While I was changing the tape you mentioned about batting against Eppa Rixey.

A. Yes, the big left-hander Rixey was pitching for the Phillies in my first game with Cincinnati. I was a left-handed hitter. Of course, it didn't make any difference to me whether he was a left-hander or a right-hander. Well, I got three base hits in four times up in that game. I came up in the ninth inning, we're two runs behind with two men out. I got a three-base hit and tied the score. I didn't score and we beat them in the tenth inning, 5-4. Heck, Cincinnati thought I was a great ballplayer. Of course, I could cover ground; I had no trouble with that.

Q. Didn't you mention before the tape was on that you had trouble with "Greasy" Neale?

A. Yes. Greasy was a football player in college and he wanted to play center field. I didn't know that when I went over to Cincinnati. So I went in there to center field. Now when a ball comes out my way I holler three times -- "I got it, I got it, I got it!"  And I hollered loud. He wouldn't say anything. Now I didn't have to watch that ball, I knew where it was going. I'd take a look at him and if I could catch that ball and get out of his way, I'd do it. If I couldn't, I'd cut behind him. We went along about eight or ten days that way. He wouldn't say anything, wouldn't even talk to me. I was catching the balls because I was faster than he was. He was fast, but I was faster. He sat down by me on the bench one day. He said, "Roush, I guess you know I've been trying to run over you ever since you've been here."  "Well, I knew you were trying to do something, but I'm pretty hard to run over."  He found that out [chuckling]. "Well," he said, "from now on I'll holler. I'll go along with you and holler."  We got on fine from then on. And Greasy was a good outfielder, one of the best I ever played alongside of, as far as covering ground was concerned. I know in 1919 we won the pennant over there and we only had three outfielders because Sherwood Magee got sick.

Q. Wasn't Pat Duncan an outfielder for you then?

A. He was a first baseman. He started out as a pitcher and then they tried to make a first baseman out of him. Pat Moran was our manager and he said to me. "With Magee sick we only have three outfielders; what are we going to do.?" I said "Put him in left field and Greasy Neale and I will play the outfield."  He said, "You mean you and Neale will play the outfield?"

Q. That would be Duncan in left field then?

A. Not Duncan. He didn't join the club till late in the 1919 season. We had the pennant won before he joined the club. No. it was Rube Bressler, a pitcher, I told him to put in left field; he could hit, but couldn't play outfield. I told Moran to put Bressler in left field. I said to Greasy, "Greasy, you play right field and I'll play center and left" [chuckle].  Now I said to Rube, "You watch me on every pitch. If I want you to move back, I'll do this [moving his hand backwards], and if I want you to move up, I'll do this."  So that's what we did. I said, "Rube, you're just like all pitchers; you back up till you fall down. I never saw a pitcher yet who could turn around and go after a ball."  Well, sure enough, that's what he started to do, back up. But I knew pretty well where they were hitting off the different pitchers. And I had him pretty well set so that he didn't have to go too far. Finally, one day he backed up until he fell down and he caught the ball just as he was going down. I told him, "Well, you finally caught one." He said later, "That's when I realized you had to turn around and run after the ball." He made a pretty good outfielder afterwards.

Q. Why did Greasy Neale try to run you over at first?

A. He wanted to play center field... Matty didn't know he wanted to play center field and McGraw had told him to play me there. I guess by running me down Greasy thought he would make me not want to play center and he could have the position himself. But he wasn't going to get me out of there that way.

Q. What kind of a manager did Mathewson make?

A. Matty was just like all pitchers as managers. Well, they know about hitters, yes, they know if they're good hitters or not. But they don't know how to talk to you and tell you you're doing this wrong and that wrong. It takes a hitter to tell a hitter what's wrong with him.

Q. You're saying that a pitcher's experience is too narrow to be able to lead and teach players on all parts of the game?

A. Well, they only play once every four days. So what do they know about hitting? They know the opposition hitters, but not the art of hitting.

Q. Was Matty tough enough to be a good manager?

A. He was easy going, but he had a ballclub over there... Matty had an automobile; he was the only one there that had one. That was in 1917, the year the baby was born and my wife was here at home. I stayed in the hotel a lot of time. Matty would come by in his car while I might be standing out in front of the hotel talking to somebody. He'd call for me to come and get in the car. We'd be driving and he'd ask we what I thought of a certain player. "Well," I answered, "he ain't worth a dime in my estimation." "That's what I wanted to know," he answered. "I can get him for practically nothing." "Well, that's all he's worth." [We chuckle.] Then he'd ask me about somebody else. And I might say, "He looks like he's going to make a pretty good ballplayer, that fellow."

Q. He put a lot of trust in your judgment, didn't he? But you were still pretty young for that, weren't you?

A. Well, I came from New York with him. And this was now in 1918. I played with him in 1916 and 1917. And he had to have some ballplayers and I guess he didn't know anyone else to ask. I came with him and I didn't say anything to anybody that Matty was asking me for my opinion on players. Some guys would broadcast it. Maybe he liked that. In 1918 we had the short season that year and I think we finished fourth. Matty didn't come back that year. [Mathewson started the 1918 season as manager, but was replaced by Heinie Groh after he entered the army.]  That was the war year and Matty went across. And when he came back from over there in 1919 he didn't come back to the club. You might say that Matty put that ballclub together that we won the pennant with in 1919.

Q. He did a good job at that in a rather short time, it seems like?

A. He didn't put it all together, but most of it. We got Bill Rariden from New York. And we got the first baseman Jake Daubert from Brooklyn. Rath was already there; he was already there when I joined the club. He came up from the minors. He had Heinie Groh at third base, but we had trouble at second base and shortstop, Rath and Kopf. They finally settled down, but they weren't worth a dime except that one year. Greasy and I were in the outfield and we made an outfielder out of Bressler. He could hit and turned out to be a pretty good outfielder. He asked me one day, "I don't understand how come you put me in one place and then after a couple of pitches you tell me to get back toward the wall?  Why don't we stay in that same place for that same hitter?"  "Well," I said, "I play the outfield like I hit. That is, if the first two pitches are balls, the hitter is liable to go for a long one. He's likely to hit that ball harder; that's why you move back. If it's 2-and-1, he's still likely to go for a long one. But if it's 2-and-2, you move over toward center field; get away from that foul line over there because he's just going to meet that ball."  He asked me if that was the way I hit and I said it was. "Well, that beats anything I ever heard," he said.  "I knew I was in the right place, but I didn't know why." [We chuckle.]  Later on Greasy said, "I learned more about playing the outfield when I was alongside you out there than anybody else."  In that book, *Glory of Their Times*, Bressler tells about that in his portion. He tells about learning to play the outfield from playing alongside of me.

Q. Tell me about Hal Chase.

A. I knew Hal Chase from the Federal League; we were in there together. When I went to Cincinnati from New York, he was the Cincinnati first baseman. That was in 1916. I hit third in the lineup and he hit fourth. I was on there a lot and we played hit-and-run. I'd go from first to third on a hit  And he was hitting to beat the band in 1916; in fact, he led the league that year. Well, we go to 1917 and I led the National League in hitting. Along in the middle of the season they started talking about Chase betting on ballgames.

Q. Who was talking?  Did you hear this in the clubhouse?

A. Why, sure. Different fellows were talking about this. Heinie Groh, our third baseman, was raising cain about this. A ball would be hit to him and he would throw to first and Chase would be late in arriving there and the ball would go by him. The ball would tip the end of this glove and go past him. The ballgames he'd lose, no wonder Groh was raising cain. He would say, "The ball went right across the first base bag belt high."  Then it got so Groh would say to Chase, "Who are you betting on today?  I want to know how many errors I'm going to have today."

Q. Unbelievable!  What would Chase say?  Would he slug him or deny it?

A. Oh, Chase would never say anything. He'd just ignore it. In 1918 it became terrible. I told my wife, "There's one thing about it; we've got to stay away from Chase and his wife. There's something going on here. I can't tell whether he's throwing ballgames or not, from the outfield."  It seemed to me that we were losing ballgames we should have won. He was batting behind me and driving me in, but in the field, balls were going by him and I didn't think those infielders were that bad throwers.

Q. Well, Chase is considered by just about everybody as the outstanding fielding first baseman of all time. Everyone I have talked to who saw him play, agrees on that. So when catchable balls were going by him, it had to raise a few eyebrows.

A. Yes. Now he didn't bet against us all the time; part of the time he bet on our club.

Q. Now Mathewson filed a protest with the National League office about Chase, didn't he?

A. Well, in 1918, Matty's last year with us, we are playing in Boston. The last game in the series over there that left hander we had -- I can't remember his name; this dang stroke -- was pitching, he threw the "shineball."  In the ninth inning of the game, the last half of the ninth, we had them beat, 1-0. They had a man on first with two men out. Hod Eller, that was his name; he was our pitcher. The batter hit a ball to Lee Magee at second base and instead of him throwing the ball to first base, he threw it to second base and there was nobody there. Greasy Neale finally got the ball out by the fence and threw it in, but by then the tying run had scored and the winning run was on third. In the tenth inning of the ballgame Lee Magee was hitting ahead of me. We had two Magees, Lee and Sherwood; they were not related. So Lee hit a groundball to the left side of the infield which hit a stone or something and bounced up and cracked Johnny Rawlings in the nose. They had to take him out.

Q. What position did Rawlings play?

A. He was the shortstop. Matty said to me that he was going to send Magee down on the first pitch and that if I then got a hit we might win the game. I had a habit of standing up in the front of the batter's box and as the pitcher got ready to pitch I'd step way back and bring the bat back and be ready. Half of them damn catchers didn't have sense enough to stay back. They'd crawl up under me. My bat was in their face. Gowdy, I think, was catching, and he threw the ball out into center field. He got the ball, jumped back, and just threw. I'll take that back. It wasn't Gowdy because he was in the army. Magee got to second base and stopped. Hell, he wasn't even running; he was just trotting down there. Then he saw the ball in center field and he lit out for third and was caught about halfway to third. But then the ball hit something and then cracked the third baseman on the knee so Magee got to third base. On the next pitch I hit the ball over the left field fence for a home run which gave us a lead of 4-2. Well, in their half of the tenth inning, they got a man on first base with two men out and the batter hits a one-bouncer to Lee Magee. Well, he caught it and threw it over second again. Our shortstop, who thought he might do it again, ran over and knocked the ball down before it got into the outfield. So the runner got to second and there were now runners on first and second. The next fellow hit a long foul to left field and Greasy Neale run about a mile to catch it. So we won the game. We left there to go to Brooklyn. Well, I never go out on the field early before a game because I don't need any hitting practice or anything like that. As I went from the clubhouse under the stands to the dugout I ran into Magee coming the other way. I asked him where he was going and he said into the clubhouse. So I went on out to the field and the fellows were all talking about something. I asked what it was about and somebody said, "Greasy Neale knocked the hell out of Lee Magee." I asked what about and they said, "Well, they got into it about trying to throw that game in Boston yesterday." Well, that's the last we ever saw of Lee Magee. He packed his clothes and went on back to Cincinnati and we never did see him again.

Q. He was suspended, wasn't he?

A. He was suspended because he left the ballclub. They did get him later on for other things.

Q. Was Chase still with you now?

A. Yes, he was playing first base. He and Magee were betting on Boston in that series. Well, we played three or four games in Brooklyn and then we moved over to New York. After that first game in New York, I was standing out in front of the hotel; I think Bill Rariden was with me. A fellow came up and asked me if my name was Roush. I said yes and he said he was from Boston and asked if we knew where Lee Magee was. We said no, that he left us in Brooklyn and we hadn't seen him since. He said, "I'm looking for him because he owes me $500." "What for?" we asked. He said, "You know that ballgame you won over there in Boston?  Well Magee and Chase both bet $500 on Boston. Chase paid his $500, but Magee never paid his. If I can get ahold of that so-and-so I'm going to take it out of his hide."  We told him that Magee had gotten into it with Greasy Neale and we hadn't seen him since. This fellow told me that I had gummed up the works by hitting that home run. He said, "We knew better than to say anything to you; you might hurt somebody" [chuckling].

Q. Did any of the players say anything to Chase during these days, like Heinie Groh did?

A. We went from Boston to Brooklyn to New York. The first day in New York, Chase kicked the ballgame away in the ninth inning. Our pitcher came into the clubhouse after the game, tore his uniform into shreds and swore he would never pitch another game for Cincinnati as long as Chase was on the club. The next day out there, Chase didn't come out to the field until the game was ready to start. As he took his position at first base, Matty walked out to him and handed him his suspension, the papers which said he was suspended for the rest of the season. Chase turned around and walked right out to the clubhouse in center field and we never saw him again. They put Sherry Magee on first base and Rube Bressler in left field and we beat the Giants a double-header that day. I think we may have won three of the four games, or maybe we won all four.

Q. Maybe it felt good just to get rid of those two guys?

A. Well, they were throwing the games. We should have won the pennant that year, 1918. [There must be some error in the sequence of events described above. The record shows that Chase played only seventy games for the Reds that year, which would make sense if he was suspended sometime in the middle of the season. Lee Magee, however, played 114 games at second base and several more at third out of the 128 game schedule. This means he must have left the club just before the end of the season, long after Chase was suspended. The suspensions could not have occurred the same week as Roush indicates above.] We had a good ballclub, but good God Almighty, you couldn't tell if they were on our side or the other side. The next year we wound up with the pennant and won the World Series.

Q. Why didn't Matty do something about all of this earlier?

A. Well, I don't know. He was easy going and maybe he didn't know what was going on; I don't know. That's one reason pitchers aren't worth a dime as managers.

Q. But didn't Matty file a formal complaint with the National League office recommending that Chase be forever barred from baseball?

A. No, that was McGraw who did that. You see, Matty was McGraw's right-hand man. He played with him for fourteen years over there. He knew what was going on. He's the one who filed the complaint and who told Matty to get rid of Chase. [There is a flaw here, too. To set the story straight, someone, maybe McGraw filed a complaint against Chase with National League President John Heydler late in 1918. Heydler conducted his own investigation of the matter and in February 1919 completely exonerated Chase of any wrongdoing, despite what seems to me to be overwhelming testimony that he was throwing games. Once cleared of guilt, Chase was signed for the 1919 season by, of all people, John McGraw. He had played 110 games at first base for McGraw in 1919 when one day in August he was very quietly released and banished from the game by I'm not sure whom.] McGraw knew what was going on because he saw him kick away that game in New York; McGraw told me afterwards, "I couldn't let that guy ruin Matty."

Q. Then Chase was investigated by Heydler, cleared by Heydler, and came back to play again in 1919.

A. McGraw thought he could handle Chase so he took him. Well, he got into it over there; he got doing the same thing and in the latter part of the season McGraw got rid of him. He got rid of him and of the center fielder, Benny Kauff.

Q. Was Kauff throwing games too?

A. Sure. At least, they said he was; that's all I know.

Q. How about the 1919 World Series now?  Did you suspect the Chicago players were throwing games?

A. I found out about it after the first ballgame. We beat Cicotte 9-1 in the first ballgame. [Interruption and train of thought slightly disrupted.]  One thing on the ballclub. Everybody cussed on the ballclub. I had a hard time when I got back home in the fall. Going to church, it got so I didn't say anything. I was afraid to say anything, if I could get out of it. One time there in Cincinnati, there was a preacher who liked Matty. He used to put a uniform on and go out there and run around with the players. One of the pitchers we had, Reuther, didn't know he was a preacher. He turned around to him once and yelled, "Hey, guy, do you know where I can get some whiskey?"  "No, I don't" [chuckles].  When Reuther found out who he was he went over and apologized to the preacher, who just laughed about it.

Q. O.K., we were talking about the Series. Now after the first game you said you heard something?

A. Oh, after the first game, well I didn't hear anything then. We beat them 9-1. Now after the second game we travel to Chicago. The first two games were in Cincinnati. We beat them 4-2 in the second game. I caught a ball in the temporary bleachers they had there. The ball was going into those bleachers when I caught it. It would have won the game for Chicago if I hadn't caught it. After the game we all congregated at the Metropole Hotel and then caught taxis to go down to the railroad station. Then Jimmy Wigmore, once known as the "million-dollar newsboy" in Cincinnati, came over. He knew all the gamblers in town. He was a man by now, older than I was, but he worked there for many more years. Anyhow, he called me over to one side and said, "Did you hear about the squabble the White Sox got into last night?"  No, I hadn't and I asked him what it was about. He said, "They were in with the gamblers and were supposed to lose the Series to Cincinnati. They were supposed to be paid after each game, but after the first game they didn't get their money. So they had a meeting up in Cicotte's room. The manager, Kid Gleason, found out about it and he went up there. They had a heck of a go-round. I heard it all because my room is right next to Cicotte's."  He said that since they didn't get their money they decided to go out and try to win the Series. Well, I didn't pay much attention to it. You hear anything at a World Series. Anyhow, we went on to Chicago. We got beat 3-0 in the first game by -- I've forgotten who the pitcher was [it was Dickie Kerr] -- then we came back the next day and beat Cicotte, 2-0. The next day we won, 5-0, and then we go back to Cincinnati. They beat us, 5-4, in ten innings. The next day they beat us 4-2, so we had to go back to Chicago for the next two games. That year was a nine-game Series and you had to win five games. So we're standing in front of the Metropole Hotel with the other fellows waiting for the taxis to take us to the station when Jimmy Wigmore came over again. He called me over and said, "You know I told you that the gamblers had gotten to some of the players on the White Sox. They also have gotten to some of the players on your club." "Is that so?" "Yup." Well, I didn't ask him who they were because he wouldn't tell me anyhow, so I said I'd see about it the next day. The next day we were in Chicago and we're all dressed and manager Pat Moran called a meeting. I spoke up and said, "Before you start this meeting, Pat, there's something I want to say." "O.K., what is it." "Well, I'll be damned if I'm going out there on that field, and run myself to death trying to win the World Series when there's someone on this club throwing the games." You could hear a pin drop in that room. Pat told me to come with him and Daubert, too. We went into the shower room and he asked me what I knew. I said I didn't know anything for sure, but that I had been told that the gamblers had gotten to some of our players. I'd seen some funny things out there, but I didn't know if it was pitchers or what it was. He called Hod Eller in. He was pitching that day. He asked him, "Hod, did anybody offer you anything to throw today's game?" He said, "Yup." "What did he offer you?" "He had five $1,000 bills and said they were mine if I'd lose today's ballgame." Pat asked what Hod had told him. He said, "I told him if I ever saw him again I would hit him right on the end of the nose. I don't like those kind of guys."

Q. This was just you, Daubert, Moran, and Eller in the shower room still?

A. Yes. Pat told Hod that if he saw anything out there in his pitching that didn't look quite right, he would pull him out of the game. So we go out on the field and we score four runs in the first inning. We wound up beating them 10-5.

Q. You got those four runs in the first inning off of Claud Williams, wasn't it? [I had been told by writer Fred Lieb, who was on the scene, that gamblers had threatened Williams' life and family if he didn't throw the game in the first inning. He was a twenty-three-game winner, but was hopeless in this game.]

A. Yes, he started, but there were several others. We had one run in. I was hitting fourth with two men on and don't think there was anybody out. He was a left-hand pitcher and I was a left-hand hitter. Now I hit a curveball right over the first base bag. Those things were lucky. I could just as easily have had the ball go foul, or I could have popped up. The pitcher certainly didn't intend me to hit the ball over the first base bag. That's for darn sure. So there's no question in my mind that they were trying to win after the first ballgame. Hell, I caught balls out there -- I was pretty fast that day... Well, that was the end of it; we won the Series five games to three and we didn't have to play the ninth game. I never thought that much about it once the Series was over.

Q. You really felt the White Sox were doing their best to win the series after the first game?

A. I'm satisfied they were. Cicotte spilled the beans in August of the next year. He said, "We were playing to win after the first game."  But all the writers picked the White Sox to beat the hell out of the Cincinnati Reds. So when we won they had to look for some excuse to explain why they were wrong. But we had the best pitching staff in either league that year.

Q. Weren't there any strange plays by the White Sox, after the first game, that might have caught your eye?

A. We beat Cicotte 2-0 in the fourth ballgame and you know how they scored their runs?  A man was rounding second base and the ball was thrown -- well, it was not thrown exactly to the catcher; it was to his side. Cicotte was moving back to the plate and he tried to jump up and stop it. Well, all the writers wrote about how Cicotte should have done this or that or shouldn't have done this or that. Well, I knew different than that. Those writers were just looking for excuses because they all picked Chicago to beat the hell out of our ballclub. I knew they wouldn't beat the hell out of us because we had too good a pitching staff. Chicago had a better hitting club than we did.

Q. Now would you say that the Reds had a better club than the White Sox?

A. I didn't say that.

Q. I know. But your pitching was better than theirs and their hitting was better than yours. Now, overall, which club do you think was the stronger one?

A. Well, they say that pitching is 70 percent of the team.

Q. So you were better. [We chuckle.] They were both good ballclubs then and it could have been a great Series.

A. On top of that, Greasy Neale was the best ground-covering outfielder I ever played alongside of, and I was one of the best in the National League. So what are you going to do with that?  I was all over the place. In one game I think I caught nine flyballs.

Q. Do the fielding averages we see in the baseball guides, do you think they accurately reflect what an outfielder can do?  For example, you covered more ground than other center fielders. That really doesn't show up in the statistics, does it?

A. It doesn't make any difference. An outfielder is an outfielder and nobody pays any attention to him. Now an outfielder can save many a ballgame out there if he knows what he's doing. You go out to the game and all you watch are the pitchers, catchers, and infielders. You don't look at the outfield unless the ball is hit out there. Even then you don't look at where he's playing or what he's doing until the ball gets out there. When I watch I look at the outfielder and the moment the ball is hit I want to see if he's moving. I always started moving when the ball was hit. Two-thirds of them stand around until the ball's halfway out there and then they start moving.

Q. I heard that Tris Speaker was classed a great center fielder even though he played a short field. But he was fast and was able to go back quickly and get the balls hit over his head.

A. He was great. He was one whom I saw and tried to style myself after... We'd play Cleveland in the spring sometimes as we came north and I saw him play. We played Cleveland every spring. Writers would write in the papers that fans should come out and see the greatest center fielders in the game. I played a short center field too and I could go back and get them. When a ball was over my head, I knew where it was going.

Q. Did you ever make any unassisted double plays the way Speaker did?  He would play a short center field with a runner on second base. The batter would hit a low line drive over second which the runner thought would fall for a hit and he started for third. But Speaker, moving in swiftly, caught the ball and raced on in to touch second base before the runner got back.

A. [Disbelievingly]  No, I never made any like that. If that ever happened, something was wrong. Somebody didn't know what he was doing. [We chuckle.] But many a time I covered second base.

Q. How were you on assists?

A. Oh, I was up near the top on assists. I didn't have as good an arm as some of the other fellows had. But most of those with strong arms threw the ball away a lot of times. When I threw the ball it went exactly where it was supposed to. I got a lot of errors at third base. With a runner on first the ball would be hit in my direction for a hit. I would get the ball and throw to third, but it often hit a spot where spikes had dug a hole and it bounced to one side. I'd get the error though the throw was straight.

Q. Did it make a difference if you threw the ball on the fly or bounced it in?

A. Always bounced it in for the simple reason that the man has a better chance to catch it. If you throw it on the fly there's a chance it may go over the third baseman's head or to one side. If you bounce it, he has a chance to position himself and make the play. That's one thing they kept telling us: "Throw it on the bounce." The catchers would say, "Don't throw the damn thing on a fly; even if I catch it I can't do anything with it since the runner's sliding in."

Q. Were there any people who gave you tips on playing the outfield when you came up, or did you have to pick it all up yourself?

A. Oh, in those days, sitting around the hotel after supper, you'd talk over plays and go over different things that happened. They don't do that today. You go to a hotel today and you'll never find a player. I don't know where they're at.

Q. Did you take part in that double-no-hitter in 1917 between Chicago and Cincinnati?

A. No, I was out with a charley-horse. I wasn't even there. Jim Thorpe, the Indian, took my place. Kopf got the hit and scored on a swinging bunt by Thorpe. But I wasn't there.

Q. I interviewed Larry Kopf and asked him if that wasn't a great thrill getting that one hit in the game and he looked at me oddly and said something like, "Not particularly." [I chuckle.]

A. Well, I get cards and letters from people and they ask me about thrills. Thrills? What do they mean? Baseball was a business to me. You might call playing baseball a thrill, but it was business with me. When you play amateur baseball it was fun. But when you get into professional ball, it's like any profession, it's business. You've got to produce or somebody has your job.

Q. But hitting home runs, winning that game with your homer there or making a great catch, that seems to me that has to be fun and thrills.

A. Well, it's like going out here and working for someone and getting paid for it. It's a business and I think that's the way most ballplayers viewed it. [I could not get him to concede that playing baseball was fun. I don't think I had this kind of reaction from anyone else. I tried to stir him up.]

Q. Well, I just wish I had been gifted enough to have been a ballplayer.

A. I got tired of traveling all the time. It was all right the first few years, but after awhile you had seen everything. Those long trips from St. Louis to Boston. We'd get on the train in St. Louis at about five o'clock in the evening and we'd get off in Boston at ten-thirty the next night. We'd ride all night, all the next day, and get in at ten-thirty. I never had any trouble sleeping on the train.

Q. That home run that won the game was hit to left field. You were a left-hand hitter. Could you hit to all fields?

A. Yes. In batting practice I worked at hitting the ball to all fields. Then when the game started I knew what I was going to do... Back in those days we were able to hit with power, but we didn't have a lively ball. I led the league in 1919 with a .321 average with the dead ball and in the next couple of years I hit around .350 with a lively ball and I wasn't even close to leading the league. Hornsby started leading the league.

Q. Did you play with Hornsby?  What was he like?

A. Sure I played with him in 1927 at New York. He was a fellow who loved to shoot craps. He didn't smoke or chew; he might take a drink once in awhile. But he'd sit and shoot craps all night. That's the reason he didn't have any money. He was always broke.

Q. It strikes me as rather strange that he was so strict in some respects, yet he was an inveterate gambler.

A. Yes. We played together in New York where I hit third and he hit fourth. He was hard to get along with if you tried to cross him or do something. I got along with him because I just went along with him. He's Hornsby and I'm Roush. You're no better than I am and he knew that and we got along all right. Like over there in 1927. McGraw got erysipelas in his face and was out of there for half the season. Hornsby ran the ballclub. I had played against him so damned often. I never will forget one time over there in St. Louis. Come the eighth inning. I was playing right field. I told the pitcher to throw Hornsby nothing but fastballs and he'd hit to right field. So he hit to right field. He wasn't doing too well against us with the whole defense shifted toward right field. He would get hits through the infield all right, but we were playing him pretty well. He told me one time, "Hit one down to me and I'll give you a base hit." I said, "I'll never hit one your way at all." I knew what he wanted; he wanted me to give him a base hit in right field. "I don't want none of your base hits."

Q. He wanted you to play out of position so his line drives would start falling in?

A. Sure. Fizzle on that. Now don't misunderstand me. He was a great hitter and he didn't have to do anything like that. But some fellows do some damn things that they're probably sorry for later. But he was just having a hell of a time getting a base hit against the Cincinnati ballclub. Rogers was all right. He was managing New York there when McGraw was out and we were in fourth or fifth place when he took over. We had the best club in the league. McGraw wouldn't pitch Grimes, saying he was a hot weather pitcher. When Hornsby took over, he pitched Grimes. Back to McGraw. We'd go into Chicago and that center-fielder they had there -- Hack Wilson. When we went over their batting order before the game and we got to Wilson, McGraw said, "We'll pitch high to Wilson; high inside or high outside." After he got through he asked for any ideas and I said I had one. "You're not going to pitch high to Wilson in this park or he'll hit them over the right field fence all day on you." He said, "I ought to know how to pitch to Hack Wilson; we had him on our club." "Yes," I answered, "and we ran him off your club pitching low to him." He hit seven over that right field fence in that series pitching high to him. Grimes got him out and he was a spitball pitcher. So McGraw was a good offensive manager, but on defense I didn't think he was very good. Next time we were in Chicago, Hornsby was now managing for McGraw. We went down the lineup and got to Hack Wilson and Hornsby said we were going to pitch high to him. I interrupted him and said, "You're going to pitch high to Wilson when last time we were here he hit seven over the fence when we pitched high to him." "Well," Hornsby answered, "that's the way McGraw said. If you fellows know how to get him out pitch the other way." We didn't have any trouble pitching low to him. I never could figure that out. When I went over to McGraw he said to me, "You have a guy over with Cincinnati who we can't get out?" "Who's that?" "Bressler." I said, "You're pitching high to him. Pitch low to him and you won't have any trouble." He said, "You can't pitch low to him because he crouches down over the plate like that." I said, "He crouches like that because he's near-sighted. He can't see that ball down there. So that's where you should pitch him."

Q. Didn't it bother him out in left field being near-sighted?

A. It didn't bother him too much. I don't really know about that. All I know is what he told me, that he had to crouch down low at the plate because he couldn't see the ball.

Q. Who was your manager in Cincinnati after Moran?

A. I can't remember his name; that's where this dang stroke comes in. He was a lawyer and then got into baseball and managed the Indianapolis club over here for awhile. [Moran managed through the 1923 season, then Jack Hendricks took over for 1924.]

Q. Now after you had won those batting titles in 1917 and 1919, did you have any contract troubles for the next year?

A. I had contract troubles all the time. [We chuckle.]   I'll tell you, back in those days they didn't want to pay anybody anything. Of course, when I went over to Cincinnati, everybody there had a share of stock in the club. They just kept selling stock to get somebody to run the ballclub. In the fall of 1918 over there, after I won the batting title in 1917, and we almost won the pennant in 1918, people began to come out to the game; they began making a little money. In the fall and winter of 1918 they reorganized the ballclub over there and got more people to put some money into the club. On top of that we won the pennant in 1919. They had some money to buy a couple or three ballplayers, which was all we needed. And we won the dang pennant. Now we had plenty of people coming out. They were making plenty of money. But like everything else they didn't want to pay it to the players. That was all right with me. "If you don't want to pay it, I'll be down in Oakland City, Indiana. When you're ready to pay, you know what I want and where I live, you call me up and I'll join the ballclub." Fizzle. I was out one year until the 20th of July, I think.

Q. What year was that?

A. It was 1922.

Q. That would be about right. You played forty-nine games that year.

A. Yes, that's what it was. I came back the next year and in 1923, 1924, and 1925 -- wait a minute now. In 1923 I had a one-year contract for $18,000. In 1924, 1925, and 1926, I had a three-year contract for $19,000 a year. That was good money back in those days.

Q. Did you ask for the three-year contract or did they offer it to you?

A. They offered it to me. They were having trouble with me every year so they thought it would be a good idea to give me a three-year contract. Heck, they're going to have to pay me anyhow and I'm up there hitting about .350 every year. And on top of that I could go and get that ball. A lot of times you get a good fielder who can't hit or a good hitter who can't field. Then when you can get a fellow who can do both things and besides that, I was a good baserunner. I wasn't a good base-stealer. There was a lot of difference in those days in stealing a base and today. Those pitchers half-balked and everything else to keep you on base. Today a pitcher can't hardly look over there. These guys today couldn't steal against what we had to put up with. And you talk about hitting. Up here was the zone, now it's from here to here. Why good God Almighty. I had many a ball called on me up here [high-high]. As long as it wasn't a third strike it wasn't too bad. But from here to here was the strike zone. Fizzle.

Q. I understand you didn't have a very high opinion of spring training? [We chuckle.]

A. Back in those days the outfield was full of sand. We'd have to run around in sand that deep.

Q. But didn't you have to get in shape; get your batting eye in tune [knowing what he would say, but wanting to have him say it].

A. I was always in shape. You give me a couple of days and I'm ready to open the season.

Q. Do you think spring training is too long?

A. For these guys today maybe, but what are they doing with their time; what do they know? They can't hit anyhow so what's the difference. Why, fizzle. I watch them and good God; they ought to go back where they came from.

Q. Why did Cincinnati trade you?

A. Sure, there was a reason. The three-year contract was up. I'll tell you the truth, what the real reason was. The board of directors of the Cincinnati club didn't like me. Garry Herrmann owned the club and his son-in-law Sidney Weil was in there, too. And after I was traded to New York and we were playing Cincinnati, I got to talking with Weil. You know what he told me? He said "You know something?" "What?" "You know what Mr. Herrmann told me to do?" "What?" "He told me to sell my stock in the club." "What for?" "He told me to get rid of my stock while it was still worth something. They got rid of Roush and this ballclub is going to the bottom. He kept this ballclub going and in no time they're going to be on the bottom." I tried to console Weil by telling him that "You're not going to finish on the bottom right away. You'll be fourth or fifth this year, and sixth or seventh next year, and then maybe in 1929 you'll get down there to the bottom." He said, "Do you think so?" I said "I know damn good and well you will. You don't have any ballclub. Nobody wants to play for Hendricks."

Q. That's the guy we were trying to think of who came after Moran, wasn't it?

A. Yes, he's the one I couldn't remember. He didn't know anything about baseball.

Q. Why did they make him manager then?   Nobody liked him.

A. Just between you and I, I don't know what your religion is or anybody else's, but he was a Catholic and one or two of the players on the Cincinnati directors were Catholics, and that was it. We had trouble on the ballclub one time over there, the third baseman and the shortstop and six or seven others, were Catholics. And they done to suit themselves, and the rest of us were out there trying to win ballgames. Finally we got into it one day. I said, "I'm going to tell you guys something. The backbone of this ballclub are all masons and you don't hear anybody say a damn word about the masons, do you?  We don't brag about it, but you guys are Catholics and you brag about it. And I want to tell you something. Now unless you get out there and start playing baseball and stop bragging about being Catholics, this ballclub is going to go to hell. And it won't take long."  Hendricks was a Catholic, see.

Q. You mean he was favoring Catholics on the team?

A. Sure, he was!  The thing changed right then and there. They went out and went to hustling. "If I opened my mouth about you guys in this gol-danged town, you'd be in a hell of a mess. The German Protestants in this town would run you out of town. Things like this shouldn't even come up. We're here trying to win baseball games."

Q. And you think Hendricks was the reason it came up?

A. Why, sure. He made a remark there one day about me. And don't think the fans didn't raise hell about that. I don't know what he said.

Q. I've talked to a couple of people who played under Jack Hendricks and I got the idea that he must have been a terrible person to play under.

A. He didn't know anything about baseball, in my estimation. He was just out there and couldn't tell you what to do. He never played it himself. He got into baseball in Indianapolis up here in the American Association. He was a lawyer. And then they got him over there at Cincinnati as a coach and the manager died that spring. So they put him in as manager.

Q. I wonder who was responsible for that?

A. Someone who was there quite awhile, a Catholic, was responsible for that. I can't remember his name... No Garry Herrmann wasn't a Catholic. He was all right; he was a Shriner. He was what I call "a playboy."  When he was young he had lots of money and was a big playboy. That's what he still was when he was running the ballclub. The only time those kind of fellows ever talk to you is in the spring of the year, at contract time. If the club would send you a contract you would --

Q. Send it back?

A. Well, I didn't send them back; I just threw them in the waste basket. I'd write them a letter saying I expected so much money this year. They'd write back and say they weren't going to pay it. I wouldn't answer that one. That's what happened in New York. I didn't want to go back to New York in 1927, but they sold me over there. New York sent me a contract for $19,000, what I had been getting in Cincinnati. I threw it in the waste basket. I wrote Stoneham and told him I wouldn't play in New York for that kind of money. I didn't tell him what I wanted or anything else. So he sent me a contract for $20,000 and I threw it in the waste basket. I wrote him and said I wouldn't play in New York for that kind of money. He wrote me a letter and asked me how much I wanted. I wrote him back and said I wanted $30,000. He wrote back and said, "We won't pay it."  I didn't have to answer that one.

Q. This was 1927, your first year with the Giants?

A. Yes, 1927. So I stayed home and the team went south. On their way back I got a telegram from McGraw to meet him in Chattanooga. So I went down there to see what he wanted. The bellhop told me McGraw wanted to see me up in his room. The ballclub was due in at about 11 o'clock and I knew he wanted to talk to me before the club got in. So I stayed around the lobby until the ballclub came in. I never went up to see him. I sat around and talked with the players and then went for a walk with some of them. When we got back one of the coaches spoke to me and said McGraw wanted to know why I didn't come up to his room. I said I'd see McGraw when I got good and ready. He didn't say anything to that and I asked him what time the team went out to the ballpark. He said you had to be in uniform at quarter after one o'clock. So at 12:30 I went up to see McGraw. I knocked on the door and he opened the door wearing his dressing robe. He said, "What the hell's the matter, Roush, don't you want to play ball for me?" He said, "I'm not near as bad as I used to be." I said, "Yeah, I've heard that one before." So we went into the room and he said, "You know this game as well as I do. You can play your own game out there and I won't say a word to you." "Yeah, I've heard that one before, too. After you get signed up it's a horse of a different color." I said, "I want to tell you something: send me to another ballclub because I don't want to play for you. The first time you start calling me a so-and-so, somebody's going to get hurt. It might be you and it might be me. I won't stand for it so you might as well send me somewhere else." He said, "I've been trying to get you back ever since I sent you to Cincinnati. You're either going to play here or you're not going to play. You can play your own game here and I won't bother you." "O.K.," I said, "if that's the way you feel about it, I'll give it a try. But I still say I'll be back in Oakland City in ten days." "No, you won't. What do you want?" "$25,000," I said. "Can't pay it." I picked up my hat and started for the door. Just as I was opening the door, he said, "Where are you going?" "Back to Oakland City, Indiana, where did you think I was going?" He said, "Shut the door and come back in here. I'll tell you what I'll do. I'll give you a three-year contract for $70,000." Well, three years; that didn't sound too bad, so I said, "All right, I'll take it." He said, "I've got to call up Stoneham." I said, "You don't have to call up anybody; you know what you're doing." He said, "Well, come back in about ten minutes and I'll have the contract made out." So I went down and got my uniform and equipment and took that to my room then went back to see McGraw. He had the contract all ready and I signed it. I found out later that he had been talking to the writers. The writers had been giving him hell because he wouldn't sign me.

Q. You're speaking of the baseball writers now?

A. Yes. They told him that he'd been trying to get me for years and now that he had me he didn't want to pay me. Well, he had a meeting with them in between times and told them he had signed me up and that I was going to play six innings that afternoon. Well, I hadn't seen a ball or had a uniform on yet. And he told those writers, "I signed that damn Roush and he's going to play six innings today. I hope he goes out there and breaks a leg." One of the writers told me that afterwards.

Q. Why would he say that?

A. He was mad at me, I suppose, or something. Anyways, I go out there and I hadn't had hold of a baseball since the year before. Well, I got two base hits in three times up and played a heck of a game in the outfield. That just shows you that I didn't have to go there and practice and do all that stuff. I was in shape all the time. I kept my legs in shape by hunting and all that, and all I needed was a couple of days to see if I was leveling that bat. Luckily, I was leveling that bat because I had to play every day from then on [chuckling]. The writers told me later that, "McGraw hoped you'd break a leg and dang if you don't get two base hits and are all over the place out there."

Q. Did he leave you alone that year?

A. He never said anything to me. It was just one of those things. I went ahead and played my game. I knew how to play the game better than he did. He was good with the rest of the ballclub in hitting; he was good that way. He was a good manager, yes. Well, he was a good manager in this respect. He knew ballplayers and half the managers don't know ballplayers or the club doesn't have the money to buy them. McGraw was over in New York there where they had the money. That's the reason they could win so damn many pennants. A lot of the other clubs didn't have the money. McGraw was a good manager on the offense, but I thought he was a dang poor manager on the defense.

Q. Had he mellowed like he said he had?

A. Yes, he had. He wasn't near as bad as the first time I was over there. Of course, he'd had a heart attack or two. Once in awhile he cut loose, but he never said anything to me. One day he said to me, "What are you playing that man over there for?" I said, "Well, that's where he hits; why shouldn't I play him there?" He never said another word. He left me alone because he knew if he didn't he might get in trouble. And I knew that game as well as he did. I made a study of hitters and pitchers, and I told him when I went over there that it would take me a little time to learn how his pitchers pitched to different hitters. I said that his pitchers pitched differently than pitchers in Cincinnati did to the different hitters. And that I would have to learn to play my position a little different. "All right." After one trip around I knew how they pitched and how I should play the hitters.

Q. Do ballplayers make a study of the game and the hitters the way you did?

A. They did back in those days. Sure, they all did.

Q. They had great natural talent, but they added to that by carefully studying the game and the players?

A. That is true. I don't know if they do that as much today, but I'm not in the game. The way some of them play today, I don't think they do too much studying [chuckling].  Back in those days they did because it was a business. Today they're making too much money and they don't care if they win or lose, judging by the way they play sometimes. They draw big crowds and the people who go out and watch them play don't know any better.

Q. Tell me, what happened in 1928?  You only played forty-six games, I see.

A. I pulled a muscle in my stomach. It kept me out most of the year. I believe it was April or early May. I came in for a flyball and if I don't catch the ball we lose the game. I caught it just above the grass. And when I caught that ball it felt like somebody had stuck a knife in my stomach and pulled it all over to one side. Well it didn't bother too much, but I couldn't lie on my bed and come straight up and I couldn't run. At least, I couldn't run very fast. I fooled around with that thing all summer. They had specialists from all over New York looking at me. And they didn't know as much about it as I did. I went here and I went there and they couldn't find anything in the x-rays. I told them that the muscles were torn in there and it was bound to show up on the pictures. They didn't know how I could tear a muscle in there and they didn't think I knew what I was talking about. Well, we fool around all summer and finally Stoneham had a meeting before our last western trip. He had McGraw and me up there and he was drunk. He said he wanted to send me home. I said, "With pay, or without pay?"  "Without pay."  "I ain't going. Give me ten days with pay and then I'll go home. Ten days notice."  McGraw got disgusted with it all and he left. He said there wasn't anything wrong with me and that I could play. I said, "Let me tell you something. When it gets so I'm trying to beat somebody out of something, I don't want anything to do with it. If there isn't anything wrong with me then I'm nuts."  When we get over to St. Louis and [Dr. Robert] Hyland is over there. I said to McGraw that we should see if he could find anything wrong with me. The last day we were there he looked at me and said, "I can tell you what's wrong with you. These two muscles come down in the front of your stomach here. You tore those muscles there and when you tear them they stick out like that. They have got to go back in like that before you can do anything. It's the same thing on your legs, except that it takes two weeks for the leg muscles to heal, while it takes a year for your stomach muscles to heal."  I asked him to tell McGraw that because he and McGraw were great beer-drinking buddies. So he told McGraw. I went down to the train because we were leaving town and Mac was drunk. Oh, here we go. Well, we get over to Cincinnati and out at the ballpark I asked McGraw if Hyland had told him what my trouble was and he said yes he had. He said he would call Stoneham and tell him, but later changed his mind. He told me to get out of uniform, get dressed, go home to Oakland City and call up Hyland and get this thing attended to. He said "I'm not going to call up Stoneham; he won't understand anyhow." So that's what I did. The next year I came back and hit .325.

Q. What did you do after the operation?  Just go home and rest?

A. That's all I could do. I was in the hospital in St. Louis for seventeen days. Then I came home and lay around. There wasn't much I could do or was supposed to do.

Q. Did you go to spring training more willingly in 1929, since you hadn't played for awhile and had that operation?

A. Well, yes. They trained in San Antonio, Texas, that year. Since I wasn't sure what I could do I thought I should get out there a little early that year. So I arrived about a week before they broke camp that time. [We chuckle.] I got in there on a Friday and it was raining. And it rained on Saturday. On Sunday, the "B" team was going on a barnstorming trip around Texas. So I told McGraw I didn't want to stay in the wet there, that I wanted to travel with the "B" team and get some playing time in. So I went with the "B" team and he told me to rejoin the club when the two teams met the following Sunday. So I played outfield there with pitchers on each side of me. We never lost a game. We had a lot of fun.

Q. You said McGraw was drunk that night when you got on the train?  Was he a drinker?

A. Who, McGraw?  Every night.

Q. Remember, this was Prohibition.

A. Fizzle on that. I knew a brewery in every city. They had to make good beer so they could take the alcohol out and make "near beer."  Near beer was legal and you could get that at regular bars and taverns. But we'd go to the breweries for real beer if we wanted to. I'll never forget one time there in New York down there on 42nd Street, off Broadway about two blocks, there was a bar. The first time we went in there, five or six of us, we had good beer. The second time we went in there, we hadn't played that day because it was raining. We had our hats and raincoats on. We busted in there -- the last fellow paid the bill. I was last one there and paid it, but we would divide it up. As we sat down at the bar, the fellow was messing around in the sink and liked to never wait on us. There were only two other fellows in the place, sitting at a table and I didn't know either one of them. One sat with his back to me so I couldn't see him and I didn't know the other one. Finally the bartender came over to us, after messing around there for about five minutes and we said we wanted some good beer. So he gave us some beer. It was near beer. I took a taste of it and said to him, "This is nothing but near beer. Don't you have any real beer?  We're from the Cincinnati ballclub and the last time we were in here you gave us some real beer."  He said, "No, that's all I've got."  Now one of those fellows sitting down heard us say we were with the Cincinnati club and he turned around and he knew me. I said, "Well, let's go some place where we can get some real beer."  Then this fellow turned around and said, "Wait a minute, Roush."  And then he turned to the barkeep and said, "Give these fellows some good beer."  So he gave us some good beer. Later the barkeep said to me, "You doggone so-and-sos, you come in here, right after I come up from the basement with a pitcher full of whisky, you guys come in here  and if ever I saw five or six guys who looked like the police, you were it. I poured every damn bit of whisky down the sink." [We roar with laughter.] I said I was sorry he did that, even though I don't drink whisky. "If ever I saw a bunch of cops," he said, "you guys were it."  We stayed there the rest of the afternoon and had a good time.

Q. Was there a lot of drinking among ballplayers in your time?

A. No, not a lot of heavy drinking. On an off day like that we'd sit around and drink some beer. We probably had seven or eight beers apiece. By the next day it was all gone anyway. Some of them were real whisky-drinkers. Well, when you drink a lot of whiskey --. [Interruption when Mrs. Roush, their daughter, Mrs. Allen, and my wife come in from the front porch and Mrs. Roush said, "We are having the nicest time out there."  Edd interrupts her to call out, "Is anybody telling the truth?"  As a free-wheeling discussion goes on, he says "You'd better watch it; he's got this thing on."]

Q. Were the breweries nice to the ballplayers during Prohibition?

A. Well, the Cincinnati ballclub had about six of eight fellows who drank beer. They knew us and invited us down to the brewery. So from time to time we'd go down there for an hour or so and then we'd go to the hotel. But we had a lot of fun out of it.

Q. What were the names of some of these breweries?

A. Well, in Cincinnati we had all kinds of them. In St. Louis it was Budweiser, but I didn't like that, it was too strong. I didn't like Rupperts. I was in there once and had one glass full and that was enough; I didn't like that... Oh, yes I met Jake Ruppert. I had to laugh one time when we were coming up in 1920. We were coming north from spring training with the New York Yankees. We had played in some town. My wife was with me and so was Bill Rariden and his wife. We were together and went out to the ballpark. We went down to the man and the gate and said these were our wives and did he have a box for them to sit in. He said they didn't have any boxes and that they could sit any place back up in there. "Where's 'back up in there?'" I wanted to know. He pointed it out and I said, "My wife ain't going to sit back up in there, I'll tell you that goddam quick." He was with the Yankees. He said, "They'll sit up there or they won't sit." I said "they'll sit down here in the boxes or there won't be a ballgame today. You're one of those smart guys. I don't give a damn who you are or where you come from, and if you want to fight, we'll do that." I went back to where the two business managers for the teams were and told them Rariden and I were going back to the hotel. And I told them that the Yankees had all the box seats and didn't have any for our wives. "You either give us some box seats, or there won't be any game." Don't think they didn't hurry around and get some tickets. Because if I wasn't in that game, which had already been advertised that I would, somebody would get in trouble. They thought "They were the Yankees," and I didn't like that.

Q. Did you ever have a chance to hit against Ruth when he was pitching during spring training?

A. No, he was in the American League. But he never pitched against us in spring training.

Q. How about the toughest pitcher you ever faced? Does anybody stand out?

A. Oh, they were all bad. They were all alike to me. I'll tell you the truth: I didn't have any trouble with any of them... My favorite pitch? That depended upon where I wanted to hit the ball. If I wanted to hit to left field I liked the ball waist high. If I wanted to pull to right field I liked it from the waist down. Any kind of a ball was good to hit straightaway. Things were a lot different with me and other players who were straightaway hitters. They just swung and didn't know where the ball was going or anything else. Fizzle, I always knew where it was going. The third baseman had to play in close because I was a good bunter. They had to play in close because I could bunt and I was fast. I hit line drives past any number of third baseman who were playing in close. I used to hit the balls right at them.

Q. Did you ever hit a third baseman in one of those situations?

A. No. But one night down in Florida, some fellow who played third base with St. Louis, said to me, "Roush, I'm not playing in on you anymore." "Why not?" I asked him. "You're going to kill some third baseman sometime. That ball you hit by me I never even got my hand up on it. It just barely missed my face." I told him, "Don't come in like that; stay back where you belong." "I am from now on. You can bunt all you damn please; I'm not coming in."

Q. Did you like to drag bunts just past the pitcher?

A. No, I didn't do too much of that because the odds are against you. But when you bunt down the third base line they've got that long throw and they're apt to throw it away.

Q. Say you had planned to bunt down the third base line, but as the ball was being delivered you would see the third baseman charging in. Could you change your mind while the ball was in the air and slap it past him?

A. Wait a minute now. You know if he's coming in or not. Now here, I'm going to show you something. [He stands up with a bat to demonstrate this.] Man on first base, nobody out. If I bunt the third baseman is coming in and the first baseman is coming in. The second baseman is covering first base. The shortstop is covering second base so there isn't a damn soul out there in the shortstop's spot in the middle of the diamond. So all you've got to do is pretend you're going to bunt and then slap it -- like that, see.

Q. That takes quick reflexes though.

A. Well, I'm not trying to knock it out of the ballpark like they are today. All right, what happens. There's nobody there to field the ball. You put on the hit and run in that case. I can hit that ball no matter where it was pitched, as long as it wasn't behind me. There in New York one time when I was with the Giants, it was a close ballgame, 1-1 or 0-0, or something, late in the game. McGraw put on the hit-and-run. This guy gets on first and they put on the hit-and-run on the first pitch. I was next up. I always told them to make no move to leave first base until the pitcher had let go of the ball. Stay close to the bag; don't get out there like you're going to steal. Then they know you're going to steal. I'll get a piece of the ball. You know where that damn pitch to me was? Right over the top of my head, about like that, see. I swung at it anyhow and you know where the ball went? Right down that right foul line about three feet fair all the way and into the seats. I was just trying to get a piece of that ball so the runner wouldn't get thrown out, so I swung like that, see. [Obviously, it was a tommyhawk-like chopping swing over his head.] McGraw said, "That was the goddamdest hit-and-run I ever saw." [We chuckle.]  He said, "Nobody else would have swung at that."  "Well," I said, "when I put on the hit-and-run I intend to hit the ball."  I hardly had anybody thrown out at second when I put on the hit-and-run.

Q. Did you strike out much?

A. No, I could get a piece of that ball. Oh, you do once in awhile against a left-hand pitcher.

Q. Do you find much difference in batting against a left-hander and a right-hander?

A. Sure. But what bothers a left-hand hitter against a left-hand pitcher is that you only see them every four or five days. If you see them more often... Now in 1919, we saw as many left-hand pitchers as right-hand pitchers. And I led the National League in hitting. Fizzle, I don't care who's pitching except that you don't see the left-handers that often.

Q. How did you get along with the umpires?

A. I never had much trouble with the umpires. Oh, once in awhile. Bill Klem was one we had in the National League. If he called a strike and you started to look around, he'd yell, "Don't you look around here."  Well, one day there he said that to me. He called a bad one on me. [Interruption while Roush's daughter leaves. As tape picks up Edd says]  Half the people around here don't even know I played baseball. I never talk much about it. Somebody might drop in and say, "Didn't you play baseball?"  I'd say, "Oh, a little bit."  They ask what I've been doing all the time and I'll say, "Oh, I do a little hunting."

Q. I was going to ask you if you had done much hunting?

A. Oh, yes, when the season's over. I had a bird dog and I'm training another one. The two bird-dogs I had for a long while, were pretty fast and were good "covey" dogs. I had one at one time and the other later.

Q. While I was changing tapes you were talking about catchers blocking home plate.

A. When you come into the plate the catcher has the plate blocked like that. Now when I came into the plate I had one foot up here and the other foot up here. I never had a catcher ever bump me off more than once. After that they would stand in front of the plate and then dive for me. I would hit them so damn hard -- and my spikes were sharp.

Q. Did you learn this from Cobb?

A. I learned it for myself. Dammit, they weren't going to run me out of the league. No catcher ever tried to bump me off twice. I hit them so hard the first time that that was it. There was no padding in the thigh area so that's where I hit them. I told them I was going to do it. The infielders the same way. I told them the base line was mine. One time with New York when Cincinnati came to town, they came out to watch me hit in batting practice. McGraw was up in the stands watching everything. After I was through hitting I sat down with those Cincinnati players. I told them that once the game started not to get in my way on the bases or they would get hurt. They all said, "We know that; we know not to get in your way."  After the game McGraw called me to his office. He said, "I saw you out there socializing with the opposition."  I said, "Yeah, what are you going to do about it?"  He said, "I don't like it."  I answered, "I don't care if you like it or not. Those boys are friends of mine; I've played with them for years. But I told them one thing: 'Don't get in my way; all friendship ceases when the ballgame starts.'"  He was going to give me the go-round, but he didn't after that.

Q. Did you sharpen your spikes in the dugout as the other team walked by, like Cobb did?

A. No, my spikes were always sharp. They were so sharp they cut through many a catcher's shinguard. I slid with one foot up in the face and the other a little lower down.

Q. Did you get into any fights over that?

A. Well, they had to get up to fight. [We chuckle.]  When I hit them they went down. No, I never had a fight. Well, they knew damn good and well they were wrong.

Q. And you probably weren't one of the bigger players. [He is listed at 5-feet 11 inches and weighing 175 pounds.]

A. Well, I was a pretty good size for those days. They're much bigger now. But I was pretty big for then. And they knew I could handle my feet. I never cut many, though, unless they were smart-alecks. There was one catcher there who used to keep hollering, every time the ball was pitched, "hit it, hit it, hit it."  I didn't care how much he hollered; I didn't pay much attention to it anyways, but it got a little monotonous. So I finally decided that the next time I came up with a man on base I was going to move up in the batter's box, and I knew he would follow me up, than I would make my backswing and hit him right across the mask. But dang it, nobody got on base ahead of me. So my last time up I told him, "Here's what I was gonna do."  And I showed him. I moved up in the box and he followed me up, shouting "hit it, hit it."  Then as the pitch came in I made my backswing and he jumped to one side and the ball hit the umpire in the mask. He yelled at me and I said it was the catchers' fault and the catcher said it was my fault. "I know who did it," he screamed. [We laugh.]  It wasn't my fault; I was just trying to teach the catcher a lesson. I didn't think that he might step out of the way. I probably shouldn't have told him that I was going to do something.

* * *

My wife had a terrific interview with Mrs. Roush during the five hours we were there. She was shown every room in the house, all the closets, told about the "dust hole" in the kitchen floor, etc. The Carl Mayses and Roushes were good friends, and Mrs. Roush told how bad Carl Mays felt after killing Ray Chapman. The pitch was totally unintentional... She said that Edd made $2,000 the first year they got married, the next year he made $4,000, the next year $8,000, and then they were on easy street... I added a couple of stories Edd told me after the tape was off.

One was about the batting titles he won. In 1916 Hal Chase won the batting title and in 1917 Roush won his first title. In 1918 Heinie Groh was leading the league late in the season and everyone thought it would be great to have three Cincinnati players in a row win the batting title. Then Groh fell into a slump and Roush told him, "Heinie, if you're not going to win that batting title I'll get in there and start hitting."  Heinie said, "You might as well; I can't hit anything."  Then Zack Wheat of Brooklyn began moving up. Roush and Wheat then became involved in a close race for the title when Roush got word that his father had died. He returned to Oakland City for the funeral and stayed home for a couple of weeks, I guess. Wheat apparently had been quite a bit above Roush in batting. Wheat fell into some kind of a slump while Roush was at home and his average dropped until it was about two points above Roush's. Then he learned that Roush was at home so they took Wheat out of the lineup at Brooklyn for the last week or so of the season so his average never dropped any lower. So Wheat won the batting title over Roush by two points, .335 to .333.

Roush didn't play any more after he had gone home. I asked him if he felt that Wheat really wanted to win the batting title that way, but he didn't know. Roush won it again in 1919...

[My wife picks up and talks about their picture gallery and Mrs. Roush's fabulous collection of piano sheet music, which she gathered while playing piano at the local movie house during silent movie days. She goes on.] Mrs. Roush told me that when they were first married, just as he joined the Giants for the first time, they had a little apartment on the Jersey side and they saved every penny he made because they didn't know how long his career would last. And you can tell, by looking around their house, how well set they are. It's just beautiful. [She describes some of the trophies, artifacts, and such, since I didn't have a chance to look around... Now I remember another story.]

I asked him about Baker Bowl in Philadelphia. Did he like to hit there with that short right-field fence?  He said it didn't matter much to him where he played, but there they would pitch to him on the outside since he was a left-hand hitter. So he would just hit to left field. He could place the ball pretty well so it didn't matter where they played. But he said he had seen many a hitter thrown out at first base by the right fielder. He would line the ball off that short fence for what should have been a hit, but it was so close that the right fielder could throw the batter out. He said that he himself was never thrown out that way because he was so fast. But a couple of times he barely beat the throw. In his first game in the league with the Giants in 1916, they played at Baker Bowl. McGraw told the new players before the game that if they hit the ball safely to right field and thought about trying for two bases, they should be very sure they could make it because the fielders could get the ball in so quickly.

Since Roush was fast he felt confident that he could make it easily to second on a hit to right-field. He tried it twice and was thrown out both times by the Philadelphia right fielder, Gavvy Cravath. McGraw spoke to him after the game and, in effect, said, "I told you so."  He didn't try that again very often. I asked him about playing in the Polo Grounds with the short fences there. What I gathered was that the ballparks and the pitchers never seemed to make much difference to him. He could hit just as well against anyone in any place. I asked him if ever kept track of his own batting averages. He said no, no one paid much attention to those things in those days; everyone was out there to win. He said he could have hit for a higher batting average if he wasn't using the hit-and-run so much. That they played to win, so you gave yourself up. "I could have had higher batting averages if I had tried to hit for average, but I didn't. We played to win." I said, "But don't higher averages put you in a better bargaining position come contract time?"  "No," he replied, "I never thought much about that. I just said 'you pay me this,' and that was it."  He said that his batting average was high enough, that he didn't have to remind them of that...

In reflecting on the interview, I noted something that was mentioned on the tape, that I could not get Roush to admit freely and enthusiastically that he loved to play baseball just for the sake of playing baseball. This is a theme I have tried to establish with all of these interviews, and I think that I have established it. But he would not admit that. To him it was a business. That was why he held out in spring training. And if he couldn't get the money he wanted, he would just stay home. Several of his stories illustrated that. He had a good business sense. So he liked baseball and made a study of it, but if the money wasn't there, he wouldn't play. The $70,000 he got in 1927-1929 was tremendous money, yet if he hadn't signed he would have gotten nothing. But he got it. And they invested wisely because they are very well off.

[My wife notes that the Roushes became something like civic leaders in Oakland City and mentions half a dozen civic organizations that were actually founded in the Roush home. They are the oldest residents in town now and get called upon for all kinds of information about the old days. For example, Edd Roush had handled the cemetery records there for years. Church, girl scout, garden club activities -- and many others -- all seemed centered in the Roush house.]

# Carmen Hill
## *Indianapolis, Indiana, February 21, 1975*

"An Early 'Mr. Four-Eyes'"

I interviewed Carmen "Bunker" Hill Friday afternoon, February 21, 1975, at his modest Indianapolis home. It was part of a weekend trip, which included interviews with Oral Hildebrand and Dominic Dallesandro, and a day with fellow collector Paul Frisz, at the spring meeting of the Indianapolis baseball collectors group. While the Hill home was a pleasant one, it was in a deteriorating section of the city. Carmen and his wife had lived there for a long time, however, and were too advanced in years to think of moving. Hill was one of the first major leaguers to wear glasses, but despite the "four-eyes" chiding he took, you did not want to get him too mad; he was "one tough hombre." Standing well over six feet and weighing close to 200 pounds, he was one of baseball's big men between the wars. He had a checkered career, up and down, and in and out of organized baseball, but he did put together two fine seasons with Pittsburgh, 1927, a pennant-winning year, and 1928. The Hills were pleasant company and the afternoon raced by. He brought out his scrapbooks and a number of those long panoramic pictures, two of which he gave me. He was animated, expressive, full of fun, and frequently stood up in the middle of the living room to explain points by vigorous demonstrations. In good health at age seventy-nine, he lived another fifteen years, dying on New Year's Day of 1990, at age ninety-four.

[CH is talking as tape picks up.]  I am pitching for Oil City. Their pitcher was a big left-hander and he pitched one ball. Then they sent out and got Scott. [laughs]. They got Scott Perry in there. I beat him 1-0 [laughs].

Q. This was 1921?

A. Yes. Oh, that really broke things loose. I'll bet there was $100,000 on that game that day.

Q. This was played in Oil City?

A. Yes... It was hard for all the fans to get in there... No, it wasn't a big grandstand, maybe 3,000-4,000.

Q. Why did Perry jump the A's?  Didn't they give him enough money?

A. Why they doubled his salary. I did not know how much he was getting, but I heard that they doubled whatever it was.

Q. Who were some of the other players on your team?

A. I've got a list of them here. I don't know if you recognize some of these players [he has brought out some pictures -- I think], a good many of them were ex-big leaguers.

Q. O.K. These are members of the Two-Team League, 1920-1921.

A. Just Oil City and Franklin... I think we played every day; we just played each other. No, I'll take that back. We would play them a series of games and then we would go on the road and play other independent clubs. Then we'd come back, but our main series was between Oil City and Franklin.

Q. I recognize a few names -- Walter Kimmick and Bunny Fabrique, who I think played with Eddie Onslow at Providence.

A. I knew Eddie Onslow... Jake Pitler was our manager... Yes, that's Joe "Moon" Harris, who was with me at Pittsburgh...

Q. I notice the date is August 26, 1939; was this some kind of a reunion?

A. I don't think so; let me see. [We get off the subject and on to a number of things, he insisting that Eddie Collins in the picture was *the* Eddie Collins, who had also jumped from the major leagues. Great confusion.]  Bill Evans was from Pittsburgh, Jimmy Hicken was with Brooklyn, he jumped from Brooklyn; Fred Hershey is another one. Jimmy McEvoy was another one; Johnny Meader [?]; Ollie O'Mara -- you certainly remember Ollie O'Mara, don't you?

Q. [Chuckling] I'm afraid not.

A. Ollie was quite a ballplayer. Third baseman. Bob Seale [?] was another big league ballplayer. Joe Harris. They had a Hill-Harris Day for us over in Pittsburgh in 1927.

Q. Very interesting. But I tell you what I would like to do now. I'd like to start at the beginning with where you were born and raised and how you broke into pro baseball.

A. Here's a picture that has quite a story behind it. That's the 1922 pennant-winning Giants. Irish Meusel jumping on home plate. I'll tell you that story a little bit later. You'll get a kick out of that.

Q. I have your record here -- Oh, that's a good picture; what's that?

A. That's Lee Meadows and I at Pittsburgh -- we were the only two players in baseball at that time who wore glasses... Yes he was "Specs"... Now here's my Corry High School baseball team. We went undefeated, I think, for seven years... This was in Corry, Pennsylvania. It is up near Erie, Pennsylvania. That picture, I think, was in 1915... Here's a story for you. I started pitching for the high school when I was in the seventh grade. I was probably about 5-feet, ten-inches by then. That gave me seven years [shouldn't it be six?] with the high school team. They used to call me "the old man of the hill" [chuckling]... No, they had no eligibility rules then... Yes, I won a lot of games as we were undefeated. And then the following year, I had had such a sensational record in high school -- yes, in 1915 -- a lawyer in town contacted the Pittsburgh ballclub. They sent him a contract for me to sign. I wasn't of age, of course, so my mother had to sign it with me. They immediately farmed me down to Warren in the old Inter-State League. Warren, Pennsylvania. I was undefeated there in six or seven ballgames that year.. The next year -- this picture is at spring training in Dawson Springs, Kentucky, spring training 1916. These are the Pirates; there's Honus Wagner and here I am. I don't remember the names of too many of the others.

Q. When did you start to wear glasses?

A. Oh, I wore glasses all the time. I wore glasses since I was fourteen.

Q. That was rather unusual for anyone wearing glasses in those days, wasn't it? Did anyone have any questions about your wearing them?

A. Oh, there was comment at different times; nothing detrimental... No, I didn't have special glasses; they didn't have safety glasses back in those days... Yes, I had several accidents with my glasses... Well, in 1916 I went with Pittsburgh in spring training and then they farmed me out to Youngstown in the Central League... Yes, my record was 19 and 12 that year with Youngstown... Here's something I want to show you. This is the Athletic Department of the high school; they dedicated the year book to me. I was pretty tall and skinny then [as we look at the picture]. I suppose I weighed around 175 pounds then... Here's the lawyer that got me the tryout, Gary Kincaid. He was quite a fan of the team.

Q. Tell me, you were born in Minnesota. Tell me about your family.

A. In Royalton, Minnesota. My father was a builder and contractor. He was raised there in Minnesota. My mother and her parents left Corry and went out there. That's where he met mother and married her. I was three years old when we left there.

Q. [I restate all of this:  Your parents were from Royalton [correct] and your mother's parents were from Corry. They met in Royalton and got married. Soon after you were born, your mother, not liking the cold there, moved the family to Corry, where you were raised.]

A. [Another picture]  Here's a ballclub where you will recognize most of the players. You'll recognize the first one there?... Yes, Dazzy Vance. That's the same year, I think, 1916. Either 1916 or 1917. [I speak about Wilbur Cooper, who was a native of my area.]

Q. How was Fred Clarke as manager?

A. A good manager... Yes, fair... Yes, he knew his baseball. He sure did.

Q. So you grew up in Corry, played seven years on the high school team, and then Pittsburgh. Did you pitch any with Pittsburgh that first year, 1915?

A. I should say I did. I don't remember the first hitter I faced, but I remember the first game I was in. Cooper was pitching and they got three runs off of him in the first three innings. Grover Cleveland Alexander was pitching against us for the Phillies. That was when he was at his very best, you know. I held them the rest of the way. We didn't score and they didn't score and we got beaten 3-0. Up to that time I considered myself a pretty fair hitter. I'll have to tell you that hitting against Alexander was something in itself. That man had the best fastball and the best curveball that I have ever run on to since. His curveball was just as fast as his fastball [chuckling]. It would just come up there and it was gone, that's all!

Q. Some pitching by you!  How did the players treat you, a young rookie coming up and entering his first game?

A. Oh, not too bad, although I had a run-in with Max Carey. Well, that was in spring training... That's right, that was the following year, 1916. I was out in the outfield chasing flyballs during batting practice. Here was a flyball coming out to me and I am waiting to catch it. Then here comes Carey racing across and reached up in front of me and caught the ball. It made me madder than hell and I jumped him. He said, "Aw go to hell, you damn busher" [chuckling]. Outside of that everybody was all right. They knew that I was just a farm boy who didn't know from nothing and they were all right.

Q. What did Fred Clarke say after that good showing against the Phillies?

A. I don't remember.

Q. Why did they farm you out if you did so well?

A. Oh, you haven't heard anything yet [chuckling]. They sent me over to Youngstown that year. [He's looking over pictures of the Youngstown team, I think.]

Q. Who kept the scrapbook?

A. My mother. Of course, she only got what was in the Corry papers.

Q. They really worked you in Youngstown -- 291 innings!

A. You know we only had three pitchers there? Usually we worked every third day and sometimes it was every other day... The manager was -- I can't remember. Anyway, Pittsburgh came over there for an exhibition game and -- this was in 1915 -- and I beat them 1-0 in twelve innings. [He's going through the scrapbook trying to pick out stories about certain games.] July 27, I pitched a game against Grand Rapids and it went nineteen innings, 0-0 to the nineteenth, and in the fourteenth there was an attempted bunt, a little flyball between first base and home. The first baseman and I went after it and we couldn't see each other. We collided as we reached the ball. I caught the ball and knocked him unconscious. He remained unconscious for two straight days. We hit pretty hard. That happened in the fourteenth inning and then in the nineteenth inning -- I thought I had the resume of that game in here -- anyway they scored three runs in the nineteenth and we came back and scored two. One of our boys hit a double and was out trying to stretch it into a triple and that ended the ballgame. So I got beat 3-2 in nineteen innings.

Q. No relief pitchers to help you out, I guess?

A. You either pitched or you didn't... Here's the story. The manager was named Blount. The first baseman was -- I can't find it. He recovered all right.

Q. What kind of a ballpark did you have in Youngstown?

A. It wasn't such a bad ballpark. The ballparks weren't too good, but they weren't bad. They would seat about 4,000-5,000... We drew pretty well in Youngstown, although I don't remember exactly. We traveled by train some of the time and by bus some of the time. You carried your own suitcases too... You roomed out on your own in Youngstown. You had to find your own quarters. I rented a room just by myself. We dressed in our rooms and went to the ballpark. I didn't get home until the season was over... Anyway, I beat them 1-0 in that exhibition game and later Barney Dreyfuss came over -- I guess to see me and he was there when I pitched that nineteen-inning game. After the 1916 season, I went back in the fall. At that time a major league club could keep you past the date when you could be drafted. They had a spring date and if they keep you past that date no other club can draft you. Then they can send you out. And they could call you back in the fall before a certain period and that could go on and on and on, for five years. And that's what happened to me. In the meantime I went back that fall... To go way back to 1914, the Giants played an exhibition game in Erie. This same lawyer made a trip to Erie and talked to the acting manager of the Giants. McGraw was not with the club; he had gone back to New York. Mike Doolan had the club. The lawyer talked to him and asked if I couldn't pitch their batting practice, which I did. Then, after I had pitched the full batting practice -- Larry McClain was a big six-foot two-inch catcher of theirs, tall, lean, and lanky -- he took me down on the sidelines and I pitched to him for another ten minutes. After we finished he came up to me and said, "Kid, I'm almost tempted to take you on to New York on my own. If McGraw was here I know he would. When I get to New York I'll tell him about you." I was up in the air after that. So, I don't hear a thing. So I made this boast or brag to all my friends that if I ever got to pitch against the Giants I was going to beat them. In the fall of 1916 when I went back up I pitched a couple of relief games and then the Giants came in. I'll never forget this because it was really funny. Bill Klem, the old umpire, was behind the plate. They had called in all their rookies from all over the place for this game -- I think the Giants had about fifty players on their bench -- and they started riding me. What I was doing was that I was coming up off this toe of my right foot, just like that. They tried to get my goat by complaining to Bill. He stood it for a bit -- they were really hollering -- and then he came out and said, "My boy, you're going to have to quit that." I said, "Mr. Klem, what am I doing wrong?" He said, "That's all right, my boy, just go ahead," and he patted me on the shoulder [chuckling]. He walked back to the plate and the next squawk that came up, he went over to the Giants bench, took his mask off, and said "Get outa here!" [Laughing.] He cleaned the whole bench. Everyone was sent into the clubhouse. And I beat them 2-0 and gave them four hits. My first full game against a big league club. Yes, the fall of 1915.

Q. Why did he tell you stop what you were doing and then tell you to go ahead?

A. Well, it was nothing I really shouldn't have been doing. He just tapped me on the shoulder and said "go ahead." And then he cleaned out the bench. [It still is not clear quite what Klem was doing and why.] I can't tell you if it was the next year or the year after that, that I became fully disgusted. I came back in the fall as usual, they called me back, and I pitched forty-six and two-thirds innings with one run being scored on me. And that run was a ball right through the shortstop's legs. That was a winning run. And I don't get to stay with the club. It was either 1917 or 1918. Then in 1919 the same thing happened. When it came time to release you -- Dreyfuss called me up and said, "Hill, I'm going to send you over to Indianapolis." You don't have that thing on, do you?

Q. Just a little bit [chuckling].

A. I said, "You lie like hell; this is one year when you don't send me any place." What do you mean?" "Just exactly what I'm telling you. I've put up with this every year since I joined your club. I've had enough." He said "I'll send you home." "All right, send me home." He waited until the team was about to go on an eastern trip. I reported to the ballpark every day. And the following week -- we had two trainers; one would go with the club and one would stay and I would chat with him awhile and I'd leave. This went on for a week or maybe longer. Dreyfuss then told the trainer he wanted to see me. His office was clear up in the top of the stands. I went up there and he said, "Well, what are you going to do, stay around here all summer?" "It suits me fine; I like it here." "When are you going to go to Indianapolis?" "When I have my outright release right here in my hand." "You won't go any other way?" "No." "I'm not going to give it to you." "O.K." I started to walk out. He waited until he saw that I was really going then he called me back. "Well, if you won't go any other way, here it is." He handed me my release to the Indianapolis ballclub. I didn't find out until later how they manipulated that. And it shows you just how crooked baseball can be. What they do if they want to get someone out of the league, they'll put in their whole ballclub on waivers and if anybody claims anybody they withdraw them. They had been doing that for some time. The other clubs knew that there was somebody on that list that they wanted to send out. Finally they don't claim anybody and that's where they get you. That's when you're eligible to be transferred out of the league. I wasn't smart enough to know that then; I didn't find it out until much later.

Q. Why didn't they keep you?  You had a good record in the minor leagues?

A. They were waiting for one of their old pitchers, I think, to drop out and they weren't willing to carry an extra one.

Q. You had a good record. With Birmingham in 1917 you won 26 --

A. 27. 27 and 12. By the way they've got a hall of fame down there and they've got me in it... No, I never asked them why they didn't keep me. I got my release and then I came out here. Now here's what happened... I had neurosis of the liver [?] in 1920, having played here at Indianapolis in 1919. Jack Hendricks was my manager. I'd hate to express my opinion of him. He was no damn good... I don't know why they kept hiring him. I just don't want to talk about the guy... No, he didn't know baseball in my book.

Q. Then you got neurosis of the stomach that winter of 1919-20?

A. Yes. Boy, I was in bad shape. I don't know what that doctor gave me, but he brought me around. In a month I was back on my feet and feeling good again. Indianapolis put me on the ineligible list when I didn't report, when they found out I was with Oil City. The following year I was out [1921 with Oil City] so the next year -- 1922 -- I came back out here. And I had a good year in 1922 [15-12, I interject]... Yes, Hendricks was still around. That year Jack and I really got into it over in Toledo. He sent me home. I went up and told the old man -- named Smith, the owner of the Indianapolis club -- that I had had enough. So in the fall, late fall of 1922, New York was fighting for the pennant. The old man -- a nice old guy, I liked him -- and McGraw were real good friends. The old man wired McGraw and told him he had a pitcher who could do him some good. He can help you for the rest of the season. McGraw wired back to send me on. It was the 31st of August that I got into New York and the first time I'd ever really been on my own there. So I was dilly-dallying around and walked all the way from 42nd Street down to their offices downtown. I walked into the office at about ten minutes before twelve. The "squirrel" said "Where in the hell have you been?"  Anyhow they had to have me signed by 12 o'clock to be eligible for the series. So I signed up with them. McGraw asked me what I was getting at Indianapolis. I told him and he said he'd double it, just like that.

Q. What were you getting, do you remember?

A. I don't remember, but it wasn't too much. That made me feel good. We go out to the ballpark and I sat on the bench with McGraw. We were playing the Dodgers over in Brooklyn. As they came up to bat he would say that "this is so-and-so and I want you to pitch to him such-and-such." He went right down the line. I didn't know any of them. The story is funny really. He said that we were playing a double-header back in New York the next day and that he wanted to work me one of the games. This was my introduction to Earl Smith.

Q. "Oil" Smith?

A. I didn't know at the time that he and McGraw were feuding. Oh, did they hate each other. In fact, McGraw had fined Smitty $2,500 already that year. I walk out there and Smitty comes out there and says "Hill" -- you better not put this on that tape -- "I want to know something. Do you pitch your own ballgame?" "You're damned right I do." "All right. If I call for something that you don't want, you shake me off. Don't hesitate. Pitch your own game. As for that little pot-bellied son-of-a-bitch on the bench, don't look at him and neither will I." I said that suited me [chuckling loudly]. So the game goes on to about the seventh inning, nothing to nothing. I made a bad pitch to Andy High and to Zack Wheat. The ball that Zack Wheat hit, our fielders today would have had an easy putout. But Ross Youngs was playing centerfield and he ran back and turned away from the ball. He should have turned toward the ball and would have had an easy catch. But it went for three bases [chuckling]. They beat me; they shut us out. [I presume High got a hit before Wheat and scored the only run of the game on Wheat's hit.] When I came into the bench McGraw called me over. "What did I tell you to pitch to Wheat?" "High." "You didn't do it, did you?" "No." "Where did I tell you to pitch to High?" "Low." "You didn't do it, did you?" "No." Everything O.K. If I hadn't remembered what he told me, I would have got it [chuckling]. As he did very shortly after that -- [getting out the picture of Irish Meusel jumping on home plate] -- that's Irish Meusel, who had just hit a home run up into the left field stands. We won the game 2-0 since there was a man on... No, this was not the World Series. This was one of the games while I was there in 1922 in September. Meusel came into the bench all smiles, jumping up and down. McGraw says, "Irish, come here. What did I tell you to do?" "You told me to take one and I took it right out of the ballpark." McGraw said "That'll cost you $200." Irish says "Make it $400." "It's $400." Irish went over and sat down. A madder human I never did see. Oh, he was hostile. And that was what that picture was all about. He got fined $400 for hitting that home run even though it won the ballgame.

Q. That's the way McGraw was, I guess.

A. Yes, now I'll get back to McGraw and that ballgame. Of all the antics you ever saw! He'd walk back and forth and motion like this and like this. Smitty and I wouldn't look at him [chuckling; roaring]. After the game that's all he said to me -- about those pitches. It's a good thing I remembered. Then I won my next three ballgames for him and that helped decide our winning the pennant. Because it was very close then. So I won three and lost one. I had trouble with the secretary -- no, not Brannick or Bondy -- I can't remember his name right now. The ballplayers were allowed two sets of tickets for the World Series. One for at the Yankees and one set for at the Giants. Different players came to me, Bancroft was one of them, and he asked me what I was going to do with my tickets. I said I didn't think I'd be using them because I didn't have anybody who was coming. He said he'd buy them from me at the regular price. He had people he wanted to give tickets to. I said I hadn't any tickets. He said "Why don't you? You're eligible for them. Go up and see the secretary and find out why you haven't got any tickets." So I went up there and the secretary said "I don't have any tickets for you." I said "the boys tell me that I'm eligible for tickets and I want them." He said "I haven't got them." The son-of-a-gun had sold them already. He'd sold my tickets. I told him that -- it was about 10 o'clock on the morning of the first game -- I wanted the tickets by game time and that if he didn't have them for me I was going straight to McGraw and tell him what he'd done. Oh, he started cussing me -- "You goddamned busher," etc., -- and I said I might be a busher and all that, but I wanted what I was entitled to. But he got tickets from somewhere and gave them to me and I turned around and sold them to Bancroft or one of the boys that wanted them [chuckling]. So I came back home and, I think it was along in January, I got a letter from the Giant office signed by this secretary, who said "It is with great pleasure that I return your contract to the Indianapolis ballclub." [Chuckling; Hill had quite a sense of humor, or an appreciation of humorous things long after the fact.]

Q. That's something! What do you have to do to stay up there?

A. McGraw never pitched one of my ballgames because Smitty worked them all and we never looked at him. And he couldn't squawk as long as we were winning. But that's why I never went back; I know that.

Q. Because you followed Smith and not McGraw on calling the pitches?

A. Because I pitched my own ballgame. He pitched all the other pitchers' games for them from the bench. As long as I played ball I wasn't about to let somebody else pitch my game for me. There are too many little things you can see at the last second as you're delivering the ball, which you can see what to do.

Q. I was going to say that with his longer experience, maybe it would have been a good idea -- at first -- to let him call them?

A. No, not if you always did your own pitching. There are too many little tricks in baseball -- the way a man stands at the plate, and the way he'll shift his feet -- that will change what you're going to pitch. Right at that last second. I did that later after I went back to Pittsburgh, to Bill Terry over in New York. I never seen a madder man in my life.

Q. What did you do?

A. Bill was an unusually good hitter, you know. A left-hand hitter, he was up there at the plate and took his regular stance. As I was about to let the ball go, he dropped his foot back like this.

Q. He dropped his left foot back.

A. Yes, he pulled back his left foot. He was going to push that ball into left field. Two men on at the time. Right at that last second -- I'm right here with it -- I just loosened my fingers and threw a lobber up there. Bill swung all the way around, swung again and pooped a little popper straight up in the air. He grabbed the bat in the middle and came running out at me and said, "You four-eyed son-of-a-bitch what was that; you never threw one like that in your life?" [Roaring with laughter.]

Q. You could actually change your delivery at the last instant?  Great coordination.

A. Yes. You had to be able to do that.

Q. How was your spitter [chuckling, knowing it was illegal]?

A. I never used one. I could throw one, but I never used it. The greatest pitch in baseball is the screwball. If I do say it, I think there was only one guy who had one as good as mine. I can't remember his name. My mind is getting faulty, but after all I'm pushing eighty... Yes, it was Hubbell. Hubbell and I, I think, were the only ones who truly had a screwball. The way they do it today -- one or two of them are fairly good -- but most of them, all they do is turn it over like this. They just turn their wrist the opposite way [counter-clockwise]. But the way to throw that is to snap it, just like you would your curveball. You snap it the other way from the curveball. I've heard so many say that "it hurts the arm."

Well, it doesn't hurt nearly as much as throwing the curveball. I've had them swing at that thing and the ball hits the plate.

Q. Tell me about that 1922 World Series. Did you get into it?

A. Oh, yes, I pitched the last ballgame.

Q. How did you do?

A. Well, no, I didn't get into the 1922 World Series. I was speaking of the 1927 series. But I did learn a lesson in the 1922 series. Jess Barnes, I think, pitched that first ballgame against the Yankees. Ruth came up there -- you'll laugh at this. Jess was standing out there, holding the ball in his glove like this, and then he stepped forward like a girl would throw -- like that -- and Ruth can't take it. When somebody does something like that to him, he starts dancing. Just dancing at the plate. And he sees that slow stuff coming he starts doing that. [Hill mimics Ruth's dancing, pigeon-toed at the plate, laughing.] He started calling Jess names, I think Ruth cussed him. Jess walked in and, I think, called Ruth "a nigger son-of-a-bitch." Well, after the ballgame, here comes Ruth up into our clubhouse and he's going to fight Barnes. He's twice as big as Barnes. He was going to whip Barnes because he said "he'd gotten personal" [chuckling]. No one could find Barnes. Anyhow, that taught me something. In later years, after that, in spring training I pitched several games against the Yankees. All I would ever throw Ruth was the slowest slowball you could ever get up there and the slowest curve. It started way up here and came down like that. It would keep him dancing. His favorite call to me was, "Put somethin' on the ball, you four-eyed son-of-a-bitch." [He is laughing so loudly he starts coughing.] And I'd throw him another one just as slow. That's all I'd ever throw him and that's all I threw him in the 1927 World Series.

Q. Did he hit you well in the Series?

A. He got that home run off me on a slow curve that was -- here's the bat and he hit it right here, just above his hands. It's 296-feet down the right field line in Yankee Stadium and they had a big screen up there. Paul Waner ran up the screen trying to catch the ball before it went over the screen. It went over just fair. In our ballpark in Pittsburgh the right fielder would have had to come in 15-20 steps to catch the darn thing... I'll tell you something about Ruth. He's the only batter I ever faced that you could hear his bat when he'd swing it. That is the God's Truth. You could hear it go [some untranslatable sound] and you could hear it all the way out to the pitcher's mound.

Q. Does that mean the wrist action was so great?

A. He could really swing a bat and he could hit a fastball a thousand miles [chuckling]. I've seen him do it. He hit one in the World Series over in St. Louis. He hit if off of Hi Bell. Bell ducked on the ball it went right by his ear and -- you know how a golfball will start low and rise? -- well that ball started to rise and kept rising and went clear into the center field bleachers right near the top. I was there and I saw that. He didn't like to hit off me at all.

Q. Did anything else of interest happen to you in that 1927 Series?

A. Yes. The first three men, Ruth was one of them, hit little poppers just out of the first baseman's reach. Joe Harris was playing first and he had a bad hip and could hardly move. These balls went by him, within eight- or ten-feet of first base, and he just couldn't get to them. The first three men up got base hits in the same spot. Then I struck out Gehrig, Meusel, and Lazzeri, all in the first inning. But any other first baseman -- to tell you the truth, I think our fielding today is much better than it was in my time. The infielders, especially.

Q. They have bigger gloves.

A. No, they're quicker. Much quicker. They get balls now that were easy base hits back in those days.

Q. Now getting back to your career chronologically, you went back to Indianapolis in 1923 after your stint with the Giants?

A. Yes. Hendricks was gone and Donie Bush took over.

Q. How was he as a manager?

A. Well, Donie was all right when you got to know him. But he always had to have somebody to jump on. I wasn't winning at all and he started picking on me. In fact, he bothered me no end. He kept riding me and I went up and told the old man. I said, "Mr. Smith, you had better get that little Irishman off my back or I'm going to tear him apart. I mean I'm going to tear him apart." He said, "What do you mean; aren't you getting along?" "We aren't getting along nohow! If he rides me one more time, you're not going to have a manager." He must have called Bush up there and had it out with him because from then on Bush left me alone. He started picking on another player we had, Cal Crum, an infielder. But that was the only bad year I had in baseball and I had a terrible year.

*Carmen Hill, pitcher for Pittsburgh, 1927. Hill had a checkered career, spending most of the early years either as a marginal pitcher for the Pirates or in the minor leagues. Suddenly, in 1927, he burst forth with a 22-11 record, helping Pittsburgh to the National League pennant. He came back with a strong performance in 1928, 16-10, but after that fell again into oblivion. (Photo from author's collection.)*

Q. How do you explain that? Bad arm maybe?

A. Nope. Things just didn't go right. I lost eight straight games and the most runs off of me in those games was three and most hits was six. How you gonna stop that? I think I lost twenty-two games that year.

Q. The book says 12-21. Who were some of your teammates that year? Was Eddie Sicking with you? I've interviewed him.

A. Yes, Eddie was with us. He and I were buddies. We went on a fishing trip way up in northern Wisconsin in 1925 and the World Series was on at that time.

Pittsburgh was behind the last we heard on the way up there, three games to one, and by gosh if they didn't turn around and win that World Series. We got up there and got to camp -- oh, we were up in a wild area -- and it started to snow. It snowed for four straight days without a let-up. I'm telling you the snow was that deep!  I went down to the lake a couple of times and cast out. When you'd bring it in the line would be frozen. We didn't do much fishing [laughing]. We stayed a couple of more days and then got out of there and came back home.

Q. Did you visit much back and forth?

A. No, I never saw Eddie after he left here...  After my bad year in 1923 I had a good year in 1924. Have you got them down there?

Q. In 1924 you were 17-14. In 1925 16-15. In 1926 you were 21-7. That was a good year.

A. Yep. That's when I went back to Pittsburgh. But you know, it's a funny thing. They were selling ballplayers all around me from the Indianapolis club, and I didn't find out until I went back to Pittsburgh what was the matter. So I went up and asked Dreyfuss, "How come I've been down there all this time?" "Well, it was the pricetag they had on you. That's what kept you there. You know what I had to pay for you?  I had to pay $50,000 and two ballplayers for you" [chuckling]. That's when I found out what had been going on.

Q. How were you notified, and when, that Pittsburgh bought you?

A. Hump Pierce, our trainer, came into the clubhouse and said "Get your things together, you're going to Chicago."  You know about Hump Pierce, don't you?

Q. No.

A. He was a honey [chuckling]. I asked why I was going to Chicago. "To join Pittsburgh."  I went into the office and the old man said "Pittsburgh went and bought you. They want you to report immediately."  So I got on the train and went on to Chicago. This was in the late fall of 1926. I won my twentieth ballgame that year, 1-0 against Minneapolis on the first day of August. So you know I had a pretty good year. The train was a little late getting into Chicago and the team had already gone out to the ballpark. Bill McKechnie was the manager. The boys were coming down out of the clubhouse. The clubhouse was underneath the stands, but you had to go up steps, and McKechnie says "Where the hell have you been?"  I said I had been trying to get there. "Go in there and get into a monkey suit." I got two-thirds up the stairs when he called out, "Wait a minute." He reached down into the ballbag, got a brand new ball and tossed it up to me [chuckling]. I was pitching! I said, "You don't even give me a chance to meet the boys." "I'm not even going to give you a chance to get scared" [roaring].

Q. How did you do?

A. I beat 'em 2-1 in ten innings.

Q. How did you feel about going up this time? It's now over ten years later from when you first were up.

A. I was glad to get back up.

Q. How about Dreyfuss, after he had optioned you out all those years and never kept you, then he released you and now you are back with him. Must have been rather strained situation?

A. Oh, he said, "You'd have been up here all the time if you hadn't been so contrary." But I wasn't about to be sent down to the minor leagues when I knew I could pitch in the big leagues and had proved it. If I hadn't proved that then I wouldn't have thought so much of it. But I knew I could pitch up there. You can believe this or not, it's easier pitching up there than down here -- especially if you've got control.

Q. Why is that? Better support?

A. Better support and -- by that time I ran my ballclub when I was out there. Bush never told me a thing. He'd say "Watch your outfield." The boys got to writing on all my mail when it came in, "Watch your outfield; watch your outfield." It's the truth. If a pitcher has excellent control -- and I'll have to pat myself on the back, I did have; I could throw that ball in a knothole most of the time... The greatest compliment I ever had was when Smitty told me -- my nickname was "Bunker" -- "Bunker Hill" -- "Bunker, I've caught all of them, and you're the best. I could sit in a rocking chair and never get out of it. I consider that quite a compliment from him when he had caught all of them -- Mathewson and the rest... Yes, this was when I was [with] Smitty again in 1927. He had come to Pittsburgh and he and I were roommates and buddies. We were buddies all that year and up until we were separated. I was sold to St. Louis and then he came right behind me. We buddied up again over there.

*Carmen Hill, pitcher for Pittsburgh, 1927. Hill was one of the first players to wear glasses. They caused him trouble only when they fell off his nose and got stomped on before he could find them. He took a lot of ribbing about being "Mr. Four-Eyes," but the ribber always smiled when he called him that. (Photo from the author's collection.)*

Q. Where did he get the nickname "Oil?"

A. The Brooklyn fans gave him the nickname. They couldn't pronounce the names very well. So "Oil" from Earl... I never quite forgave Bush for not pitching me in Pittsburgh. [McKechnie was with the Pirates when Hill was called up in August 1926, but over the winter of 1926-1927 McKechnie moved on to Boston and Bush was brought up to manage the Pirates in 1927.] I had won twelve and only lost two in the Pittsburgh ballpark in 1927 and one of the losses was a giveaway, it was kicked away. So I figured I should have been one of the starters at home. Wouldn't you figure that way? I had the best record of anybody at home. That rankled with me and then I don't get to start until that last ballgame of the World Series. And I came out of that in the seventh inning for a pinch-hitter. We tied the score 3-3 in the seventh and John Miljus went in to relieve me. He got through the eighth inning and in the last of the ninth inning he got a wild streak. I think somebody got a basehit and then he struck out a man and then he walked two men. He struck out the next man. Now the score is tied in the ninth inning and bases are loaded for the Yankees. The umpire had just announced that if nobody scored they would play the game over the next day. It gets terribly hazy in New York in late afternoon. Just a haze. John had two balls and two strikes on the hitter and Earl Combs, the fastest man on the Yankee ballclub, was on third base. Smitty had come out for a pinch-hitter the same inning I did and Johnny Gooch had come in to catch. So John did something he never did before, in fact, I never saw a catcher do it before. He motioned to Miljus that he wanted a curveball. He got down on one knee and got behind the hitter and motioned like this, that he wanted an overhand curveball. Well, to this day Miljus couldn't tell you why he did what he did. At the very last second, he starts his windup, and then he comes from way down here, in a sweeping side-arm curveball. And Gooch couldn't get up off of that knee fast enough to catch the ball, if only to knock it down. He did knock it down and it rolled, well, only about ten-feet away and here comes Combs. He slid in there -- smack -- just like that, under the tag. Gooch got the ball and tossed it to Miljus, but Combs was under the tag and the game was over. The crowd couldn't realize what had happened. We started to cross the field from our third base dugout and I was clear over to first base before there was a sound out of that crowd. But then it just broke loose. They were stunned. It seemed like you were in a vacuum until they came alive.

Q. Why did Miljus do that?

A. He didn't know why he changed [apparently from an overhand or three-quarter delivery to a side-arm one]. Maybe he thought he could strike him out. But he wouldn't have. He had a good overhand fastball.

Q. Tell me, on that 1927 Pirate team, one of the great mysteries had been why Bush benched Cuyler, a fine hitter, about midway through the season. Can you shed any light on that?

A. Didn't I tell you he had to have somebody to jump on? He picked Cuyler.

Q. You mean he'd pick on a .340 hitter for frivolous reasons?

A. It don't make any difference. He was that way. But I shook him off of me, I tell you.

Q. I can see getting on someone, but to bench a star hitter like Cuyler when the team is in the thick of a pennant fight, makes no sense to me.

A. It didn't make any sense to anybody. I'll tell you something else. Cuyler had an awful lot of friends in Pittsburgh and at the ballpark they would call him over to the side and want to talk to him. Bush jumped him about it. Well, if you know people and know them real well you just can't ignore them, can you? So he continued to do it and Bush set him on the bench and kept him there. It got so that if he said anything to me I'd let him have it right back.

Q. Over all, did Bush get along very well with the players?

A. Do you want to know something? That ballclub ran itself. That's a fact.

Q. It takes a good ballclub to do that. There must have been a leader?

A. Carey? Not necessarily. Traynor? I'd say Traynor came the closest to being a leader. Glenn Wright? He was quite a ballplayer. But he cost me one of the games in Pittsburgh. A little pop fly was hit just over his head, he went back and turned this way instead of that way. The ball dropped right along the side of him. It cost me the game. That was one of the few games New York beat me. In fact, the only game New York beat me that year. I beat them every time we played against them.

Q. After a play like that what does the pitcher say to the man who made the error, if anything, or the player to the pitcher?

A. Well, what happened in that game, Wright went back and got the ball. I think there were two men on at the time. He got the ball and threw it badly to third base. Traynor got it and the two men on base scored and the man who hit the ball was going into second. Traynor threw to second, but threw it badly into right field [chuckling].  So the runner scored from second. The ball came back in and they threw it over to Traynor. He starts walking over towards me. I put both hands behind me. He kept coming and I kept backing. I backed him up clear over to first base. He said, "What's the matter?"  I said, "Spit on that son-of-a-bitch and put the fire out before I'll take it" [roars with laughter].  It was too hot to handle.

Q. You say the team ran itself. Can you give any examples of that?

A. Well, I ran my ballgame. Hornsby got one hit off of me in seven ballgames. And he talked me into that one. He actually did. He was the last out one inning and he came by me as I was coming in to the dugout. He said, "I see you're pitching low and outside to me today, aren't you?"  I said, "I didn't notice, Rog, is that where you think I'm pitching you?"  "That's where you're pitching me." I got thinking about that. The next time he came up I thought he's expecting me to change. But I didn't change. I pitched that ball low and outside and he got a base hit right by the second baseman. Hit like a rifle shot and he laughed all the way to first base.

Q. And you hadn't been pitching him low and outside at all, had you?

A. Yes, I had. But he thought he was trying to get me to change. To pitch inside to him. The more I thought about it the more I thought I would continue to pitch him the same way. He figured that's what I would do and I did... Yes, he was a smart ballplayer... No, I didn't know him very well. He was a loner.

Q. Did you ever have arm trouble?

A. Oh, gosh, yes. I had arm trouble in 1918. I was sent down to Birmingham and they had a short season because of the war and they closed early. And Pittsburgh sent me to Kansas City. I had a terrible arm. We had a manager named Ganzel. A big heavy-set guy with a squeaky voice. I could barely throw that ball at all and after about five or six innings my arm was all swollen up like it was infected. After five or six innings I wasn't able to bring my arms up. They just dropped. I'd turn around and walk out of there. "What are you coming out for?" he'd ask in that high, squeaky voice. I'd just look at him. We had a short season there, too. Did you ever hear of "Bonesetter" Reese of Youngstown?

Q. I certainly have.

A. I stopped to see Bonesetter. He looked my arm over and said, "My boy, I won't touch that arm with all the swelling that's in it. You go home and get that swelling out and come back." I went home and we had a little old chiropractor there. I went to see him and he started giving me treatments. He worked on that arm and that swelling went down. I was feeling pretty good so I went out and started throwing a little bit. We had a little city league there at home back in Corry. So they wanted me to pitch a game for them. One of the clubs did. I went down and pitched six innings. Then here comes a telegram from Pittsburgh -- they were in New York. It said, "If your arm is in shape, join us immediately." So I went home, packed a suitcase, and went to New York. I got to the hotel and there was a note to catch the train for Bridgeport, Connecticut. The Pirates were playing an exhibition game there against Baltimore. That game went to thirteen innings, a 3-3 tie, and I pitched the whole game. My arm was all right the rest of the year. But it had been in miserable shape; like a piece of raw beefsteak.

Q. What had happened?  Had you any idea?

A. It was something in the elbow, I think, but I really don't know what it was. The result was that it looked like that -- that's as far as it would come out, but I didn't have a sore arm. I couldn't straighten it out at all. You know what happened?  That winter I had bought an old Henderson motorcycle -- one of those four-cylinder jobs that you cranked like an automobile. I tore it down, put new rings in it, new pins, and fixed it all up. I started to crank it once and that crank slipped off -- my wife was in the other room and she heard that arm "snap" just like that. It didn't hurt, but what it did, it started to jerk, just like that. And it came clear up here like this.

Q. It was bent right up to the shoulder.

A. Right up tight here. After the third day it started to come back and when it came back down it was straight. So that's what happened.

Q. Were you worried about your pitching?

A. Oh, I thought I was through. Yes, I was worried, but that thing straightened out like a string. And then I had another funny occurrence. In 1927. I won my first ballgame on the third of May, I think, that year. I didn't have a sore arm, but I couldn't throw hard; I couldn't break a pane of glass. I would throw as hard as I could, but I couldn't throw hard. Through Joe Harris I heard about this guy named Guy Green of Lyonsville, Pennsylvania, about 150 miles from Pittsburgh. I was telling Joe that I didn't have a sore arm, but that I couldn't throw. He told me to go see Guy Green. I did. I built up a friendship with that fellow until he died here a few years ago. I never knew a human that could do what he could. He could run his hand down your back and tell you your life history. It's a fact. He sat me down on a piano stool and I told him that I had arm trouble. He run his hand down my back and then came over here on this shoulder and -- his hands were that big; he had huge hands -- he'd dig down in there and get ahold of a tendon and flip it. Then he got another place back in there and flipped it. Then he came over here on this side of the shoulder and --

Q. The right arm.

A. -- and he says "Now, this ought to do it." He dug down in there and got hold of a tendon -- you could feel it when it would go -- and he says "Now straighten your arm out." I straighened it out and he felt all over and said, "You're all right now, but don't pitch for a couple of days." So I went back and told Bush that this doctor had told me not to pitch for a couple of days. "What doctor?" I told him. So I didn't throw any that day and don't you know but on the next day Bush put me in there. But I'm telling you it was no effort to go out there and pitch nine innings at all. I started in and won fifteen out of sixteen straight. I haven't told you much about Bush, but I'll tell you one thing. We were in New York and the Dempsey-Sharkey fight was coming up at Yankee Stadium. I had pitched that day and Smitty and I wanted to go see that fight. Well, Bush was having supper with a couple of big shots there in New York; I didn't know who they were and didn't give a damn. I went over to him in the dining room and said "Ownie, the Dempsey-Sharkey fight is on tonight and Smitty and I would like to go see it. Have you any objections?" "You can't go." I said "You just go plumb to hell" and turned around and walked off. About an hour or two later he came looking me up. He said "You shouldn't ever have done a thing like that with those people at the table." I said "I meant every word of it and I mean it now." He said "Well, you and Smitty go ahead and go." So we went to the fight.

Q. You would have gone anyway, wouldn't you?

A. Yes. We would have gone, but I would have preferred his consent. Now here's the one I was going to tell you. I pitched a game in New York on a Saturday and we went to Brooklyn for a Sunday game. He said "I'm going to take you along." I said "You had better not." "Well, you better be at the train." "Don't hold the train, I won't be there." I'd pitched that day, you see, and he wanted to take me over there, so he could use me. And that's what he pulled down the stretch. I had to relieve an inning or two even when I was working my own turn. I told him. I said, "Bush, what have you got seven or eight other pitchers for? I'm not the only pitcher on this club." So we go over to Philadelphia. I pitched the opener there and won it. The following day -- little Mike Cvengros, I don't know if you remember him or not, was pitching this game. He was in hot water from the beginning right up to the seventh inning. The score is tied at three. He walks the first three men and Bush sent me down to the bullpen. "I want you to pitch to just one man." I was down there at the start of the inning and begin to warm up. Mike walks these first three men. There were three balls and no strikes on the next hitter and I get the wave-in. I'm kicking dirt all the way in there, calling him everything I could lay my tongue to. It just shows you [chuckling] that Bush and I weren't on the same team. I go in there and Bernie Friberg, a right-hand hitter, was up. They took out Friberg and brought in Cy Young -- that good left-handed hitting outfielder. Now we're at Baker Bowl, that bandbox park where the second baseman played the balls off the right-field wall. That's a fact. I had pitched to Young before and knew what his weakness was -- right here, inside. I'll bet you I pitched three balls that didn't vary a quarter of an inch all in the same place on the inside and struck him out. The next man fouled out to Smitty, and the next man fouled out to Traynor at third. The game went fourteen innings and we won it in the fourteenth. That was my pitching to one man. Not that he picked on me all that year, but it seemed that if there was a pinch, I was in it. We had a couple of pitchers that had a tendency to go out and get lit up the night before they pitched. Ray Kremer was one of them. I don't know how many times I had to pitch with two days rest. Bush would say "Well, Kremer's got a sore arm" or "Kremer doesn't feel good." He was the one rotating just ahead of me. I think I backed up Kremer about three times that year and somebody else a couple or three times with only two days rest. I wouldn't have refused if you'd have killed me, I wouldn't have refused to go in there. When he called on me I'd go.

Q. Did you pitch differently to batters at Baker Bowl because of that short right field fence?

A. My main pitch in that ballpark was the screwball. Just keep throwing that. They couldn't hit the darn thing. In one ballgame over there, this same Cy Young, after I got two strikes on him, he tried to bunt the third strike twice in one game. Because he couldn't hit the screwball and he fouled it for the third strike both times.

Q. Did you hit many batters? Probably not with your good control.

A. No. I brushed them back. When this feud with McGraw and Smith was going on, if the occasion arose, McGraw would have his pitcher walk Smitty by throwing at him. And I mean they would really throw at him because those were their orders. The pitchers had nothing against Earl, but they were ordered to throw at him and Smitty knew it. This one day it happened twice. About the fourth or fifth inning, Smitty walked out and said, "Bunker, are you my friend?"

I said "Shut up, go back there and catch."  The first three men up in that inning, I really downed them. One fellow, his hat went one way, the bat another, and he went still another way [chuckling]. I was throwing at him and I was throwing at the next two. That ended the shooting game; there was no more shooting and I had an easy ballgame.

Q. When you threw at them what did you aim at?

A. You could never hit a man in the head throwing at his head. If you wanted to hit a man in the head -- I never did it intentionally, but I knew where to throw it. You aim for his left shoulder if he's a right-hand hitter and you'll get him. He'll duck into it. But throwing at a man's head, you'll never hit him. You'll come close. I've turned their caps around. I have hit some intentionally, but not the way you think. I've put them out of a ballgame by breaking a curveball onto their knee. If you hit a man on the knee -- smack! -- and he isn't going to play any more. I called a shot one time on somebody. He was walking up, taking a couple of steps and I told them on the bench that he'd taken all the steps he was going to take in this ballgame. "What are you going to do?"  "I'm going to hit him on the knee."  I hit him on that knee and you could hear it pop all over the place and they had to carry him off [laughing]. But to deliberately throw to hit somebody in the head, no, I never did that.

Q. Do you think many pitchers did or do?  How about Carl Mays?

A. No, I don't think so. As for Mays, I can understand that because I got hit by a similar pitcher down in the Southern League. An underhand pitcher down there hit me in the head. I got hit right back of this ear. It can happen because his ball will duck -- and underhand ball will duck. If he gets it up high enough you'll duck right into it.

Q. Did you ever get thrown out of any games?

A. Uh -- no. Hendricks took me out of a game up in Milwaukee one time that I wasn't willing to come out of. He put Pug Cavet in there to relieve me with a man on third base and two men out. There was no reason for him to take me out of there. Pug Cavet, do you remember him, a tall, skinny guy? Pug came out there and got the ball. He looked around, started his windup -- a very big, awkward guy -- his arm came down and hit his leg and the ball dropped out behind him. The man on third scored and won the ballgame for Milwaukee.

Q. But you never got thrown out of a game by an umpire?

A. No... I got along pretty well with umpires. I think Bill Klem was great. If that ball was on the corner you got it. And Smitty, in my estimation, was the greatest catcher in baseball. He had to be for the simple reason that he did all his catching one-handed. He never had a bad finger on his right hand. His fingers were just as straight as they could be. Every other catcher I ever saw had banged up fingers.

Q. So you're saying he had to be good to be able to catch everything in his gloved hand?

A. Yes. And I'll tell you something else. Here's home plate. Smitty would catch a low ball with his glove up. Which brings the ball up. The same on an inside ball -- he'd catch it with the glove towards the plate, never out here. The same over here on an inside pitch. Well, he could do that with one hand. The glove always toward the plate. Well, the ball could be an inch or two off the plate and the way he'd catch it, it would be over the plate. He got me many a strike that way. He was a wizard at it.

Q. So the glove was always in the strike zone while the ball might be a little bit off. And the umpire would go with the glove.

A. The umpire would have to go with the glove. I don't care how good a man's eyesight is. He was the only catcher who could do that. He was the greatest catcher -- they didn't make them any better.

Q. Have you any Federal League stories?

A. Well, I pitched against the Federal Leaguers one game. No, I take that back. I was thinking of the Black Sox; we played them an exhibition game. Benny Kauff had been with the Feds and he was with them there. He was quite a hitter... [Back to Smith]  Earl was a heavy drinker; yes, he drank a lot.

Q. Was there a lot of drinking on that Pittsburgh club?

A. All of them [chuckling].

Q. Not Pie Traynor?

A. You wouldn't be sure of that, would you? [Chuckling.]  Well, as a rule, Pie was pretty decent, but... A bunch of us were out one night in spring training and I can't for the life of me remember where we were. We went into this restaurant which had a real long counter. All along that counter were the nicest pies that you ever saw. Somebody bet Pie that he couldn't walk the full length of that counter without stepping on a pie [laughing]. He tried it and I don't think he missed one [roaring].

Q. Who paid the bill?

A. We did. We all chipped in $2.50 to pay for the pies.

Q. Is that how he got his nickname?

A. No, he had his nickname before that, but he confirmed it there.

Q. What were these accidents you had with your glasses?

A. Oh, I had a fellow trapped between third and home and he just shoved me in the face like that and broke my glasses all to pieces. It happened here in Indianapolis... Oh, he did it intentionally. I swore up and down I was going to get him for it, but before he left he came and apologized. It was the catcher for the Toledo club. It was a good thing he apologized because there was one guy I intended to hit. I mean really hit him... No, I don't want to mention his name. Then another time I was standing behind the batting cage or just to the side of the cage talking to someone. Somebody was up there hitting and he fouled the ball which came back, hit the ground, and bounced up, hitting me right here breaking the lens all to pieces. It pushed my nose clear over to here. I grabbed my eye and rushed into the clubhouse and started dousing my eye with cold water and kept that up for awhile and never got a cut out of it. It cut around the edges, but not in the eye. Oh, I was all right. I went down to a doctor who sat me down in a chair. He took a steel instrument and he went up in there and pushed my nose way back. It's still a little out of line, but it had been way over here. He pushed it all back.

Q. I imagine that felt pretty good?

A. I was gripping both arms of the chair and I pulled them both out... I have had some trouble with my nose, but not a great deal.

Q. When you got punched in the face, did you get any cuts that time?

A. Yes, I got cut. I did the same thing that I did this time. I ran into the clubhouse with my hand over the eye and washed it all out. I got cut around the nose and around here where the glass broke. Outside of that, I was very fortunate. I used to play in pepper games all the time.

Q. Did you ever think much about your glasses during a game or did you just forget them?

A. I'd just forget them.

Q. Did you ever try pitching without them?

A. Well, what would have been my twenty-third ballgame here with Pittsburgh -- it happened in Chicago -- this news article gave the game to me. I had two men out in the fourth inning. I had Chicago beat 1-0 at the time. I broke my glasses, though I can't remember how. All I had was a pair of nose glasses, the kind that clamped onto your nose. Well, I started that game and about every second pitch, away they'd go. I'd go get them, wipe them off, and put them on again. I had gone four and two-thirds innings when they flipped off again. As I went to pick them up I stepped on them and broke them all to pieces and had to leave the game.

Q. But you just fell short of getting credit for the victory, didn't you?

A. You're supposed to pitch five innings to receive credit for the win. But the paper gave me the win. See here, it says "Hill wins number twenty-three." They figured I was forced to leave for unusual circumstances so I should get the win. But it was later ruled that since I did not have a "commanding lead," they took the win away from me. Well Kremer went in to relieve me and held them and we won 2-1.

Q. What did you do in the off-seasons?

A. Whatever I could find to do. I'm telling you, jobs were scarce. Nobody wanted to hire you if you were only going to be there a few months. It was hard to find anything... Yes, lots of hunting and fishing. I did that back in Corry.

Q. When did you move from Corry to make your permanent home here in Indianapolis?

A. In 1921 or 1922.

Q. When did you get married?

A. Back in Corry in 1918. I married early and took my wife with me down south when I played at Birmingham. Our baby girl was born down there... We rented when we moved here in 1922.

Q. How about your biggest thrill in baseball?

A. Well, of course, pitching in a World Series is a big thrill; there's no question about that. I pitched a no-hitter down in the Southern League, which was a thrill. That was in 1917, my good year.

Q. How did you like living down south? Pretty hot, I expect?

A. No. I liked it. Birmingham was a pretty good place to be, but some of those other places! Oh, boy!... Yes, I remember Sulphur Dell in Nashville. I think that maybe the only home run I ever hit was in Nashville with the bases full.

Q. Maybe that was your greatest thrill. What did Waite Hoyt say was his greatest thrill? "Hitting two home runs in one game." Pitchers love to hit. Well, how about some tough hitters to pitch to. Do any stand out?

A. Well, I had a theory about hitters. I never talked to anybody about it, but any hitter who is up there swinging from his tail, I just loved those guys. But you take a man who stands up to the plate with a wide stance and takes only a short little step, he's going to hit that ball some place. But you take the guy who stands back here -- free swingers -- . Bush told me not too long ago before he died, he said, "Bunker, if you were pitching today you could win twenty-five and not try." That's what he said.

Q. What was he getting at?

A. Well, it's these free-swingers of today. They've got to take that step and my contention is -- well, I'll have to give you a trade secret [a demonstration, chuckling]. That pitcher's box out there is eighteen inches wide. When I was pitching to a right-hander I would be over on this far corner. [I presume he means the extreme right edge of the pitcher's plate as the pitcher faces the batter.] Here's where the right-hand hitters generally stand and then they step forward. All right, if you're over on this side of the pitcher's plate, as far as you can get, and you throw from three-quarters sidearm, that ball is going to cross his line of vision about here and he's got to move his eyes to follow it. Well you take a man who is spread out there like this and takes that little short step, he never loses sight of that ball. But a free-swinger can't do that. He's back there and he's got to come forward and I pitch him from this corner of the plate here -- clear over here, as far as I can go and still be on the pitching plate. On left-hand hitters I'm on the other corner and come straight overhand. That makes that ball go away from him. That was one of my secrets of pitching. All the others seem to pitch from the same place; there's one hole they stay in all the time. I've had hitters say, "Hill, I can't understand why we can't hit you."  In 1927, or 1928, the leading hitter in the National League was with Philadelphia.

Q. Lefty O'Doul?

A. Yes, I think so. He came to me in the last game there and he had a little black book, he says, "Hill, you know what I've hit off of you this year?"  "No, I don't have any idea." "I've got it down right here; .147."

Q. The league-leading hitter! He kept a book on all the pitchers?

A. He had a book on every pitcher in the league. He had a book on each one, what he hit, where it was, everything. I never knew anybody else to do that in those days... No, I never kept a book on the batters. I figured on remembering what they could and couldn't hit.

Q. How about when a new rookie came into the league?

A. He might give you trouble. I remember when Al Lopez came to Brooklyn he was hitting everybody. The pitchers all around the league got to talking about him. What were they going to do to stop him. Well, I hadn't pitched against him yet. We were in New York before we went over to Brooklyn and some of the New York pitchers were talking to us. Freddie Fitzsimmons said, "Hill, don't throw him a curveball. He'll murder a curveball." He was hitting around .400, I guess, at that time. Nobody knew how to pitch to him. I had hitters tell me they didn't like to hit my curveball, so I thought well now, we'll find out. I think I struck him out three times in that first game throwing him curveballs. It got around the league then that he wasn't a good curveball hitter... He'd just been lucky at first in hitting the curve. Those three strikeouts broke the charm.

Q. I think you won over 200 games, all told, did you ever add them up?

A. No, I never did. You know what I figured was my difference in pitching compared to the other fellows?  Just what I told you about using the pitcher's plate. It only takes about that much to miss the bat altogether. Just that small amount. And I figured I had that advantage by working from one side of the plate to the other side [pitcher's plate]. I figured that anytime I could make the batter move his eyes, I was ahead of him.

Q. You made quite a study of the art of pitching.

A. You have to. These pitchers today, nine out of ten of them are just throwers. I get so mad some times watching them. I tell my wife that I'm going to sit down and watch what he's going to do wrong. This happened in 1931. You may have to look it up to be sure. 1931 or 1932. Bush became the manager of the Minneapolis ballclub and St. Louis had sent me up there. I had gone from Pittsburgh to St. Louis and St. Louis farmed me up there to Minneapolis. We were playing in the Little World Series. We had been to Newark and we were returning to finish the Series at Minneapolis. We had a layover in Chicago of six hours. Well [chuckling], Jess Petty, Rosy Ryan, and myself, and a little outfielder -- I can't remember his name to save me, an ex-major leaguer -- we went out to a friend of Jess's there in Chicago. And boy, he really put one on for us. The result was we overstayed the layover [laughing]. We knew we had to get there, so we started calling airports to see who had a plane that could take us to Minneapolis. We couldn't get a thing in Chicago and had to go to Milwaukee. We were able to get somebody at Milwaukee who would take us. He came down and picked us up and took us up to Minneapolis. Yes, we flew up; it cost us $200 apiece [laughing]. We got up there about midnight, went to bed and had a good night's sleep. The funny thing was, as we were crossing the Mississippi River, with lights on both sides of the river, I saw something down there on the water which I wanted to look at. There were little windows in this plane that opened out. Well, I opened the window next to me, stuck my head out, and -- pphht -- my glasses were gone just like that [laughing]. So we went out to the ballpark the next morning, and you know, they never missed us!  They never knew we weren't on that train!  To this day I don't think Bush ever knew it. Anyway, we went out to the ballpark and expected to really get it, but nobody said anything; we hadn't been missed. Bush came over and said "You're going to work today."  I said, "Well, I don't know whether I am or not. I dropped my glasses last night and broke them."  He said, "You know, I did the same thing. I dropped and broke mine too. I guess you know that our uniforms didn't get here."  I said, "No, I hadn't heard that."  He said "A drunken newspaperman went back in the baggage car on the way up here from Chicago and threw all the trunks off the train."  Well, my baseball glasses were in the trunk. I told him that I didn't have another pair of glasses and that if they weren't here I couldn't pitch. So he had to call on somebody else [roaring].

Q. What did you use for uniforms?

A. We used make-shift outfits. And there's something that happened in that ballgame that I never forgot. Did you ever hear of an umpire's decision being changed five times before they arrived at a final decision?  Well, this little center fielder came in on a flyball and dove for it. When he dove he turned sideways with his back to the stands and the infield, and for the life of you, you could not tell whether he caught that ball or not. The home plate umpire called the man out. Well, the Newark team started squawking, saying he trapped the ball. The first base umpire agreed, saying he trapped it. The umpire at second base said he caught it. The umpire at third base [laughing] reversed the decision and said he trapped it. It took five changes in decision before it was decided that the ball was caught. It was Rice, yes Harry Rice who made that play.

# Ray Hayworth

*High Point, North Carolina, March 13, 1978*

"Mickey Cochrane's Backup"

I pulled into the driveway of Ray Hayworth's large farm outside High Point, North Carolina -- an hour or so after interviewing ancient Ernie Shore in Winston-Salem -- on the afternoon of March 13, 1978. He was whacking away at a woodpile and as I parked the car he came over and introduced himself. He had been expecting me. He was very congenial and a bit larger than I remembered him to be when he was catching for the Tigers in the early 1930s. In a way he reminded me of the old movie star, easy-going Stewart Erwin. Ray owned a lot of land in the area, some of which he had inherited and some of which he had purchased with his 1934 World Series check. His son, a public official in High Point, helped Ray work out a plan whereby much of the land was subdivided and sold. But they still retained a great deal. That the Hayworths had money was obvious from a quick tour of the house. Lovely furnishings, upholstery, antiques, and pictures were to be seen everywhere. The interview lasted about ninety minutes. It was an easy exchange as Ray was knowledgable, had a good memory, and expressed himself lucidly. He talked more about his scouting career than I would have preferred in the time I had, but there is some good stuff there, too, especially about the signing of Ernie Banks. I am sure much more about Hayworth's career would have come out had I been able to stay longer. He was certainly willing to go on. But I had a long three-hour drive over unfamiliar roads ahead of me, so I contented myself with what I had and left.

A. Well, I can begin by saying that I grew up about twenty minutes from here in Springfield, a Quaker settlement. As I grew up around Springfield, baseball was everything, all the kids played baseball and we had leagues here at that time, at every crossroads and factory. We grew up with it. I might say that in my early years I grew up in a baseball family. There were four brothers, all of us played professionally and all of us were catchers. My brother "Red," the youngest one, he followed me and played with St. Louis [Browns] in the 1944 World Series. Getting back to my early days around Springfield, south of here, was really sort of a foundation of our baseball beginnings. It was so interesting. There was an old gentleman here they called Rubel Spiro, a great left-hand pitcher in this area; he was sort of our father along the way. We followed him.

Q. Did you live on a farm?

A. Yes. My dad was a tobacco farmer and also raised cotton. He was a merchant for many years.

Q. Did he play any baseball?

A. No, he never played a game in his life; he had no interest in the game until we began playing. Then he became interested; my mother, too.

Q. Did they get to see you play?

A. Yes, they used to come to Washington to see me play and then they were in Detroit for the 1934 and 1935 World Series.

Q. Now you hear about boys who were raised on farms throwing rocks at tin cans...

A. Yes, I believe that is where we developed our arms, throwing rocks at squirrels and things; I guess that does help develop kids' arms. Fortunately, for my brothers and myself, nature gave us good strong arms, we could all throw well. We never had great foot speed -- this is the kind of thing I looked for in my years of scouting, following my playing career. As time went on I went to high school and eventually went to Oak Ridge. Yes, they had a team in high school and believe it or not I pitched in high school. Then I went to Oak Ridge and began catching altogether. I was signed by Detroit after a couple of years.

Q. This Oak Ridge; was it an academy of some sort?

A. Yes, although it was more a preparatory school for college. After I finished the tenth grade in high school I went over there and finished my schooling. I decided not to go to college, but to go into professional baseball instead. I signed with Detroit. At that time they put a lot of their kids out at Bluefield, West Virginia, where I played two years. Vic Sorrell and a few others who Detroit had signed. This is the way they did it then, a few years ahead of the farm system. Then I went on to Detroit in 1926.

Q. Tell me about all these players coming out of this Winston-Salem/High Point area.

A. Yes, Colonel Holt over at the academy, was a highly regarded coach even though he was only in prep school. He sent many players to the major leagues. Jakie May, Wes Ferrell, and my brother "Red" -- in fact, "Red" was the ninth player he sent to the major leagues -- and many other players were sent out of there. It was a fine place and every kid in this country wanted to go to school at Oak Ridge.

Q. How do you account for this, just chance, I suppose?

A. Yes. When I moved out of here there were so many fellows right out of this immediate area -- Larry Woodall, Sam "Hoot" Gibson, the knuckle-baller, and a great many players, like the Ferrells; Slaughter came on a little bit later. I know at one time we sat down and counted all the fellows from here in about a ten-year period who got to the major leagues from this area; there were just so many of them. And I think it was, as I said before, that so much baseball was played here. We found out late, when I was scouting, that we could get good players from Cuba, Panama, the Dominican Republic, because down there all the kids do is play baseball. They learn that it's a great opportunity for them.

Q. What year was it that you finished up at the academy?

A. 1925. In 1926 I went to spring training with Detroit. Old Billy Dall made one trip to this country one spring, at Wake Forest he signed Vic Sorrell, he came through here and I signed with Detroit at that time. He went on out to Tennessee and signed Dale Alexander and Johnny Stone. He got the doggonedest collection of players, and everyone signed up with Detroit.

Q. He saw you play?

A. Yes; it was mainly through the coach at Oak Ridge. He visited us here. I had a chance to go Wake Forest to school, but at that time all I could see was baseball. I just lived it and read about players I admired, like Ty Cobb, Tris Speaker, and Eddie Collins, Babe Ruth, all of those fellows. I got to go up there and play against these people. I remember the first day I got into a game I got to hit against Walter Johnson; I thought that was the greatest thing there ever was.

Q. Did your parents want you to go on to college?

A. They really didn't push college that much because my interests were not in that drection and fortunately I went right into professional ball.

Q. How did they feel about that? Did they approve?

A. Yes. They had to sign for me since I was not of age. I went right up to the Tigers in 1926 and I stayed with them nearly all year. I'll tell you how this

*Ray Hayworth, regular Detroit catcher until Mickey Cochrane joined the team as manager in 1934. This did not trouble Ray, however, as he enjoyed playing for a winning team; he treasures highly his World Series rings. In his 15-year career spread over three decades, he batted .265 in 698 games. (Photo from National Baseball Library, Cooperstown, NY.)*

happened. I went to spring training and Toronto, their Triple-A club, and Detroit both trained at Augusta, Georgia. I went down with the Toronto club, Vic Sorrell and I. I caught a few games for Toronto. Then, unfortunately at that point, unfortunate for the Detroit club, but fortunate for me, Johnny Bassler broke his leg. Bassler was their number one catcher. So after that they were looking around [for a replacement] and they had seen me in spring training, and [Manager] Ty Cobb said "let's bring that kid over here and we'll keep him until Bassler gets back." But Bassler didn't get back until August. Meanwhile, Larry Woodall, the other catcher, got a bad spike wound in the knee. They looked around and [chuckling] I'm the only one sitting there and I got along real well. It was a great experience for me because after playing up there I knew that I could do the job. So the next year I went to Nashville and stayed there until July and then I went over to Shreveport. I finished 1927 there and played there in 1928 and went on back to spring training with Detroit in 1929. At the close of spring training, Bucky Harris, our manager, wanted to send me down to Toledo to play for Casey Stengel. He'll teach you to hit-and-run, to hit to right field, and do the other things you'll need to do. So I went down there with Casey and had a great year, hitting .330. I went back to Detroit and stayed there for ten years until I was sold to Brooklyn.

Q.  What was it like going up there to the big-time in 1926?

A.  Well, it was a great thrill for me. As I mentioned all these great old-timers, it was a thrill to see them and then to play against them.

Q. How was Ty Cobb; how did he deal with you?

A.  I have been asked that question many times. Ty Cobb was the fiercest competitor I ever saw on the field; he would do anything to beat you. But the nicest person to sit in the hotel lobby and visit with that you would ever want to meet. I could never put the two of them together. I used to listen to the great stories Cobb would tell, as we sat around the hotel lobbies, stories about base-stealing and how they sharpened their spikes, as they did in those days. I was pleasantly surprised. He was very nice to me, he knew I was just a young kid. We developed a friendship that lasted through the years, as long as he lived. Other people in Detroit were nice to me. Charlie Gehringer was just coming on; he had a great career ahead. The great teams Detroit had in 1934 and 1935 began to be put together in 1932, with players coming up from the Texas League. Jo-Jo White, "Schoolboy" Rowe, Tommy Bridges -- all those fellows were just coming along then; we sort of grew up together. When they were able to make the addition of Mickey Cochrane and "Goose" Goslin, along with Hank Greenberg, Charlie Gehringer, Marv Owen, and Pete Fox, and all the great pitchers we had then -- Elden Auker, Hogsett, Sorrell, Crowder, Rowe, and Bridges. And I'll tell you, it was such a great pleasure to play [chuckling], we'd win every day. How nice it was to play on a championship club. I found out later how disappointing

later how disappointing it was to play on a second division club. So I had a taste
of it all the way around.

Q. Do you remember anything about the scandal at the end of the 1926 season?

A.  I remember it, but I don't recall the details. Cobb did resign after that
season, yes, but he was near the end of his career. When I was born in 1904 he
was just joining the Tigers and I got up there to play with him before he
finished. I don't remember Donie Bush, who managed the Tigers the next year
since I was down with Nashville and Shreveport. Bucky Harris was manager
when I came back up. I played for Cobb, Harris, Mickey Cochrane and Del
Baker; I played for some great managers. I went on to play for Brooklyn with
Durocher, Bill Terry at New York, Southworth at St. Louis.

Q. What manager is at the top of your list?

A. I thought that Southworth was a great manager, although I wasn't with him
too long. Durocher was good. I remember Mr. Rickey saying at a meeting one
time that Durocher could make decisions faster than any manager he ever knew.
Situations changed rapidly in the course of a game and Durocher was right there.
That's the reason he admired him so. There life-styles were not very similar, but
Rickey thought Durocher was a great manager.

Q. Did you have much chance to observe Cobb as a manager?

A. Well, Cobb was such a great player he expected so much from his men
because he was so great himself. Other people, Southworth and Cochrane, they
had different ways of managing. It's just hard to say. They were all good
managers, but I feel that one or two were great ones.

Q.  It seems that great players were not very good managers, while less than
average players were pretty good managers.

A. I would like again to quote Mr. Rickey. I had great admiration for him. He
analyzed the game so thoroughly and he said one time about managers. He said
there is no way to tell if a fellow is going to become a good manager until you
give him a club and put him on the field and find out. Meaning you couldn't
take a great player and assume he would become a great manager. A lot of good
ones were not great players -- Alston, McCarthy. Managers are a rare breed and
you just cannot tell until, as Mr. Rickey said, you give them the opportunity.

Q. What kind of a man was Dale Alexander?

A. Great. I roomed with Dale for several years. He was a mild, easy-going fellow, but my, he could swing that bat!  He left our club and went over to Boston and led the American League in batting. He was as slow as ... [unintelligible]. But Dale was a real gentleman, as fine a character as you would want. He used to come over here and see me and I went home with him after the season one year and went squirrel hunting. He and Johnny Stone, and Tommy Bridges...

Q. There were a lot of Tenneseeans up there weren't there?

A. Yes, a lot of good players came out of Tennessee.

Q. You mentioned Johnny Gill earlier; were you with him?

A. Yes, I was with Johnny with Shreveport in the Texas League and he went up to Cleveland. I remember the day he left the club down there to go to Cleveland. He had his suitcase with two bats strapped on the outside, but everybody in baseball thought a great deal of him -- he had such a sense of humor. A most likeable kind of fellow. But along the way you met so many individuals who were so different; this was natural as they came from all over the country. But the best friends I had came along later, like Lavagetto at Brooklyn ...

Q. Tell me about Nashville.

A. Well, I went to Nashville with Jimmy Hamilton and he had an awfully good catcher named Leo Mackey, and I just didn't get to play at all. But he had a friend over at Shreveport in the Texas League named Art Baylor who needed a catcher so they sent me over there.  Let me tell you quickly a most unusual story. I went over there and it was as hot as blazes and I didn't start off too well. It was hot and I wasn't in shape. I was there about two or three weeks and Detroit called up. Jack Zeller called and asked, "How is this Hayworth boy doing?"  "Not too good," was the reply. "Give him his release." Well, we went on a road trip just at that time. Down to San Antonio and around and I had the hottest streak in baseball that I ever had. I hit home runs, several with the bases loaded. The New York Giant scout was following the team around during my hot streak and the Giants called up our club and offered $50,000 for me. They called Detroit and said "Don't release him!"  So I finished up that year and the next season I had a pretty solid year.

Q. What happened to you on that road trip?

A. Oh, I don't know. I caught up with the heat and got into shape. It's in the Texas League Record Books -- I think it was three home runs with the bases loaded, a double and triple, and I drove in just a slew of runs. I think I drove in twenty-one runs. The New York scout couldn't pass that up. So that really saved me there and gave me the opportunity to go on up. I got more experience and kind of took hold of things... But the key to my going back up was my year with Casey Stengel. He was a great teacher. I used to say that any player who wanted a career in the big leagues should spend at least one year with Casey Stengel. He was a remarkable man. He used to hold these meetings and honest I couldn't keep a straight face; I'd hide my face in the locker. He was the funniest man I ever listened to. But he'd get his points across. He came in the clubhouse one day and sat down right in the middle of the room with a newspaper reading the stock market reports. Fellows, he said, this railroad is looking pretty good. But it is going to go up. The way you fellows have been playing you're really going to be riding the rails pretty soon [laughing]... He used to get out there in the middle of the clubhouse with a fungo bat, standing right next to a big trunk. Then he'd lecture us -- and you know how he could lecture -- and every once in awhile to make a point he'd hit that trunk with the fungo bat and it sounded like a stick of dynamite going off. As I say any man who played baseball, if he could have one year with Casey Stengel --  he was such a great man.

Q. Well, he had the Boston Braves for a number of years and he was always in the second division. I guess he didn't have the material.

A. Yes, we always say in baseball that you can't win without the horses. I could see that with our Detroit team in the early 1930s. But then the players grew up and we added a few stars and oh boy, what a team we had. That's what it  takes -- balance ...

Q. Down in the Texas League was Clarence Kraft around then?  He hit a lot of home runs, didn't he?

A. Clarence Kraft?  Yes, he hit a lot of homers. He was a great favorite in that league. You know back in the minors, they had some real stars, which the people worshipped just like they do in the majors. Take Ziggy Sears; man he was some man. He later managed for many years in the National League.

Q. Tell me about Swayne Field in Toledo.

A. Swayne Field had a short right field fence, very short. It was tough to pitch in that park. The toughest pitcher I ever caught in my whole baseball career was [Leroy] Parmelee. I used to say that he was the only pitcher who could pitch one-third of the game under home plate. He hit me all over. He could throw hard. He would throw that sinker, which would hit on the front end of the plate and it would get you in the arms, and around -- he bruised me all over. He had a tremendous arm... Later when he was with the Giants -- Fitzsimmons used to tell this story -- that when they would go into a tough series, Parmelee would say "Fitz you pitch the first game, Hub you pitch the second game, and Schumacher you pitch the third game. Let met pitch the last game." He didn't want to pitch those first tough games; he'd like to come in at the end and "smoke 'em out,"

Q. Was DeWitt "Bevo" LeBourveau with you at Toledo?

A. Yes, he was. A good hitter, a real good hitter. There was Jigger Statz then and some other fellows. They had good players in the minor leagues. There were the old-timers coming down and there were so many more leagues then that there were a lot of good players.

Q. Who were other pitchers with you at Toledo?

A. Oh, Hugh McQuillen came down from the Giants, and Parmelee, and I wish I could think of the name of that left-hander we had, who was a good pitcher. We're getting back so long ago now that my memory begins to fade... I like to go back through my old scrapbooks now and then. My wife kept them for me and she has filled them with everything from the Texas League -- we were married in 1927... I say if you read those scrapbooks you would have to think I belong in the Hall of Fame. She put in all the good days; she never put anything in when "I had the collar." If I hit a home run or did something pretty good, that went into the scrapbook, naturally.

Q. How did Toledo do in 1929?

A. Not too well; they didn't have a very good club. I left there in August and went over to Toronto with [Manager] Steve O'Neill. They were right in the thick of a pennant race over there and Toledo didn't have a chance, so Detroit sent me over to help out -- for three weeks or so. Then I joined Detroit in New York for the rest of the season. I stayed there right through the 1938 season.

Q. What was it like going back up there again after having been up once and sent down?

A. Well, I felt ready this time. Bucky Harris put me right in the lineup and I was our first string catcher in 1930, 1931, 1932, and 1933. You know it was back then in 1931 that I began that streak of errorless games. I wound up going 100 games with 439 chances without an error. That was a new major league record. The previous record was held by Johnny Bassler of 285 chances. I figured when I went to 439 chances nobody would ever equal it, but Buddy Rosar went by me and went on to 600 chances without an error and that's been broken a couple of times since.

Q. And the gloves they had in those days were not as big as those of later days; how can they not catch the ball today?

A. Yes. I have the gloves I used hanging up in the basement now. The one I used during the streak, the one after that, and the one after that when I retired. The baseball Hall of Fame wants that glove I used during the streak and I may send it to them some day. And "believe it or not," Ripley had a big cartoon about it which I have around here some place. The Hall of Fame wants that cartoon, too. I think it should be up there; I haven't sent it yet, but I probably will. Even though the record has been broken it had considerable interest at the time... When I see the present day gloves I don't see how I caught as well as I did -- they're so much improved.

Q. Did you catch any spitballers after the pitch had been outlawed [in 1920]?

A. Oh, yes a lot of guys threw it. I remember [a] time against Boston, Bridges loaded the ball up and threw it and I never saw such a hard hit ball in my life. Cramer hit a rope out to left-center. But it was a very effective pitch. Faber, Quinn, and others, they used slippery elm then... When I first faced John Quinn -- I was a right field hitter -- I went two for four, hitting two singles between first and second. I hit the spitter late. A hard pitch to hit because it breaks down so quickly. But Red Faber could break his spitter down or away making it harder to hit. I heard Ty Cobb say one day when Faber was pitching against us in Detroit, "that man is the toughest man I have ever hit against; the most difficult to hit" -- because the ball just moves so fast your eye cannot adjust quickly enough to it. The same thing with the knuckleball. It is hard to hit -- and catch. I was on a team with two knuckleball pitchers -- Johnny Niggeling and Tot Pressnell; boy, could they make that ball dance down there. Fitzsimmons threw a knuckler, but they all broke down like a spitter. These other pitchers threw "butterflies" we called them and you had to have the knack of taking that ball at the very last second; you couldn't go to it and catch it. No, we didn't use bigger gloves like they do today; we used our same glove. They were not easy to catch.

Q. Did you have any pickoff plays with runners on the bases?

A. Oh, yes. we had our plays. We would use our gloves to make the signal. Or the fielders would signal us. Greenberg would hold his glove on his knee in a certain way and I knew I should throw to him. The greatest contest I ever had was with Ben Chapman. He loved to steal on me. I threw him out three times in one game in New York. Daggone if that wasn't some afternoon. I threw him out twice trying to steal third base. But he was a great base-runner. And so was George Case... But actually you couldn't shoot 'em out if your pitcher didn't help you. If the pitcher had a poor move -- good-bye. If the pitcher had a good move you could throw them out.

Q. Now about Mickey Cochrane. Here you are the first string catcher for four years and suddenly the club acquires Cochrane, a superstar catcher, who will no doubt replace you in the lineup, but will also be the team's manager. Tell me your feelings concerning this.

A. Well, I felt he was the manager and I knew he was going to do a lot of catching. But I said to myself I would rather catch behind Cochrane on a winning team than be the first-string catcher in St. Louis where I knew they were going to finish last. Of course, I hit better when Cochrane came because he hit against all the right-handers and I hit against the left-handers. In 1934 my average went up to .292. I caught around sixty to eighty games that year... Yes, it was an adjustment, to become backup catcher. But in those days we wanted to win so badly, that was the most important thing. We were young with families, the depression was on and we needed the money so we wanted to win. Also there was a lot of prestige to winning... I went in and finished the game when "Bump" Hadley beaned him [Cochrane] in New York. Oh, it was a brutal injury. The ball sailed; it wasn't a beanball. Cochrane later said he just strided into it and that's the last he remembers. He lost sight of the ball; it jumped about a foot or two and struck him right over the temple. No way he could avoid it. "Bump" Hadley was just as sorry as anybody in the world, but he too had no control over what happened. That really ended Mike's career. It just wasn't worth going through the rigors of getting in shape... Birdie Tebbetts came along and replaced me as I was getting to the end of my career. I'll explain how this happened. You go along and catch regularly and pretty soon you start catching every other day and then you drift to the bullpen and only catch a game now and then. Because if you catch today and then catch tomorrow you are still tired -- as you get older. You don't come back overnight. I remember back in the early 1930s I'd catch a double-header today and another one tomorrow. But in 1937 and 1938 I'd catch today and I'd be tired the next day. Although I stayed in major league baseball until I was forty-one years old [1945] I didn't do much playing.

Q. Are catchers' careers shorter because of this wear and tear on the body?

A. No, I think their careers are rather long because you are not expected to have great foot speed. If you can catch and throw and hit pretty well you can have a fairly long career. What I've seen over the last fifteen to twenty years is that the quickest route to the major leagues is by being a catcher. There aren't as many catchers as there are other people playing other positions; if a fellow has pretty good ability he doesn't want to go back of the plate, he wants to go to the outfield, he wants to pitch or play the infield...

Q. Don't your knees begin to bother you after awhile with all that squatting?

A. In all my career, I played twenty years of professional baseball, my knees never bothered me. It's your stamina; as I said awhile ago you don't come back as rapidly. This must happen to fighters. Ty Cobb lasted twenty-three years... I found this out in scouting that there is no way to determine in advance how well, or how long, a fellow will wear in baseball. Some wear out at thirty-two or thirty-three, most wear out at thirty-six or thirty-seven, a few will go to forty and beyond. Like Jack Quinn, and some of the colored fellows seem to have great stamina. I remember one year in Chicago I remember we had Ransom Jackson playing there. He was a young man' he was thirty-one or thirty-two, but all of a sudden he was through -- he couldn't play anymore, he wore out early. Some of the old warhorses go on right up there until they're thirty-nine or forty and keep on playing. But again there is no way to determine how a fellow will wear.

Q. Tell me about Harry Heilmann and Heinie Manush.

A. We had Heilmann and Manush in 1926 and Cobb and Bob Fothergill... You know that was a most unusual year. You know Fothergill and Manush battled each other for the league batting lead all season and Manush beat him up by the end of the year. In all my career in baseball I never saw such hitting as we had on that club. We'd go out every day and score seven or eight runs and the other team would score ten. We didn't have much pitching. But I'll tell you, those fellows, Heilmann, Manush, Fothergill, Cobb, Gehringer, and some of the others, they could really hit that ball. But unfortunately then we didn't have the frontline pitching.

Q. Did Heilmann and Cobb get along?  I understand there was some kind of a feud between them.

A. Heilmann and Cobb got along great, but I don't think Cobb and Blue hit it off too well; they were different personalities. Luzerne Atwill Blue, he was our first baseman. Johnny Neun came along and replaced him. Other players were Marty McManus, our third baseman; Harry Rice; Donie Bush had already left us, but Jackie Warner was our shortstop in 1926... I have a copy of the first *Who's Who in Major League Baseball* [1933], it's down there by my resting chair, and every so often I get it down and look through it; I get the biggest kick out of that. The players look so young and they have hair; it is interesting to see how they looked then and how they look now, although many of them are gone. I enjoy looking at that book and I also enjoy looking at the *Baseball Encyclopedia*.

Q. How about Heinie Manush's personality; a friendly man?

A. Not too friendly; he was a very determined man.  He later left our club and played with Washington and then Boston. He tried to "get" me, sliding in at home, but I'd get out of the way. One day he did cut the toe of my shoe. Oh yes, they'd come right after you.  We were battling for the pennant in 1935, playing in New York. It was a knock down-drag out series which we had to win. Selkirk was on second base and somebody got a base hit. Here he comes into the plate and I'm standing about one step down the third base line. Here he comes -- that high in the air -- he's going to get me, I knew that, but I had to get him out of there. Well, I tagged him out and hung onto the ball. But he hit me! I don't think anybody ever got hit as hard on a football field [chuckling mildly], just about broke me in half; it was his knees. In those days you didn't give an inch; you didn't step up or step back. I guess you see some of it now. When the game's at stake the catchers stay right in there. But they have the best of gear.

Q. Have you a lot of scars from these encounters?

A. Well, Art Shires in the Texas League put one on my right kneecap which I'm still carrying around. He spiked me on a play at that plate. Other than that... Art Shires, he was a character. He went to Chicago and led the league in talking. He was something of a fighter, too. I saw him in a few fights, one down in Waco, Texas.

Q. How about pitching to Ruth?

A. Well, some of our pitchers handled Ruth pretty good. Tommy Bridges and "Schoolboy" Rowe. But the Babe was unpredictable; when he got his pitch, good-bye. The thing that struck me about Ruth as a hitter, he could hit left-hand pitchers. Now [Earl] Whitehill, we thought he was a good left-hand pitcher, but Ruth hit him like he owned him. He hit that curveball like it was rolling off a table. He'd step right in there and...

Q. How did you call the game with your pitchers?

A. They'd go with you most of the time; occasionally, you'd have a pitcher out there who would want to go a certain way with a hitter. Whitehill, or Marberry ... At a certain time in the game they had it in their mind that there was a certain kind of pitch they wanted to throw. I'd give them the signal for what I thought they should throw, but they'd look me off and I'd give them the sign for the other pitch. I knew what they were doing. I went with them so the second baseman and shortstop would know what was coming. Ninety percent of the time they'd go with the catcher's signal, at least they did with me. But I always thought it would be a mistake on my part, or on any catcher's part to get bull-headed and say "You're going to throw such-and-such a pitch."  Often times the pitcher is more confident in a certain pitch and you may not know that...

Q. Would you go over the other team's hitters with your pitcher before the game?

A. Yes, most clubs meet and go over the other hitters; I know Brooklyn did and Detroit did most of the time; especially in the first game of a series. You would go down the batting order, in fact, all the hitters... Some were highball hitters, some were lowball hitters. What we would concentrate on were the "holes" you could pitch to. Like a fellow might be "tight-up" or "down and away."  Some fellows were dead fastball hitters. For example, Bing Miller was the best curveball hitter of all time; we just couldn't throw him a curveball, he'd wear us out. We'd try to pitch him tight, in on the hands. Well, you watch these fellows play over a period of time and you learn where the "holes" are. And the holes are not very big for the top-notch hitters in the big leagues;  you have to draw that line very fine. Where so many pitchers in the minor leagues had great stuff, but not make it in the majors, they just couldn't draw that line fine enough. As the hitters move up to the big leagues  the holes get smaller, and as the pitchers move up he draws the line finer, so everything stays even. But looking at it in another light, the pitcher, if his control is not fine enough, or the holes on the hitter are too big, look out -- neither one of them is going to stay in the big leagues very long [chuckling]... We used to tell young players in spring training that we were sending them back to the minors for more experience as a hitter. He'd say, "What's wrong? I can hit just as well as the guys you've got out on the field." Well, we'd answer, we don't really decide that. It's the fellows on the other team that decide that. They won't let you stay up here until you are ready. Then they begin to accept it.

Q. What do you talk about when you go out to talk to the pitcher?

A. We go over what we had talked about before the game; "remember, now, in our meeting we were going to keep the ball high and tight or away; the players will be positioned that way." So we remind him and impress upon what he must do. You got to concentrate... Or sometimes you see that pitcher is "pushing" the ball, not slinging it like he should, and you go out and tell him to start slinging the ball and not push it. Of course, the manager can usually see this from the bench. But a lot of times if the pitcher is a three-quarter pitcher he may drop down to more of a sidearm and you go out and tell him to back up over the top; your ball is flattening out, it's not doing anything. Same way with the curveball; you tell him, look don't try to overpower the hitter just put more spin on the ball. It's things like that we talk about. Maybe you'll see that the pitcher is getting tensed up and a little conversation will settle them down and they come back.

Q. What about these stories you hear that the catcher goes out to the pitcher and they talk about what restaurant they will have dinner at or some such thing?

A. [Laughing] Yes, at Detroit one time somebody was pitching who had been out on the town the night before. I went out and asked him "What in the world did you have to drink last night? I can't get near you."  Then I turned around and went back behind the plate.

Q. You really get to know the other hitters, don't you?

A. Yes. They show you -- after you play against a club two or three times you remember the balls that they hit and where they were thrown. You keep it in your head. I never kept a book, but you remember these guys; they beat you in a game so you had better remember them. You stay away from their strengths amd pitch to their weakness. There isn't a player who ever lived who didn't have some weakness around that strike zone.

Q. A catcher must have to be one of the smartest players on the field; there is so much he has to keep track of.

A. Well, he is. He must know what's going on, what his pitcher is doing; he watches the infield and if a fellow drifts out of position. Things like that.

Q. I always thought a catcher like Cochrane would make a much better manager than an outfielder, like Tris Speaker, because he was so much closer to the action.

A. Yes, he is closer to the play. I remember when I managed Mr. Rickey's club at Forth Worth right after the war. I had a bunch of young players just back from the war, and boy, they wanted to play. They had great ability. I started having meetings in the clubhouse and I never had so many questions fired at me. I told them at the outset, if there is anything you don't understand about this game and you want to know, you ask me. If I don't know the answer I can sure get it for you -- from Mr. Rickey. He's one of the smartest men this game has ever known; he analyzed everything so well, every phase of the game. We used to go down to spring training and all the managers would be in the front row and the players in the background and have a meeting for an hour. He'd start out with hitting and bunting, then catching, and then he'd go around all the positions. He'd discuss all the positions and how they should be played. Then he would take the managers separately and go over specific game situations, asking them when they would play the infield in, when they would play it back, and they had to answer all this. It was good sound baseball; he'd give us all this. Then he'd come watch us play and you had better remember what he said and not play the infield in at the wrong time and so forth. It was a great education. When I got back into baseball managing I learned a lot then I had not known before as a player; I wish I had. I might have been able to contribute more. He had a great system; that's why he was so successful with all of his clubs. Look at the Dodger club -- they didn't make many mistakes, they were so well schooled. There's a way to do it; a way to play every position and a way to pitch, hit, and bunt, all those things. Baseball is a vast field in which there are many things you have to know. I have a series of lectures here that were put together back in the early 1950s when they had these coaches' clinics all over the country. The National Association gave us permission to hand them out at our coaches meetings after I went to Milwaukee. They are a great set of lectures, covering every phase of the game.

Q. Who delivered the lectures?

A. We were appointed. In North Carolina, Mace Brown and I would do them. He'd do the pitching and I'd do the catching. Yes, they were written out -- offensive and defensive play. This was put together by fifteen or twenty of baseball's top players, representing all positions. Based on percentage play that's how to conduct spring training. All written in a set of lectures; the finest thing I ever saw. We used them for years and years. I guess they still do, although I am not sure what they do today. I have been retired for five years; I retired at age sixty-eight in 1972. I had done so much special assignment scouting after I was director of scouting at Chicago, Milwaukee, and Atlanta. I went back into special assignment scouting and I tell you I was flying all over the country for years. One day I'd be in San Antone, the next day in Los Angeles, and maybe the next day in Spokane -- wherever top prospects were.

Q. You didn't travel like that in the minors. What was train travel like in the minors?

A. Well, all my travel was by train in my playing days. We had the number one car for the regulars and the number two car was for what we called "the riff-raff." The secondary players and pitchers were back there. The guys played like a bunch of kids and they had a good time. We'd ride all night in the Texas League with the windows open; no air conditioning. The fellows used to say don't sleep over there by the windows; those mosquitoes will sting you right through the screens. You really couldn't sleep because it was so hot; you rested a little bit. Later on they came with some air conditioning... Down at the Rice Hotel in Houston, we'd go in there and go up to bed and pull the beds out right under that ceiling fan; if you'd wet the sheet then it wouldn't be too bad.

Q. How about playing on a hot Sunday afternoon in Houston?

A. Oh, Houston, and Shreveport, and Waco! Waco had an all-dirt infield and you could hardly stand it. You'd see the infielders out there and they looked like prancing horses. They'd poured water into their shoes -- directly into the shoes -- between innings. It was so hot on the ground you could feel the spikes through the shoes... You could get used to that heat; you could condition yourself for it...

Q. Did you ever catch a double-header in that heat?

A. Yes, yes. You'd lose eight or nine pounds on one of those days, but you'd gain it back by the next day. Ty Cobb used to have a mix that he put together. We were playing in Washington -- it was awful hot in Washington -- he'd have the trainer take a sack and fill it full of oatmeal and put it in a bucket of ice water, and cut up a lot of lemons and oranges and put them in there, and we'd drink that. It was good and it strengthened you. It didn't make you sick like plain ice water might. A number of teams did that... But it is so much nicer today. I traveled with the Cubs -- I was with them for thirteen years, 1947 through 1959, as director of scouting -- I did special assignment scouting until the last year when I was director of scouting. Then I went to Milwaukee; I was with Milwaukee five years then I went on to Atlanta and stayed there until the end of 1969. Then I went to Montreal in 1970, 1971, and 1972, with John McHale. I did special assignment scouting for the three years I was there, but I was director of scouting all the time I was at Milwaukee. I went with the team to Atlanta and remained director of scouting through 1966 and then for the next three years,

1967-1969, I did special assignment scouting and Jim Fanning took my place as director of scouting. Then I moved to Montreal and did special assignment scouting until I retired at the end of 1972.

Q. We talked earlier about playing day ball in the Texas League. They had no lights then. When did you play your first nightball?

A. I played my first nightball with Cincinnati when I was with Brooklyn.

Q. Let me finish up with your career. You were with Detroit through 1938?

A. I went to Brooklyn in the latter part of that year, say September. I was with the Dodgers in 1939 and was traded to the Giants for Jimmy Ripple in the fall of 1939. I was in New York in all of 1940. I didn't play any; I was bullpen coach, but an active player on the roster. Harry Danning and Ken O'Dea were the regular catchers. I was released by New York at the end of the 1940 season and I went to Milwaukee with Bill Killefer. I was made a free agent and signed with the St. Louis Browns in the spring of 1942. Yes, I was with Milwaukee all through 1941. In 1942 I went to spring training with the St. Louis Browns and stayed with them through the first of May. I was released and signed by the St. Louis Cardinals, with whom I stayed for about six weeks. Rickey wanted me to go over to the Rochester club and manage it for the rest of the year as playing manager, which I did because [Estel] Crabtee was the manager, but he got sick and couldn't manage. Through the winter of 1942-1943 Mr. Rickey went to Brooklyn so he immediately took me to Brooklyn with him. I stayed in Brooklyn as an active player, due to wartime conditions, through 1943, 1944, and to July of 1945. He put [Clyde] Sukeforth and myself off the active list and we began scouting. That's when we started scouting the colored clubs. We scouted all those colored fellows -- Newcombe, Campanella, and all those fellows. He put Sukeforth and I with George Sisler and Wid Mathews, and that's when we began to learn about scouting. I continued on in scouting, except for my brief period in managing in 1946-1947 until I retired. In 1946 I was with Fort Worth, in 1947 I was with Macon, Georgia, for the Chicago Cubs. I managed there to the end of the year and then I went on their scouting staff.

Q. How did you feel about scouting for these black players?

A. I tell you that was an experience. We'd go to New York where they had a double-header every Sunday, but they had four different clubs playing. You'd see so many players. One Sunday they'd play in Yankee Stadium and the next Sunday in the Polo Grounds, depending on whether the Yankees or Giants were out of town. Sukey, Sisler, Wid Mathews and I would go over there -- that was an experience. Of course, the games were attended mostly by colored people; they danced up and down the aisle and threw stuff and bet money... They had great players on the field, the ones we were looking at. I remember old Josh Gibson in Yankee Stadium one afternoon hit a ball to right field -- and he was a right-hand hitter -- as far as Ruth ever hit one. He was a powerhouse hitter. We got to see so many of the colored players who came on and made their way big in baseball. It was a free and open market then for these players and Mr. Rickey got in on the ground floor. He got Robinson, Newcombe, and others -- they were top players and they were young. He scouted colored players down in Mexico and everywhere.

Q. Did you ever think much about this when you were playing back in the 1920s and 1930s, the fact that there were no blacks in baseball?

A. I never played against a colored player in my entire career. Never thought much about it. They all came on after I finished my career and got into the scouting field. I scouted colored players from then on. I did the special assignment on Ernie Banks. We bought Ernie Banks from the [Kansas City] Monarchs. I was put onto him by Wid Mathews. He called me in the office one morning and said, "Ray, I want you to fly to Davenport, Iowa, and see a young colored shortstop that we just had a call about. The business manager down at Macon saw the Kansas City Monarch club play there last night -- business manager's name was Gordon -- and he said somebody ought to see Banks, he's a fine young ballplayer." So I immediately went out to Davenport and that night saw Banks play. Buck O'Neill was the manager of the Monarchs. I saw Banks take infield practice and I called Buck O'Neill over. I told him who I was and asked him to tell me something about this boy Banks. He said "Well, he's a fine boy; he just got back from the service and he has good ability." So through us, and our reporting and buying Banks, it brought Buck O'Neill to Chicago and I bet he stayed there twenty years scouting. But I still have my original report that I made on Banks in my file here. We bought Banks for about $21,000 and about two or three years later St. Louis offered Mr. Wrigley $500,000 for Banks. Mr. Wrigley said "I don't want $500,000 for Banks; I just want another Banks." I followed him on into Kansas City and into Chicago where they had a Negro Leagues World Series. So I met Wid Mathews that afternoon at the White Sox Park. He said, "What about Banks?" I said get him! Some way or another, get him! We had a meeting the next morning and bought him. I told [Phil] Cavarretta, our manager, that this fellow was not too far away from playing in Chicago right now.

Q. Did he have a good night when you saw him in Davenport?

A. He hit one over the left field fence -- they have a water tank beyond the fence -- and the last time I saw the ball it was going by the water tank. I said to myself if he can hit the ball that far one time he can do it again... Oh, he was a great player and a splendid fellow. That was one of the top people I ever signed. I went out to the coast one year and signed Dick Ellsworth; saw him in a high school game and signed him. And there were numerous other players I was involved with [in signing], too many to mention, that I signed in Milwaukee and Atlanta when I was there.

Q. Back in the 1920s and 1930s, did you players think much about the fact that there were no black players in baseball

A. Oh we knew there were some great players around. Some of the players would tell me -- they played in exhibition games in the fall against them, I never did myself -- Tommy Bridges told me once that "Man, they really have got some players."  But they just hadn't broken the color line yet. And it is a pity, too, because there were a lot of great colored players -- even before my time -- there were some great players. They just didn't recognize them and bring them into the game.

Q. It would have caused too much trouble at the time, I suppose and even when Rickey broke the line with Robinson there was considerable opposition, wasn't there?

A. A great deal. But the thing that hurt me more about the colored situation in baseball, after I was into scouting and traveling around, with Milwaukee for an example -- even as late as that. Our club would go down to Houston and Aaron couldn't stay at the same hotel with us; he had to stay out in town some place. And it was hard to see some of these young colored players, that we had signed and owned, they couldn't go into a restaurant, they had to stay out. It didn't seem right to me that people should be treated that way; I was happy to see it change around.

Q. Robinson certainly put up with a lot; I guess Rickey knew his man.

A. He certainly did. Robinson had the desire and the ability to carry him over those rough spots.

Q.  How did you get along with umpires?

A. Well, I'll tell you, I got along pretty well with umpires. I had a few run-ins with them. Let me tell you about a little incident that happened in Detroit one time. Bill Dinneen was the umpire. It was an off day and I heard the umpires talking and they decided to take a little trip over to Windsor; visit around a little bit over there. Well, in those days it was dry in Detroit, but you could get beer or anything you wanted over in Canada. The next day when we were playing again, Dinneen was behind the plate and I thought he missed one. I didn't turn around; I just backed up a little bit and said "you fellows must have gotten a hold of some bad stuff over in Canada yesterday." He quickly replied, "That's all for you, get out of here!" [Laughing.] It was the meanest thing I could think of saying to him. Bucky Harris bounced off the bench came over and asked Dinneen why he had thrown me out. "And you go with him," roared Big Bill. Really, touched a nerve that day. I don't know if the man had a bottle of beer or not, but I couldn't think of anything else to say. Another time I had a run-in with an umpire: he was having a real bad night, so I backed up alongside of him and asked, "Are you feeling all right?" "Yes, I do." I came back and said "You just can't be that lousy and feel all right; you must be sick." "Get outa here!" That was down at Macon, Georgia -- I can't remember the fellow's name. But when I told him that I knew I was going to get the rest of the night off. I have gotten after umpires on hot days and right away they sense it; they see that you're irritable and that you think they have missed a strike or two and they'll say, "You can talk all you want to, but you're not getting out of this game; you're going to stay here in the heat and suffer with the rest of us." That hurt too.

Q. You didn't try to get thrown out of a game did you?

A. Nah. I'd say these mean things to them -- I thought they were mean -- thinking maybe they'd bear down a little harder. I know now, sitting here and talking, that they were doing the best job they could.

Q. Umpiring is a pretty tough job,

A. It is a tough job. There are so many pitches right on the corner or off the corner of the plate; how can you tell if a pitch is one-sixteenth of an inch off the plate or on the plate? It's a matter of seeing and judging. I really admire umpires, it's a difficult profession, but somebody must do it. I think overall they do a wonderful job.

Q. Say you have a real good hitter at bat and the pitch is right on or off the corner of the plate. Do you think the umpire is likely to give the hitter, who has a reputation for a good eye, the benefit of the doubt?

A. Oh, I think so; they don't seem to draw quite as fine a line as they did with me [chuckling]. Ted Williams had the greatest eye of anybody. He would take a pitch just barely off the plate; I couldn't do that. He wouldn't even offer at the ball; great eyesight.

Q. Do any umpires stand out above the others; or maybe below the others?

A. There were so many good umpires and there were some who didn't rate as high as the others. I really admired Cal Hubbard. Lou Klein used to tell about how he would hit the ball to the infield and run his tail off to first base and just get nipped. And old Cal was standing down there with his hands in his vest and -- umpires didn't make those gestures then that they do today -- as Klein would go by he'd just give him that little thumb, "that little thumb."  One day after Hubbard called Klein out on such a play he went up to him and said "Can't you give me a better out than that?"  But Hubbard was a good umpire; Bill McGowan was a good umpire -- I remember him from the 1934 and 1935 Series. Billy Evans was still umpiring when I broke in...

Q. What was it like playing in the World Series?

A. Well, no matter how much you play, there is something different about the World Series. You get up for it more, there's more excitement. It's different than playing the regular season; there's something about it and all the players sense this. It's extra special.

Q. But you didn't catch in either one?

A. I finished up the last game of the 1934 Series. Cochrane caught all of the 1935 Series, which went six games and we won over the Cubs. Cochrane had a great Series. People have asked me why I didn't complain about being backup, or ask to be traded, but as I said earlier, I preferred being on a winner than playing regularly for a second division team, where I worked myself to death and wouldn't reap the harvest -- moneywise -- that I did by being in Detroit.

Q. In 1934, was there a real leader on the field, besides Cochrane?

A. Well, Cochrane was our leader, but there were some other fellows like Goslin and Gehringer -- Billy Rogell? Not as much as some of the other fellows.

Q. Gehringer was so quiet; it's surprising he could lead.

A. He did so many things so well, he could lead by example. Our holler guys were Gerald Walker and --

Q. Was Gerald Walker on his own?

A. He might as well have been. He used to drive the manager crazy, but he had so much ability that he offset some of that... Yes, Harvey Walker was up with Detroit for awhile too, but he didn't stay too long; he didn't have quite the ability his brother had... Roy Johnson? he played quite a bit; a kind of temperamental player, but he had a lot of ability... Billy Rogell was a good, steady shortstop. The kind of player Cochrane would pry every now and then to keep him on his toes. A good playmaker; he could handle that glove and cover a lot of ground. Teamed with Gehringer they made a great double-play combination at second base... Marv Owen? We used to call him "shovel-hands." No matter what was hit to him he scooped it up. His hands were much bigger than mine. A sure-handed third-baseman. He didn't get beat up all over, he'd just catch them and throw them out. You know in the 1935 Series, when Greenberg got that fractured wrist, he [Owen] just moved over to first base and did a whale of a job there, and "Flea" Clifton moved off the bench to play third base. Owen had played first base earlier in his career, but he had such good hands he played a great game for us at first. But our clubs then had great depth, we had great bench strength... Goose Goslin? I remember Goslin's hit in that 1935 World Series -- a soft Texas League single right over second base which scored Cochrane with the winning run in the sixth game. They practically tore down the ballpark and downtown too. They say it was the greatest celebration in Detroit since World War I... Goose was not an overly talkative person, but a likeable one. He was nice to my boys; they just loved Goose.

Q. Did you ever catch a no-hitter?

A. No; oh yes, I caught a perfect game, once, but not in the major leagues. I caught the game in Detroit that Tommy Bridges pitched against Washington. We went down to the ninth inning and he had pitched perfect ball; hadn't walked a guy or given base hit. Walter Johnson was managing the Washington club and he brought in Dave Harris to pinch-hit with Joe Judge and Sam Rice, both left-hand hitters, sitting on the bench. Tommy threw him a high fastball -- about there -- it wasn't even in the strike zone -- and he broke his bat and hit it to left field for a base hit. That spoiled that perfect game.

Q. Do you think that Johnson sent Harris, a right-hand hitter, in there, just so Bridges might have his perfect game?

A. Well, I don't know about that. Harris just took a wild swing and got the base hit. Everybody just died with it, because he was so close to a perfect game. He got the next man out so it was a one-hitter.

Q. But you did catch a no-hitter in the minors?

A. Yes, some place I caught such a game -- I think it was while I was with the Toledo club somebody pitched a no-hitter. But I never caught one in the major leagues. I caught several one-hitters and two-hitters; if I had caught a no-hitter I think I would remember it.

Q. Who were some of the easiest pitchers to catch at Detroit?

A. Oh, Bridges and Rowe; Crowder was very easy to catch; none of them were really difficult.

Q. Did you catch any of the games in Rowe's sixteen-game winning streak in 1934?

A. Yes, I caught several of them.  I remember one year, we finished the season in Detroit and Johnny Allen had tied the all-time record. We went out there and beat them [Cleveland] and I caught the game. Bucky Harris pitched "Jake" Wade, who wasn't even a regular pitcher on our staff. Wild!  He went out there that day and durned if he didn't beat Johnny Allen. [Correction: Allen had not tied the consecutive game winning record for pitchers; he was one game short with fifteen.] That day Jake pitched a masterpiece and he beat Allen 1-0... Here's a little incident I would like to tell you about. Visiting with Charlie Gehringer and his wife down in Palm Beach one spring; I ran into him one afternoon and we got talking. Charlie and Marv Owen were always great friends. Charlie said that they had a wedding anniversary and they got this very heavy package from Marv Owen. When they opened it, it was a brick from the church in which Charlie and his wife had gotten married in out in California, where Owen was their best man. He went by this church one day and they were tearing it down, so he got one of the bricks and sent it to them. Charlie and his wife thought this was one of the greatest things that ever happened... Marv was scouting for Detroit one year and they called him into the office -- he came on from California -- but without many clothes with him and when he got to Detroit he about froze to death. Charlie loaned him an overcoat -- a real nice overcoat -- and Marv wore it and took it back with him to California. When he got home he called Charlie and said he wanted to send the coat back to him. Charlie said, "forget it, it's a gift" [chuckling].

Q. I've heard these stories about Hogsett and Gehringer -- two very quiet men who roomed together; they'd get up in the morning and say "good morning" to one another and then when they were ready to go to bed they would say "good night" and that was the extent of their conversation. How true was this?

A. [chuckling] Oh, pretty true, I guess. Neither of them talked much. I guess the "Chief" [Hogsett] got up and said "how?" -- he was an Indian... Charlie never talked much in groups, but you could sit down and talk with him -- he was very easy to visit with; I enjoyed talking with him. But they're all cut out a little differently; you meet a lot of people along the way and some stand out in your memory more than others.

Q. How about your biggest thrill in baseball?

A. Probably the greatest thrill I had was breaking that errorless record. But the biggest thrill was when Goslin got that hit in the 1935 World Series, which won the Series for us. We wanted to win so badly because we had lost the year before -- the Dean brothers had won two games apiece and knocked us out of the Series and we didn't get that World Series ring -- so we wanted that ring. It was a great thrill to win it knowing that we were going to get it. So we did and we got it. That among many other nice gifts that we got... Here's a thing on my desk you might like to see -- it's a very beautiful thing given to us in Detroit: a lovely plaque. And in the drawer there I have my lifetime pass to baseball, that you might want to see... I was awfully proud to get that.

Q. That 1934 Series; was that when they began throwing the stuff at Medwick?

A. Yes. Medwick slid hard into Marv Owen at third base and upended him and the fans were so disturbed about it that they wouldn't let Medwick come back to left field. I don't know where they got all the vegetables, apples, and oranges from, but they covered the field with them. Landis called Medwick over and asked him some questions, and of course, banished him from the game. It was a double-dose of bad feeling because everybody knew the Cardinals had us beat that day. It was a lopsided score... Yes, I was in the game at the end. Frisch beat us that day with a double or triple down the right field line, which broke the game open. He hit it off Elden Auker.

Q. Elden Auker, the submarine specialist.

A. Yes, I caught Auker a few times; I caught him in the pennant-winning game in 1935. We were playing the Browns in Detroit and Auker beat them 2-1. Auker and Hogsett were identical pitchers -- one right-handed the other left-handed --

underhand pitchers who threw sinkers all the time and climbing curveballs. They were tough to hit -- and tough to catch. We were fortunate to have them on our side; they were great pitchers.

Q. Auker really went way down on his delivery.

A. Yes, that was due to a football injury. He was a fine football player. He was a great college player out at the University of Kansas, I think it was, and he had a shoulder injury. He was also a pitcher, so this caused him to go underhanded. And from that time on he was an outstanding underhanded pitcher. Yes, he and Hogsett both threw that way. I always wanted to come across a young prospect -- in my scouting career -- who threw underhanded, but I never found any. They were all on top or three-quarters.

Q. Was there any feeling about Hogsett because he was an Indian?

A. No, no. He was a very likeable fellow on our club. He had a good sense of humor. Nothing special; he was just a regular fellow... Art Herring? Yes, he was with us. I'd like to see some of those fellows again, but our paths don't cross very often. I did see a few of them while scouting, those who had also gotten into scouting. There are several old major league scouts who come through here occasionally and some live in this area -- Gil English, now retired, scouted for many years... Mace Brown, who is still active with the Red Sox. Billy Smith scouted for us and other teams; he lives about four or five miles from here. In fact, we have about half a dozen fellows around here -- some still active, some retired -- they're all my golfing buddies... No, I didn't scout college players much, my brother and some others scout high school and college teams.

Q. How was it batting against Walter Johnson?

A. Oh, yes, I remember batting against Walter Johnson very distinctly; I should have because I heard so much about him as a kid growing up, and how hard he could throw. I got a kick out of hitting against him. Here's a little story about him you might want to hear. One day Whitlow Wyatt and I were sitting on the bench in Detroit in the early 1930s, and Walter Johnson [then managing Washington] came out through our dugout as players did then. He stopped to talk a minute and we said "Walter, back in your heyday, just how hard could you throw?" "Boys," he replied, "I could throw just as hard I wanted to; if I wanted to reach back and get it, I could throw as hard as necessaary." This meant if he had to get a fellow out he'd just strike him out. Back in those days when Washington was finishing last almost every year he'd win twenty to twenty-five games. I believe what he said because we'd sit on the bench and watch him pitch batting practice -- this while the Washington manager -- and he could still throw harder than anyone on the Washington staff, and he was retired as a pitcher. He could throw hard right down to the end of his career... No, I don't remember getting any hits off of him; I did hit a couple of balls pretty hard, but I don't think I got any hits. Now if you ask me about Bob Feller I can tell you about some of the hits I got off of him. There weren't too many. I think Bob Feller was the toughest pitcher I ever faced in my life. He had all the motions, then he had a good curveball and he threw so hard. What bothered me most, though, he was always looking out at right field; if he only looked at me once in awhile [chuckling]. That worried me, I was afraid he was going to lose sight of me at the plate -- and the way he threw I was worried.

Q. I understand Ty Cobb batted for you once.

A. Yes, we were playing a game in Detroit and -- I had faced Johnson once or twice -- we got in a situation with a couple of men on base, and Cobb pinch hit for me [and] got a double. I remember that very distinctly. I didn't feel bad about that at all. But it was a great thrill to bat against Walter Johnson.

# Riggs Stephenson

*Tuscaloosa, Alabama, August 4, 1977*

"Football Star"

The knock on Riggs Stephenson, when talking about baseball Hall of Fame material, is that he did not play in enough games and that his fielding might be suspect. Nevertheless his statistics are impressive and, in this writer's view, he should be installed in the Cooperstown Valhalla. In fourteen seasons in the big time he played in over 100 games five years and in eighty or more five other years. He played in 1,310 games in all. He collected 1,515 hits with a lifetime batting average of .336. To me anyone who plays fourteen seasons and bats .336 should have automatic admission. Particularly in this day when some lesser lights are being admitted. Stephenson was one of the better all-around athletes who played baseball. In addition to his baseball skills, he was an outstanding football player at the University of Alabama, being selected one year for the all-Southern team. He was not overly big by modern standards, but he carried a solid muscular 190 pounds on a five-foot, ten-inch frame. He was said to have been one of the hardest running backs ever to play in the south. And it was not safe to get in his way on the baseball field either, as "Rabbit" Maranville once found out. "Stevie" also played basketball at Alabama. Yet in the quiet of his Tuscaloosa, Alabama, living room, he appeared to be anything but a rough-and-tough diamond and gridiron star. He was pleasant, modest, and had little to say. This was not exactly an easy interview because of Stephenson's quietness, but nonetheless it was a good one because he had a good career and he remembered it well.

Q. Could you tell me a little bit about your background, where you grew up and when you first played ball?

A. I grew up about ten miles outside of Akron, Alabama, on a farm near Greensboro, which was the county seat... My father was a farmer then he got a job working for the government. He rode around in a horse-and-buggy and I'd go with him once in awhile. We'd go out about seven miles from Akron where we'd stop and I would ride in on horseback and meet him later. I was just a kid about fourteen years or so then... Yes, the family has always lived around that area. My grandparents lived in a little place down there called Concord Church. We were Presbyterians.

Q. When did you first play ball?

A. Well, I started playing down there in a semi-pro league. There were a lot of little towns -- Eutaw, Boligee, Livingston, and York -- and all those little towns. I started playing there. I went to high school in Guntersville, Alabama -- my brother, who was 15 years older than myself -- got a job up there teaching and that's why I went there to school. After that I entered the University of Alabama in 1917. I played on the 1917 football team at Alabama. I stayed there four years and won three letters in football, three in baseball, and one in basketball... Yes, played all those sports in high school. I played two years in high school.

Q. How did you get into baseball?

A. I always liked baseball and my brothers before me played baseball. One of them played two years of professional baseball over in the Georgia-Alabama League. His name was Sam Gardner and my older brother was Julian W. They called him "Big Steve."  He later was at Jacksonville State College and taught and coached football, basketball, and baseball there. That is near Anniston, Alabama. He stayed there thirty-five years. They named a gymnasium after him.

Q. Then your brothers helped break you into baseball?

A. Yes, but I was the only one who realized anything out of it.

Q. Did your dad have much interest in the game?

A. No, he came along before there was much interest in the game. He was something of an athlete, though. He used to ride horses in tournaments where they were required to ride fast and throw lances, like in medieval days. He was a broad-jumper and did a few things like that.

Q. Did your father go to college?

A. No, he was from Columbia, Tennessee... They understood the importance of an education, however, and wanted us boys to go to college. They sacrificed a lot so we could go to college. We all helped work our way through, though.

Q. It says here that your tuition was paid by the state?

A. I don't know what state that was [chuckling]. It must have come out of the University of Alabama. We had jobs. Sewell [Joe] and I were waiters in the dining hall. C. D. Pepper of Florida was head waiter.

Q. How did you happen to go to Alabama?

A. My brother went to Alabama. He pitched on the team and wanted me to come down here. Up from Akron, down from Guntersville. He wanted me to come here because they didn't have a very good team. Not too many players.

Q. You were a star football player at Alabama, weren't you?

A. Well, not many of us from the South made All-American in those days -- Walter Camp picked them -- but I did make All-Southern.

Q. They said you were the greatest fullback in the South?

A. [Chuckling]  That's what they said, but they may have been exaggerating a little bit.... Yes, we all had to play sixty minutes; go both ways. We'd be better if we could have gone out of the game every so often, as they do today, and get a little rest. I ran the ball, backed up the line, did the passing, and a lot of things... At first our coach was Thomas Kelly from West Point. He was there one year. Then after the war Zinn Scott came down from Cleveland and coached two years. He was a sportswriter in Cleveland and wrote about horses. We lost one game each year we played.

Q. What position in baseball did you play at Alabama?

A. Sewell and I played three years. I played shortstop and he played second base.

Q. You must not have lost many games with that combination.

A. No and we had some more good players. Joe's brother Luke and then we had a pitcher named Boone who played for Connie Mack... Joe was actually a year ahead of me at Alabama, but I was about ten months older than he was... Yes, I was an infielder in high school, college, and the early years in pro ball, until I hurt my knee in Cleveland. I was not a good defensive player. I had trouble making the double-play. So Speaker sent me down to Kansas City to learn how to play the outfield in 1925. I went down there and while I was down there, Cleveland got a chance to get a second baseman, Johnny Hodapp, from Indianapolis. So they traded me and four or five other players over to Indianapolis for Johnny Hodapp. Then the next year the Cubs, managed by Joe McCarthy, bought me and I played there nine years.

Q. You graduated from Alabama in 1921?

A. I finished up in mid-year 1922. I had to leave early to go to Cleveland. When Wamby got his arm broken I had already signed with Cleveland.

Q. Who signed you?

A. Tris Speaker. Zinn Scott took me down to spring training in New Orleans and they signed me for $300 a month. They didn't expect me to play much, but when Wamby broke his arm -- I think it was in Mobile as we started north -- so they called me up. I joined them in St. Louis just before the season began and opened up with them. This was the 1921 season. So I had to drop out of school in April 1921, missing my exams, and then came back in the fall and completed the work and took the exams in early 1922.

Q. Did you like the academic work?

A. Not much. As I have often said, the only A's I made were in football and baseball [chuckling]. I had two good roommates, both of whom made Phi Beta Kappa, so that took care of academic honors for our room... Yes, I got a bachelor of science degree, but that's about all.

Q. What did you think about going up to the big time?

A. I didn't know much about it. We had only about two balls to play with down here and we got up there and I never saw so many white, clean baseballs in all my life. Then with all the flags flying, it was quite a thrill to see all that. But it didn't seem to bother me much; I didn't get excited. I was hitting about .500 in the first week... No, the family never saw me play. My mother may have seen me play once when we came through here on the way north to spring training. I didn't do well... No, my dad never saw me play except as a kid. Oh, he was interested all right, but it just wasn't convenient for him to come up north during the season. My brothers saw me play a lot. My sister came to the World Series in 1929... The family was still living in Akron when I went up. My father passed away in 1928.

Q. So they called you up because Wamby broke his arm?

A. Yes. He was hit by a pitched ball. They had an extra infielder named Harry Lunte, but he had a lame leg so he couldn't play. They didn't really have anybody but "Doc" Joe Evans, who was a third baseman and later played outfield. He and Charlie Jamieson alternated in left field the year they won the pennant, in 1920. Sewell joined them that year when Chapman was killed. He'll tell you about that... Luke Sewell also came in 1921, but a little later in the year, after school was out.

Q. How strange that three players from the same place -- the University of Alabama -- come up to the same major league team at the same time. Speaker must have thought the university was a farm team for him. But I guess it was pure coincidence.

A. Well, maybe [chuckling]. After Joe went up then I -- although I signed with Cleveland before Joe went up, so there couldn't have been any connection there. Joe signed with New Orleans then Cleveland bought him when they had to have a shortstop.

Q. The book here says that you put in about five years with Cleveland and in none of them did you play over 100 games. Was there any reason for that?

A. Well, Wamby was the second baseman and after he came back there wasn't much room for me there.

Q. But the averages: you hit .330, .339, .319, and .371. Anyone who hits like that has to be in the lineup.

A. Well, that .371 was the year -- 1924 -- that I hurt my knee and didn't play much. Mostly pinch-hitting or in the last few innings of a game... Wamby was in there most of the time and then when they figured I was ready to play, I hurt my knee.

Q. How did you hurt your knee?

A. It was kind of a funny way to hurt it. The ground was awfully hard and I ran down to first base -- playing the Chicago White Sox -- and first baseman Earl Sheely reached way up high for the throw. He had his leg up in the air and I tripped over that leg and landed right on my knee on that hard ground. It didn't bother me much at first, but that night I couldn't walk. I wasn't much good the rest of the year. That was the year I hit .371, I think. Babe Ruth, I believe, hit just a little more than that that year. I think he led the league that year.

Q. Yes, that was one of those even-numbered years that Harry Heilmann did not lead the league [we chuckle]. How did you like Cleveland to live in?

A. Oh, Cleveland was a nice city. I enjoyed it there... I can't remember all the places we stayed at, but we started off at a little hotel named Euclid on Euclid

Avenue. Then we went to -- I can't remember the name, but Sewell will tell you, he can remember everything. Most of the players stayed in rented apartments, but a few of us who were single stayed in the hotel. Later on, Joe Sewell got married and Luke and I stayed with him in their house.

Q. How did you like Tris Speaker?

A. Tris was a great ballplayer. He was a fine fellow, but I didn't think he was as detailed a manager as McCarthy was. McCarthy was more up on the details of the game. I don't know if he was a better manager than Tris, but he did get a good bit out of his players.

Q. Perhaps Speaker was too good a player to be a good manager?

A. Well, that's what they said about Ty Cobb, too. I don't know. But he did all right. He won that pennant and World Series in 1920... As far as I know, the players got along well with Tris; liked him.

Q. Who else was on that team?

A. Steve O'Neill was the catcher. Doc Johnston and George Burns were the two first basemen; they alternated. Wamby at second, Sewell at short, and when I first went there Larry Gardner was the third baseman. Jamieson was in left field, Speaker in center, and in right field they had Elmer Smith and Joe Wood. Joe Evans, also, in left. That was a good team.

Q. Jamieson, they used to say, could bunt the ball right down the first base line and as he ran down the line he could keep the ball between his moving feet so no one could field it. [We chuckle.]

A. I don't know about that, but he was quite a player. George Uhle was a pitcher, Ray Caldwell was another one, and Stan Coveleski was the main one. Guy Morton was a pitcher who came from Alabama. Then they had big Jim Lindsey from here, who later went to the St. Louis Cardinals and pitched with them for a long time as a relief pitcher.

Q. What was it like to bat against Walter Johnson?

A. Well, Walter had a sore arm at the end and they say he didn't throw as hard as he used to. Every now and then he'd cut one loose. Steve O'Neill used to laugh about how Sewell and I used to hit line drives off of Walter Johnson. He wasn't quite as good by the time I came up as he had been. He had some good years, though. He wasn't all that bad. He used to throw me curveballs.

Q. I thought he threw fastballs all the time?

A. Well, he did most of the time. But with that big long arm and wrist -- it looked about this long -- and that ball would just scoot up there. But he threw me curveballs a lot of the time... Oh, I didn't hit him too much... I never heard that he threw at any hitters.

Q. Who were some of the toughest pitchers you had to hit against?

A. A lot of people have asked me that. For me there were a lot of tough ones. But I would have to say that Dazzy Vance was the hardest one for me and for the Cubs when I was with them. He used to strike out Hack Wilson three or four times a game. He struck me out quite a bit, too. Then I would say that Burleigh Grimes, the old spitball pitcher, was tough. Then there were some other pitchers, who were not as well known, but who were tough for me. Ad Liska of the Phillies, who threw underhand, was tough for me. I remember getting but one hit off of him and that was a bunt... Yes, I batted against Carl Mays when he was with the Giants [in 1929]. He was tough. I could hit his curveball, but I couldn't hit his fastball much. He knocked the skin off of the fingers when his hand scraped the ground with that underhand pitch.

Q. So in 1925 that's when you went to Kansas City?

A. Yes, to learn to be an outfielder. They sent me down in June, I think... Yes, I was very disappointed about that. I went down there with the intention of giving it all I had and that if it didn't do much good, I was going to quit. But I was fortunate enough to hit pretty well there -- .325 I believe and .380 the year that they [the Cubs] bought me... The Kansas City manager was "Doc" Johnny Lavan and when I went over to Indianapolis Donie Bush was the manager there.

Q. Again, how did you happen to go to Indianapolis?

A. That was when Cleveland traded us for Hodapp. They sent four of five of us -- Yoter, Speece, Cleverman, me, and maybe another one. They needed a second baseman. Joe [Sewell] said Hodapp was a good second baseman, although he played third base at Indianapolis. He was a good hitter. He was a good-natured fellow, Joe used to say. He'd come in after the game and say, "Poor John, four for no." Four at-bats and no hits. How long did he stay up?

Q. That's the question I wanted to ask him. He quit at the height of his career when he was only about thirty-one or thirty-two with a lifetime average well over .300. They had money, I guess, so he didn't have to play ball, and the time came when he was supposed to take over the family funeral business in Cincinnati, so he took it over... Kansas City had a pretty big ballpark didn't it?

A. Yes, a terribly big park. And they put me over in right field, that sun field, where the sun was always shining right in your eyes. I had a little trouble with that, but finally got used to it. I hit a few over the left field fence, but not many. Most of the time when you hit it down into that left field corner it went for a triple. There weren't many hit over that right field fence when I was there. Joe Hauser hit one.

Q. I've talked to Joe and he described his home runs in Kansas City. That's where I heard about those huge dimensions.

A. You talked to Joe?  How is he?

Q. Fine. I spent a day with him up in Sheboygan, Wisconsin, and he is busy and cheerful. He's about seventy-nine now. He told about hitting two home runs in Kansas City in successive days. They thought the first one was a fluke then he came back and hit another one the next day.

A. Funny thing about Joe. He hit a lot of home runs up there with Minneapolis and before then with the Athletics and he hurt his knee. The funny thing was that he used a little light bat. Most of us fellows used heavy bats.

Q. I think he told me that he had been using a light bat until he went to Baltimore in 1930 and someone told him to use a heavier bat. That's when he started hitting all those home runs, sixty in Baltimore in 1930 and sixty-three in Minneapolis in 1933.

A. I often wondered why they didn't bring him back up to the majors after he hit all the homers in Baltimore?  I suppose it was the bad leg and he couldn't run too well. I thought he was a good first baseman. Of course, Jimmy Foxx came along for the Athletics. But there were a lot of clubs which didn't have very good first basemen and they could have used him. I felt that a lot of good players in the minors never got a real chance in the majors because the team which controlled them already had someone at that particular position. So there was no place to put them and they stayed in the minors. Now its the other way around. In those days the owner could send you to Kalamazoo if he felt like it.

Today players have a little more say where they go. As John McGraw told one of his pitchers, "I'll send you so far away that it will take a ten-cent postcard to write back." I can't think of that old boy's name; he came from Texas.

Q. Did the reserve clause bother you? The fact that Cleveland owned you and could do what they wanted with you?

A. To tell you the truth, I was so glad to be playing ball in the big leagues -- and I was hungry; a lot of boys up there today aren't hungry -- and then, I really didn't know much about the reserve clause. I knew what it was, but that's all. We had a little union-like organization, where we could contribute $10 a year to take care of some of the players that got hurt. But it was nothing like the union they have now. These fellows now are getting a good pension. Only five years in the league and they are eligible... No, I never got a pension. I think it first came in in 1946.

Q. That bothers me. The modern players who are making all of this money have done nothing to help the older players who really built the game up.

A. They won't do a thing. They've got more money than they know what to do with.

Q. Did you have any contract problems with Cleveland? Did you ever hold out, for example?

A. I didn't hold out, but I would ask for more money. I didn't get it most of the time. At Chicago I asked for a little more and they gave it to me one year, but I never did make much money in baseball. They other fellows made more than I did. I was a little handicapped because they always seemed to have three or four fellows trying out for left field and trying to take my place. They made more than I did sometimes.

Q. Who were your contract talks with at Cleveland and Chicago?

A. At Cleveland Ernest Barnard was the president and I dealt with him. Jimmy Dunn, the previous owner, had just died, I think. At Chicago my dealings were with Mr. Bill Veeck, senior.

Q. Did you like playing in League Park in Cleveland?

A. Yes, that was a good park for me. I hit a lot to right field where they had that short fence even though I was a right-hand hitter. I hit a few up on the wall

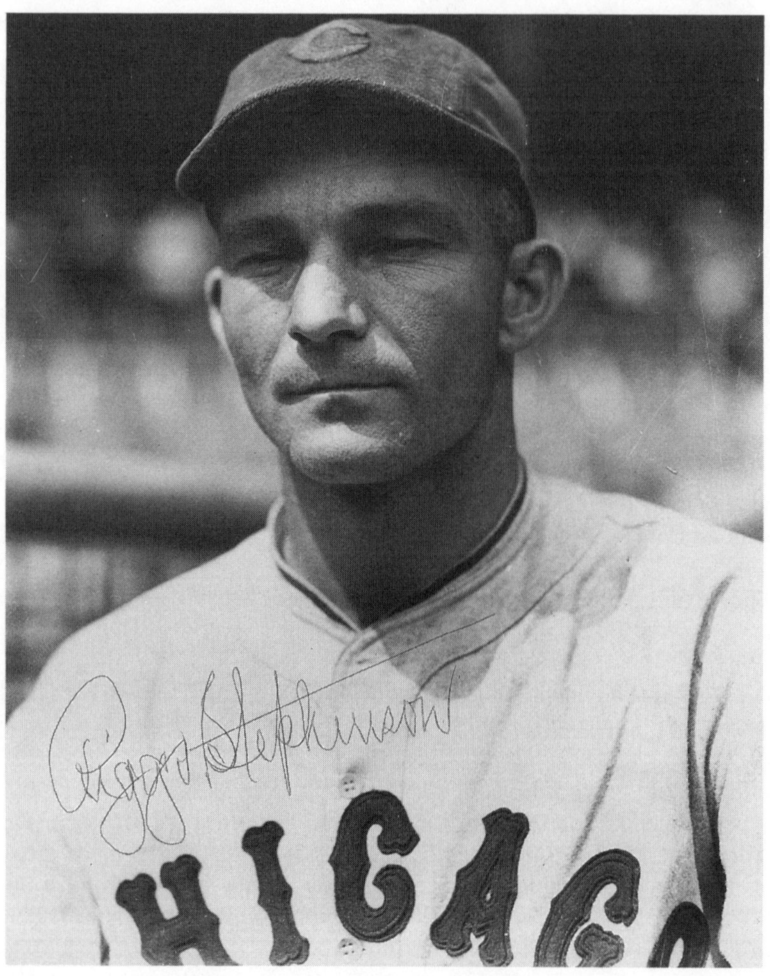

*Riggs Stephenson, Chicago Cub outfielder, 1926-1934. An infielder with Cleveland until his arm went bad, "Stevie" re-tooled for the outfield and became a mainstay on the great Chicago teams of the late 1920s and early 1930s. In spite of a .336 lifetime batting average, he has been snubbed by the Hall of Fame because he only played 1,310 games in a 14 year career. (Photo from the author's collection.)*

there. Sewell hit a lot of them off the wall. I didn't hit many out of the park in left field where they have that long distance. I never hit one over the right field fence, although I did get a lot of hits to right. I just tried to hit the ball where it was pitched. But I was usually thought of as a right field hitter. Hack Wilson was a right field hitter though he batted right-handed. He hit most of his home runs, I think, to right field. Hornsby hit to right field, or right center and left center. Cuyler was a right-field hitter.

Q. You were a line-drive hitter?

A. Yes, I hit mostly doubles. I led the league one year at Chicago in doubles. It might have been 1928 or 1929.

Q. O.K., you're in Indianapolis now under Donie Bush. How did Joe McCarthy find out about you?

A. McCarthy was the manager at Louisville in the American Association. When he went up to manage the Cubs in 1926 he knew about me and some of the scouts recommended me. I was mighty happy to go back up.

Q. I interviewed McCarthy a couple of years ago at his home near Buffalo. And I think he is a good example of what we were talking about earlier. That is, a man who never achieved much as a player, but who became a good manager.

A. Yes, he studied the game. That's why I think he was probably a smarter manager than some of the others I played ball for -- five or six of them.

Q. Your batting averages at Chicago are really something [from 1926 through 1933 he never hit under .319 and was over .360 twice]. When did you come up to the Cubs?

A. It was June 4 or June 8, 1926. I went down to Kansas City in June 1925 and came back up to the Cubs in June 1926... I broke into the Cubs outfield pretty soon after I went up. The other outfielders then were Hack Wilson and Clif Heathcote. Joe Munson was the left fielder, I think, and they sent him down and Shannon was a shortstop whom they also sent down when I came up. In the infield we had Charlie Grimm. Sparky Adams was the second baseman. Jimmy Cooney was the shortstop, and Freigau was the third baseman. In the next few years they changed around. Hornsby was second baseman for a couple of years then Billy Herman came up. Woody English was the shortstop and then Billy Jurges. Then English moved to third and later Stan Hack was the third baseman.

Q. Woody English doesn't live far from me in Ohio and I have seen him a couple of times.

A. How does he look? We tried to get in contact with him up there. The fact is we were with his former wife. I don't know if he's married again or not.

Q. I don't know if he remarried, but he lives alone with his mother now.

A. His first wife, Hilde, lives in Chicago. After the divorce she remarried a man named Fredericks. She became a big game hunter in Africa and won a lot of trophies. Later on she wouldn't shoot any animals, but just take their pictures. We went out and had supper with them one night. Mr. Fredericks is now dead, but she still lives along the lakefront in Chicago. She lives on the fifty-first floor or an apartment building... We kept up pretty good contact with her. They would stop through on the way to Florida when we were in Akron. But this last time was the first time we had seen them in about ten years.

Q. Woody has bad arthritis, but looks in pretty good shape in spite of that. He takes care of himself. He's about seventy now and his mother's about ninety. He lives in a small house in the center of Newark, Ohio.

A. Well, if you see him say 'hello,' and tell him to come to some of the old-timers affairs. I never see him. He has a funny idea about those things... Yes, he's a little shy. I did get a card from his good friend, Clyde Beck, in which he said he hadn't seen English. Beck was an extra infielder for the Cubs. He was a good little infielder.

Q. I tried to get him to come over and speak at the convention in Columbus of the Society for American Baseball Research, of which I am president, and although at first he said he would, he later backed out.

A. He's probably like I am. Our speaking abilities have not improved with age [chuckling].

Q. Well, you had some great years in Chicago.

A. Yes, everything went very well in Chicago. The nine years I spent there were very pleasant.

Q. In 1927, which I guess was your first full year, you played in 152 games, hit .344, got 199 hits and scored 101 runs.

A. Yes, that was a good year. A funny thing about those 199 hits. We were playing in St. Louis and I had a 3-and-0 count on me. McCarthy gave me the signal to hit. I didn't know what to do. I had 199 hits and one more would have been 200. But I took the pitch and then another and then finally went out without getting my 200th hit... Yes, he was trying to help me get the 200th, but I just couldn't hit a 3-and-0 or 3-and-1 pitch. I only hit a 3-and-0 pitch but once and that was in Kansas City. I hit a little bouncer right back to the pitcher... I tried to hit it too hard and hit it on the handle.

Q. How were you on an 0-and-2 pitch?

A. I got so I could hit them pretty good. Not so good at first, but later on I got better. They curve you on that pitch and you have to learn to protect the plate. Fred Maguire said I was a better hitter with two strikes. Fred played for the Braves and then for the Cubs, too, just before they got Rogers Hornsby... Hornsby and I got along all right. We had no trouble. Hack Wilson used to have a little trouble with him. No outspoken words or anything serious, but there was a little something there. They didn't get along too good. But Hack ought to be in the Hall of Fame. As I was telling some people a few days ago, if they don't put people like Hack, Chuck Klein, Johnny Mize, Lon Warneke, and Ernie Lombardi, fellows like that, if they don't put them in the Hall of Fame they ought to close the place down. They deserve to be in there, based on their records, compared to some of the fellows that have been taken in.

Q. Your credentials are pretty impressive?

A. Well, pretty good, but I don't expect to get in.

Q. The trouble is that too many of the writers who do the electing don't know much about what happened before they were born.

A. Well, they have some older fellows on the Old-Timers Committee now -- Burleigh Grimes, I think, is on the committee.

Q. Tell me about Hack Wilson.

A. I used to dress right by Hack. He and I never had a cross word while I was there. He was a good-natured fellow. He drank some at night, but I never saw him -- they all say he drank. He and Malone drank together. He was a good player. Some said he wasn't a very good fielder, but he was a good fielder. Those balls he missed in the [1929] World Series were due to the sun. He was standing ready to catch them then at the last moment ducked his head down. One went for a home run with the bases loaded and I don't know how many scored on the other one -- all in one inning. That was that bad inning against the

Athletics where we had them beaten 8-0 and it wound up 10-8 in their favor.

Q. I suppose that is an inning you wouldn't like to talk much about [chuckling]?

A. I used to know every play. I've kind of forgotten about it now. It was a strange inning. That ball that bounced over McMillan's head -- he was playing third base. All three of those plays, none of them were errors, they were just lucky plays. I remember very well how the inning started. Al Simmons hit a home run into the left field seats over my head. Charlie Root was pitching. I thought that was all right, one run wasn't going to make any difference. Then it started -- doubling, singling, bouncing balls, flyballs, and things. The next day, Guy Bush was pitching. Bing Miller, with two men on base, hit a line-drive to right center, which won that game for them. We only won one game in the series, Bush beat Earnshaw.

Q. Do you remember Fred Blake?

A. Very well. They called him "Sheriff."  He was a pretty good pitcher, too. I think he came down here and pitched for Birmingham for awhile after he left Chicago. English was kidding one day about his wife, a lovely lady. She had thirty-five pairs of shoes!... He's in Bluefield, West Virginia?  A good friend of mine on the Alabama football team lived in Bluefield, "Mother" Lenoir. His wife died awhile ago and we haven't heard a thing from him since. He used to come down here for Homecoming every year. [We talk about that fine large picture of the 1929 Cubs set against the Wrigley Field background, a copy of which Blake gave me and which Stephenson has. Joe McCarthy had one hanging in his home, too. He shows me some of his own pictures, one of which he signs and gives to me. He can't find any pictures of himself in a Cleveland uniform, which I asked about.]

Q. How did it seem to be back in Wrigley Field for that old-timers game about a month ago?

A. It was nice; it hadn't changed much... No, they didn't have all those vines and ivy covering the left field wall when I played there. It seems like they have straightened out that point in left center a little bit. Made it a bit shorter. They had a little incline up to the wall, but they've taken that out... Yes, I only played left field.

Q. I was going to ask you, in the event you played any right field, how you handled the situation in Baker Bowl?

*Chicago Cubs' "Murderers' row" of the early 1930s. From left to right, outfielder Kiki Cuyler, catcher Gabby Hartnett, outfielder Riggs Stephenson, and first baseman Charlie Grimm. (Photo from the author's collection.)*

A. I sure remember that place... No particular stories about it, except one day I hit two home runs at Baker Bowl, one over the right-field fence and one over the left-field fence. It was a pretty good distance to the left-field fence and they had a high fence in right field, even though it wasn't very far out there. Kind of like old League Park in Cleveland.

Q. Any favorite ballparks to hit in?

A. No, I didn't have any particular favorites, although I seemed to do very well in Cincinnati.

Q. Now 1929 was a good year for you. You hit .362, but I guess you didn't come close to winning the batting title, did you?

A. No. I think Lefty O'Doul hit over .390 that year and he didn't even win the batting title. I can't remember who won it. [O'Doul did win it with a robust .398 average.]... Yes, the seventeen home runs I hit that year was the most I ever hit. I never hit too many home runs. I hit a lot of line drives through the infield.

Q. In the 1929 Series, how did you like batting against Lefty Grove?

A. I only hit against him once, when he came in to relieve,  I hit the ball on the handle. I always liked to hit left-handers. Maybe a right-hand hitter has a better chance against left-handers. They checked it out once, comparing Babe Herman and me, how we did against pitchers. They found out that we both hit about the same against right-handers as against left-handers... Yes, that was when Herman came over to the Cubs. He came over from Cincinnati [in 1933]... Babe was a nice fellow. No, he wasn't crazy. He made some errors and things, but most of those were when he was with Brooklyn. [We chuckle.]

Q. Maybe it was Brooklyn and not Herman... How did the Cubs do in 1930 and 1931 when the Cardinals beat you out?

A. Well, I remember 1930. Wasn't that when Hack hit so many home runs -- 56? As I remember we left home about this time of year with two months to play, and we were a good bit ahead of the Cardinals. I may be wrong, but I think we were ten games ahead at that point, and when the season was over we were ten games behind. We had a road trip and we couldn't win anything. Well, the pitching was bad, but we'd go along and have them beaten when someone would come up and hit one and the game was over.

Q. In 1930 they have you down for only 109 games. Were you hurt then, or were they platooning you, or was there some other problem?

A. I can't remember. Oh, now I remember. That year I had an ankle broken. I tripped over first base and the man bumped me and when I hit the base I turned my ankle over. I've forgotten who it was. How many games did I play in 1931? Eighty?  Then that was the year I broke my ankle, not 1930. Augie Galan came in and took my place. He came up as a second baseman and took my place in the outfield. He was a good little hitter. He stayed on longer than I thought he would.

Q. In 1931 the Cardinals beat you again.

A. I don't remember for sure what happened. Was Dizzy Dean pitching then?

Q. I think he came up a bit later. Did you get hit by a pitched ball much?

A. I got hit a lot in the American League, but I never got hit much in the National League. I expect when I first started off they were trying to make me a little shy. I remember getting hit up on my arm -- right there -- a lot of times. Oh, a funny thing one time. We were talking about Walter Johnson. We were playing in Cleveland once when Walter threw one that bounced off my head and hit up on the screen. It hit right there -- on that hard place -- and went right up on the screen.

Q. You were hit on the head by a Walter Johnson pitch?
A. Yes, I was hit on the head by Walter Johnson, but it wasn't a solid lick. I fell down and they made me take a time-out and then I went on down to first base. I was lucky, I guess. An inch lower and it might have killed me. A helmet might have helped.

Q. Was there any talk of helmets in your time?

A. No. I never heard of any. I certainly would have worn one if they had them then.

Q. Did pitchers throw at batters much?

A. Oh, yes, they threw at them. Stengel said "Don't throw up there and don't throw back there; throw right there." [Under the chin.]... I went to Japan on an exhibition tour with him in 1922 and 1923... Yes, that was Fred Hunter's tour. Fred doesn't sound right. [It was Herb.] Luke Sewell went with us. We had a good team on that tour. Luke and Freddie Hofmann were catchers. George Kelly was first baseman. Hunter played second. Doc Lavan played shortstop and I played third base. Amos Strunk was in the outfield... He's still living! Bullet Joe Bush, Waite Hoyt, and Pillette were the pitchers. Stengel and Irish Meusel were also in the outfield. I enjoyed that trip very much, especially when it didn't cost me anything [chuckles]. I brought this kimona back from Japan.

Q. When you hurt your knee with Cleveland, did that slow you down at all?

A. I think they kind of made up their mind that I couldn't play second base. I don't think the knee really slowed me down much. Speaker said that I could run and hit and that if I wanted to prolong my career I should go down to the minors and learn to play the outfield. I appreciated that. I never could have taken Jamieson's place in left field. My arm wasn't strong enough to play right field. The right fielder should have the strongest arm of any outfielder, in my opinion. At Chicago they needed a left fielder. Luck is part of the game in baseball anyway... My arm probably was not quite average. I was accurate and could throw short distances, but I couldn't throw very well long distances.

Q. Did you ever throw anybody out at the plate?

A. Oh, yes, I threw a few of them out. I remember throwing McCurdy out in Philadelphia one time. We were kidding about it and Cuyler, you know, had a great arm. Wilson had a pretty strong arm, too. They were talking about it once and Hartnett -- a good friend of mine -- said "Stephenson threw that man out at the plate and I haven't seen you guys throw anybody out." But, you see, they wouldn't run on those other fellows very much.

Q. It can't be easy throwing anybody out at the plate?

A. No, it isn't. You have to have a mighty accurate arm. But I never had many assists.

Q. Now it's 1932 and you win another pennant.

A. Yes, we played the Yankees in 1932... No, the Series didn't last long -- they won four straight. I had a pretty good Series, though... .444? Yes, and I got a good many hits... eight out of eighteen? I think Gehrig was the only one higher than me.

Q. What happened in that Series? Were the Yankees that much better?

A. Yes. I don't think we had the power to beat the Babe, Gehrig, Lazzeri, and the rest; Dickey, Sewell, Chapman, Combs.

Q. How about the "called shot"?

A. I remember that very well. There was a lot of difference of opinion on that. Sewell, who hit just ahead of the Babe, said he really pointed. Some of them said no, but Joe will tell you about that. He knows more about it than I do. He said that somebody in Chicago, where we were for the old-timers game -- maybe an umpire -- gave the right version of it.

Q. Woody English, who was playing third on that pitch, said he was just pointing to the dugout, that there were only two strikes and that he had one more to go. And then there's the story that the Cubs gave Mark Koenig only half a share of World Series money and Ruth was riding them for that.

A. Yes, that's right, half a share. Bobby Smith and Bush were riding the Babe. And Burleigh Grimes had a towel wrapped around his neck and when Babe hit the homer Burleigh threw the towel up in the air in disgust [chuckles]. I was in left field so I couldn't see too much, but that ball went right over the corner of the scoreboard, the only one I ever saw go over there while I was with the Cubs.

The right corner of that center field scoreboard. They keep those seats out there vacant now to give the batters a better view of the pitch. They sat out there when I played and it made it tough when certain right-hand pitchers were on the mound.

Q. Should Koenig have gotten a full share?

A. Well, I don't know. I guess I voted for a half share thinking that he shouldn't get as much as fellows who had been there the whole year. He was there only a month or two, but he did help us win a couple of games. I think it was Jurges who got injured and Koenig was playing for him. Jurges didn't hit too much, but he was a great fielder. He hit about .250 or .260, which wasn't much of an average then, but it seems like a great average today.

Q. You can get a two- or three-million dollar contract now for hitting .250 [we chuckle].

A. Yes. But they must be pretty good athletes these days. They're bigger and can run faster. I don't know if they're any stronger or not. I know they can run faster because they have broken all these records.

Q. But they're not hungry like you fellows were?

A. That may be the main reason... I had average speed. Ten stolen bases in 1929 was my tops. I didn't get thrown out much. I hardly ever ran so they couldn't throw me out much.

Q. When you went up to bat with the Cubs, what kind of signals would they give you about hitting or taking and under what circumstances?

A. McCarthy would usually give you the signal to hit or take on the 3-and-1 count, but usually on 2-and-1 or 2-and-0 you were on your own. If we were behind we generally took the first pitch, hoping to get a walk. Of course, the other team soon found this out and they would pop the first pitch right in there. That would be when you're leading off the inning and only a couple of runs behind. With men on base, you were usually on your own. He wanted you to hit with men on and the count in your favor.

Q. With men on in a close game and less than two out would you be ordered to bunt?

A. Most of the time... You're right, they don't bunt much any more to advance the runners because they don't know how to bunt. We practiced bunting quite a bit and I was a pretty good bunter when I first went up. Later on I didn't bunt so much. Then I began to lose my ability to bunt fair and often bunted the ball foul. But in Cleveland a couple of people remarked about how well I bunted and wanted to know where I learned how. Hughie Critz of the Reds and the Giants was a good push-bunter. He'd push the ball by the pitcher and with the second baseman covering first there was no one to field the ball and it would go for a hit. Yes, he's over in Greenwood, Mississippi. I had a card from him. Then there were drag-bunters as opposed to push-bunters... Speaking of cards, I also got one from "Footsie" Blair over in Texarkana, Arkansas, who was an infielder with us on the Cubs.

Q. What was it like going out to Catalina Island?

A. That was great. I really enjoyed that out there. Lots of nice places to walk and lovely scenery to see. Later on we trained in Los Angeles and that was nice too... Mr. William Wrigley used to come out to the island with us, but after he died I don't remember seeing his son, P.K., out there. When I left there, P.K. gave me a watch. I think that was the first time I ever saw him. P.K. was mechanically inclined and liked to tear things apart and put them back together again rather than go to the ballpark.

Q. Did you see Bill Veeck senior much?

A. He was out there a lot. He was all right, but he was pretty hard. You know how he got his job don't you? When he went to work for Mr. Wrigley? Well, the Cubs were having a tough time back in the early 1920s and Bill Veeck was writing for a paper there in Chicago. Mr. Wrigley got after him for some of the stuff he had written which was critical of the way the Cubs were being run. Mr. Wrigley asked him, "Do you think you can do a better job?" "If I couldn't, I would quit," he answered. So Mr. Wrigley gave him the job of president [chuckles]. I don't know if that's true or not, but that was the story that was going around.

Q. Fred Blake gave me a menu card that you people used on the train to Catalina. It looked like you ate very well?

A. Yes, I remember that. We did eat well. That's one thing I liked about it, you could eat all you wanted... If you see Fred say "hello."

Q. Yes, I will. That's one of the fun parts of this interviewing. I see a lot of you fellows who were teammates long ago and bring you up-to-date on what the others are doing. And then it is very interesting to hear different people describe the same thing -- like Ruth's "called shot."

A. We have old-time get-togethers here of Alabama football players. Those who played in the late teens and 1920s get together and talk about the old days. Then the younger players, those who played in the 1930s and 1940s are there having their own get-togethers and they don't pay a bit of attention to us old-timers. That's the way it was at the old-timers game in Chicago. Those who played in the 1930s, 1940s, and 1950s, didn't pay a bit of attention to us who came before them. I don't understand why they didn't come around and speak to us. Maybe we were the same way, I don't know. It seemed a little unnatural. [This well illustrates, I think to myself, the attitude of modern players in excluding the old-timers from their lush pension program.] At the football homecoming they'd give us tickets in the end-zone. I told them to keep their tickes, I wasn't coming anymore. I couldn't see a thing from the end-zone.

Q. How about your relations with umpires?

A. Oh, I never had any trouble with umpires. I might say a little something once in awhile. Remember Ernie Quigley? Well, if he called a strike, which I thought was a ball, I'd just say something like, "That was a little outside, wasn't it, Ernie?" I seemed to get better results from that approach. I said that to Ernie one time -- he was a fraternity brother of mine -- and he said, "My boy, I'd rather call them on you than anyone else." I said, "Yes, but if you keep calling them like that on me, I won't be here very long" [chuckles]. After that I got good decisions from him, I thought. You know, on pitches like that, it's always an inch-off or an inch-on and you can call them either way. Like that old umpire who came from Cajun country around New Orleans -- who was a good umpire, too. He was in the American League. He said, "There ain't any close ones: they're either 'dis' or 'dat'" [chuckles]. [That was Bill Guthrie.]

Q. Was Billy Evans umpiring in the American League when you were there?

A. Oh, yes. Billy was a nice fellow. You could always talk to Billy. Some of the umpires you couldn't talk to. Eddie Ainsmith, the old catcher for Washington who later umpired in the Southern League. I said to him once, "Eddie, you missed that one." "Stevie," he replied, "I'm allowed to miss eleven" [chuckles].

Q. Who were some that you couldn't talk to?

A. There weren't any in particular that I remember, but there were some who had a chip on their shoulder or for some reason wouldn't talk. Brick Owens was pretty hard. Tommy Connolly was all right; he was nice. There was a good little one who came but didn't stay long. Dolly Stark. I don't know why he didn't stay long.

Q. I don't suppose you ever called Bill Klem "Catfish," did you?

A. Not me. One time I hit a ball right on the end of the bat and rolled right down the first base line very close to the foul line. He called out, "Foulball!" I ran about four or five steps and quit running. The ball was spinning wildly and hit a piece of grass and bounced back and hit the first base bag. Klem shouted, "You're out!" I protested. "Bill, you called that a foulball?" He said, "I'm sorry, my boy" [chuckles]... No, he never missed many. He was great on balls and strikes. That's the hardest thing to call, I always thought.

Q. What do you think of this modern practice of appealing to the first or third base umpire whether a batter has swung too far or not?

A. Well, I think that's all right because you can't always tell from behind the plate if the batter has gone too far. I think that's all right; they've got to help each other.

Q. Did you ever hear of that colorful old umpire, Tim Hurst?

A. Yes, Jimmie Burke, the coach for the Cubs, used to talk about Tim Hurst... It's a funny thing about a lot of players up there that I never had heard of. There was an old fellow up there in Chicago in the fire department, Harry Steinfeldt. He was part of that Ticker to Evers to Chance infield.

Q. How long were you with the Cubs?

A. Nine years, including part of that 1926 season. 1934 was my last year. I was released. I went down to Indianapolis and played another year there. Played there on the way up and on the way down... Yes, they had Eddie Sicking, Schreiber, and Walter Holke. Guy Bush was there. And that old left-hand pitcher was playing right field. After Indianapolis I came to Birmingham where I managed two years. I played the first year there, in 1936. I think I hit .355 that year.

# Walter Miller
## *Novelty, Ohio, October 29, 1974*

"The Civil Engineer"

Walter Miller, pitcher for the Cleveland Indians in the 1920s and 1930s, may have known my father, although neither of them would have remembered it. Dad was a civil engineer for the city of Cleveland for over forty years. Miller was a civil engineer who worked for the city in the off season and after baseball became an executive with Universal Concrete. He knew Frank Lander, with whom my father was a business partner at one time. I always had a warm spot for engineers. Both of my older brothers, as well as my father, were engineers and I often thought I should have been one. I liked Miller, not only because he was a bright, urbane, and courteous gentleman, but also because he was an engineer. And I never realized until lately that he pitched the first major league game I ever saw. It was from Walter Miller that I had a first-hand account of the unusual circumstances surrounding Emil "Dutch" Levsen's double-header wins one day in 1926. It was an amazing performance, yet it got relatively little media attention. Although he had only a mediocre career -- slowed down by sinus trouble -- Miller was able to handle "Babe" Ruth pretty well and utterly frustrated "Goose" Goslin. But his biggest thrill?  "Just playing baseball."

[As tape picks up we are discussing a former Marietta College basketball coach. Walter is speaking.] Oh, yes, I knew Don Kelley. He and my son went through Ohio State together. My son, John, captained the 1955 basketball team, and Don captained the 1956 basketball team.

Q. We started talking awhile ago and the tape wasn't working. I wonder if you could go over some of that again?

A. I was born in the little town of Wagram, on old route 40 about fifteen miles east of Columbus. It was a crossroads with a grocery store, a church, and an old wooden school building. The school building burned down when I was about five years old. I used to go to school with my brothers in order to get away from the farm. I guess my mother didn't want to take care of me during the day. After the new brick schoolhouse was built, I guess we all went to school there. My oldest sister was Martha, then came Edgar, then came May, then Stanley, then Guy, then Hazel, then Ray, then myself, then Russell, then Les and Chester, the twins, were born in 1902, three months after my father was killed in an accident. We all stayed on the farm and ran the farm with our mother's help; she was the boss.

Yes, after my father died. We had quite a dairy herd and did most of the farm work by hand. It seemed natural that every time we had a spare minute we'd be throwing things, the girls included. There were always plenty of stones and apples, and when we didn't have chickens to throw at, we'd throw at the birds and the glass insulators on the telephone poles. My uncle worked for AT & T at that time, back in the early 1900s, and he spent more money putting new insulators on the poles there than anywhere in the state of Ohio. And we eleven kids kept breaking them every night coming home from school. But that's the way we grew up. My oldest brother kind of took over running the farm when my father got killed.

Q. That would be Edgar?

A. Yes, that was Edgar. He was still in high school, seventeen years old at the time. After he got out of high school, he taught for four or five years, then started in at Ohio State. He went through Ohio State in three years. He was quite a star in the family. But then Martha taught school when she became old enough, and then May taught school. Then Stanley, Guy, Hazel, and Ray, then Les and Chester, all taught school, either grade school or high school.

Q. Did they all go to college?

A. All but Stanley and May went through Ohio State.

Q. How was all of that financed?   That was not an easy thing to do for a widowed mother with eleven children.

A. Well in 1900 your tuition was about $30 a semester, I think. They used to have dormitories there on the old campus. My brother lived in a dormitory there close to Mirror Lake; he lived in the basement. That was in 1908 to 1910, I believe. The rest of us roomed around in dormitories and rooming houses. We worked our way through mostly. Of course, the boys and girls all taught school, which brought in as much as $100 a month.

Q. They put this back into the family kitty to help the others along?

A. No, they kept that. We made the farm self-supporting. We had no hired help and our milk bill was $200 to $300 a month. We sold twenty to thirty fat hogs every year. We sold a little wheat, a little corn, a little hay; so we were mainly self-supporting. What each one earned teaching school, they kept for their own college expenses, so they made their way through pretty good.

Q. You didn't have to have a college degree to teach school then?

A. No, these were all county schools and all you had to do was take the county examination. I was the only one who never taught school. I could never figure that out because the other ten were all school teachers. One brother became an engineer and another one finished up as a professor at Ohio State before he retired. He was an agricultural economist. He just retired -- well, he is eighty-two now, so he's been retired several years. [Walter was born February 28, 1898, so was seventy-six years old at the time of this interview.]

Q. Tell me again that your grandfather, who I think it was, received a land grant here from President Monroe, maybe?

A. Oh, yes. This niece and nephew of mine are fanatics on family trees. They started working on our family tree about fifteen years ago. It was rather easy, because over there in Woodstock, Virginia, where the family farm was, my great grandfather on my mother's side, and my grandfather on my father's side, were brothers, so they all grew up in Woodstock in one family. And these two brothers, Isaac and Alexander, left the Virginia home and emigrated here to Ohio. We don't know how they got here, probably on horseback and wagon. We think they got dissatisfied because after their father died, they wanted the estate settled and didn't want to wait. They left right away and I guess the folks gave them $100 apiece. That's what we hear from the neighbors out in Woodstock -- the old-timers. That's how they got to Ohio. So it turned out that my mother and father were first cousins once removed.

Q. Then this grant of land?

A. Yes. Isaac Miller, my grandfather, got 180 or close to 200 acres all together. And when he died each person got twenty to thirty acres, something like that. My father bought out three other shares so he wound up with close to 100 acres. We had the typical old log barn, which you see on some of the colonial places which have been preserved. We had an old log house, which we lived in, with rough siding. In about 1906 we rebuilt the house. We left those logs, some of them were 8 by 14 inches, we left those logs in place and sided over them, then added a couple of more rooms for the big family. I was kind of sorry when the old place burned down seven years ago. I wanted to get a couple of logs out of the house. There was nothing left at all.

Q. You were pretty young then when your father passed away.

A. I was only four years old. I don't remember him at all. The twins weren't born until June and my father died the 29th of April, 1902... He was born in 1860 so he must have been around forty-two or forty-three years old when he died. My mother was born in 1863 so he was a couple years older than she was.

Q. Tell me about life and Ohio State when you went there.

A. I started in 1917. Three other brothers and sisters had been there off and on. Two other brothers were already enrolled when I entered, but they enlisted in the war right away. I stayed around until 1918 and then I got in that student army. I spent fifty to sixty days fighting the "Battle of the Olentangy," as we used to call it. [Chuckling. The Olentangy River runs along the campus.] We lived on the campus and didn't get uniforms until the day before we were discharged. That was the SATC, the Student Army Training Corps. We had it rough [chuckling]. We trained and I was training for the air force, or getting ready to.

Q. Did you play baseball at Ohio State?

A. We kids played baseball from the time we were old enough to throw and it seemed like every Saturday and Sunday there were enough of us to have our own baseball game. The young ones were too young to hit much while we babied them along, but we all played together. Of course, it was a pretty rough game. We made the baseball out of an old unraveled sweater or sock, or something like that, wrapped around a walnut or a stone. We cut the cover out of an old shoe and sewed it around the baseball.

Q. How about your bats?

A. Somehow we got regular bats. I remember once when I went to Columbus to get my first suit, the salesman at Lazarus gave me a ball bat. And we would go out in the woods and cut our own bats out of a young ash tree. If they were too heavy, we would use a linden tree, which is kind of a bass wood. We had pretty good bats, of different weights. I had been preceded at Ohio State by my brother Ray, who made the varsity in 1920 or 1921, I guess, after he got back from the army. I know he was on the pitching staff for two years. I came along in 1922 and 1923. I made the freshman team. In those days Director St. John was the football coach, the basketball coach, and the baseball coach, also the director of Athletics. We'd start spring training along in March. We'd have indoor sessions, training and coaching sessions, and that's where I think I learned a lot about baseball. In those sessions St. John would go over every phase of the game. He did a real good job, I thought. At the time I was on the squad they had a couple

*J. Walter [Jake] Miller in a 1931 photo taken by Charles M. Conlon, the celebrated baseball photographer. Miller, who pitched for Cleveland, 1924-1931, and for the Chicago White Sox in 1933, had a lifetime record of 60 wins and 59 losses and an earned run average of 4.09. He had a successful professional career outside of baseball as a civil engineer. He pitched the first major league game I ever saw in August, 1929. (Photo from the National Baseball Library, Cooperstown, NY.)*

of left-handers and three good right-handers, so I never really had much of a chance. I would work out with them, but never took a road trip with them. But I learned a lot and gained valuable experience from the coaching I got there. St.

John said later -- he was asked by some of the Cleveland newspapers why Miller didn't pitch any for the varsity. He said that I could have if I had a little more experience, but that I wasn't far enough along. I guess he was right.

Q. Did any of those fellows who were ahead of you at Ohio State, ever make the big time?

A. Only one, Wayne Wright, who was ahead of me. He pitched for St. Louis for a year or so, but he didn't last too long.

Q. Now you said you entered in 1917, but you were pitching in 1921 and 1922?

A. Well, I lost a year on account of the army and in 1918 after the war I got the brave idea of going to Kansas and working to make some big money. So when we got through in Kansas that August, we went to the University of Minnesota. I studied one year there, 1919-1920, and then came back to Ohio State in 1921.

Q. How did you get into engineering at Ohio State?

A. Well I got into electrical engineering because my older brother Edgar -- when I was planning to go to college; we all planned to go to college somehow, it seemed the natural thing to do -- Edgar said there ought to be an engineer in the family, someone who knows how to build dams and things like that. I entered into electrical engineering, but after a year of that and some of that detailed laboratory work, I decided to shift over to civil engineering. And while I was at Minnesota, they had a freshman team there, the first one they ever had, although it was strictly intramural. We won the championship at the university, and someone induced me to go up there on the iron ranges that summer and work and play ball. That's where I really got started.

Q. You played up there in the summer of 1920?

A. Yes. It was a semi-pro league. I had a job on the state highway and I helped with the transit and surveying instruments. They listed me on the engineering crew as a rodman. We lived out in the woods and surveyed roads during the weeks and on Sundays we would come in and play baseball. That's where I got started into civil engineering. That was just about the time they were beginning to build the first paved highways in Minnesota and they had a tremendous highway improvement program.

Q. How did you happen to go up to Minnesota?

A. Well, I had a roommate who was a rather ambitious guy and he didn't want to come back to Ohio State. We debated whether we should go to Colorado or Minnesota. We finally decided upon Minnesota, which turned out to be a real good thing. He went through the law school there and became an executive with Procter and Gamble. I kept playing ball up in that Minnesota iron range for the next couple of summers. In 1923, that was the year I finished college, I left at the end of the winter quarter -- around the first of April, I went out to Terre Haute, Indiana, for spring training. I had been approached by a scout from Terre Haute, so I went there after finishing at Ohio State.

Q. Had you graduated by this time?

A. Well, I had more than enough credits, I had 115 when I only needed 105, but I didn't graduate because I didn't stay to write my thesis. I'm the only one in the family who didn't get his or her college degree... Yes, baseball interfered.

Q. How did this Terre Haute scout hear about you?

A. Well, up in Minnesota, every year I got a little better, and I got a better job each year -- I worked in the mines part of the time and part of the time on the highways. A chap came up there from Terre Haute to play first base -- he didn't last too long -- but when he went back he got in touch with the Terre Haute officials and they telegraphed me right away and told me to come down and join the club. This was in the fall of 1922, so I signed up with them for 1923.

Q. If you had played with the Ohio State varsity in the spring of 1923 you probably would have finished your thesis and graduated, wouldn't you?

A. Oh, no. I had the thesis about half-finished when the winter quarter ended. We started on it in January. There were three other fellows helping me. One of them, John Dowler, turned out to be the big engineer down at Athens. He graduated in 1923 as I should have... But I wouldn't have been able to pitch for Ohio State that last year [1923] anyhow because I had taken money for playing summer ball up in Minnesota.

Q. How did things go for you at Terre Haute in 1923?

A. I had a varied career in 1923. I went through spring training with Terre Haute and just before the season began the manager came to me and said, "We've got a good job for you; we're going to send you to Hamilton, Ontario." They had just acquired a great big left-hander from St. Louis that they had had the year before. St. Louis couldn't keep him so they sent him back to Terre Haute, which was a farm club for the St. Louis Browns at that time. So they sent me to Hamilton. I reported up there, but I had a little trouble getting started.

Q. Who was your manager at Terre Haute?

A. I can't remember and I can't remember the manager at Hamilton either. I do remember that we had a tail-end club with a lot of ex-big leaguers who had been playing as far back as 1908. It was quite a get-together gang, I'll tell you. Some wild ones, and some not so wild... No, no big names. The catcher [chuckling], I wrote his letters home to his wife; he couldn't read or write. They had a great big first baseman they called "Wobbly" Kuhn. They called him Wobbly because I guess he was under the weather most of the time. But I had a pretty good year up there once I got started. I'd pitch seven innings of just wonderful ball, then they'd beat me up for awhile. I had to learn to pace myself. Then in the middle of the summer Terre Haute decided they wanted me back. I came back to Terre Haute and pitched some darn good games back there.

Q. You were 7-3, it says here.

A. Yes, and then when their season closed, the president of the club, Ross Harris I think his name was, a banker in Terre Haute, he told me he wanted me to go to Rochester and join that club, which had three or four weeks of the season to go yet. At the same time they sent two other ballplayers from Terre Haute to Rochester. I went up with them and we finished the season with Rochester. That was George Stallings who was the manager there.

Q. George Stallings!  I've talked to more people who played under George Stallings.

A. Yes, old George Stallings. He owned the ballclub... No Eddie Onslow wasn't with them; he was with Baltimore. He had a fellow named Lake catching. Do you remember that New York Giant player who pulled that World Series boner?

Q. Fred Merkle?

A. Yes, Fred Merkle was our first baseman. He was a wonderful chap... No, I never heard him mention that boner. He was a quiet chap. He played a lot of bridge. One of the quietest fellows I have ever run across. But at that time in 1923, Rochester was --

Q. How about Fred Blake?  He was with Rochester for awhile.

A. I can't remember that. I knew Fred Blake. I met him when he was with the Cubs. But I can't remember any of the other pitchers who were with Rochester then, except maybe one little right-hander.

Q. This stay with Rochester doesn't appear here on your record.

A. No, I only pitched in part of one game. They decided they didn't want me so they turned me back to Terre Haute. Then the next year while with Terre Haute, Cleveland bought me.

Q. Was there a working agreement between Hamilton and Terre Haute and Rochester?  In other words, how did you happen to go to those clubs?

A. There was no link with Hamilton. Hamilton was just a lousy ballclub, which needed players. Hamilton wrote around and got me. They assumed my contract and paid me. And the same was true of Rochester. The other players who went with me up there were pretty good and might have stayed, but I just went along for a tryout. At least, that's what I thought it was... In 1924 Cleveland sent several ballplayers to Terre Haute and they kind of arranged a working agreement with Terre Haute as a farm club. The St. Louis Browns dropped out of it as far as Terre Haute was concerned.

Q. What did you do that winter after your first professional season?

A. Well, I considered myself an engineer and I came to Cleveland. These other two players from Terre Haute who went up with me to Rochester, one of them had an open roadster. After the last game of the season at Rochester, we got into that car and drove all night to Cleveland. They let me out in Cleveland and I stopped at my brother's. I got a job down at the court house working for the county sanitary engineer. After I was playing ball in Cleveland I used to get down to the Court House quite a bit and I knew a number of people there... That was my older brother Edgar where I stopped. I think he was principal of West High School at the time. He taught up in Michigan for awhile and then came to the Cleveland system through a Mr. Lake, who had been county high school superintendent in Licking County where we lived. Edgar taught there for forty years or so and was principal at West High for about the last twenty-five years. I lived with him in 1923 and in 1924 went back to Terre Haute. I had a fairly good record there in the first part of 1924, then when Cleveland bought me I came back and lived with Edgar again.

Q. When you came to Cleveland did you get a pretty big raise?

A. No, I didn't. Salaries weren't too good for a rookie, I'll tell you that. They had a salary limit in the Three-Eye League [Terre Haute], which was a Class B league and a darn good one at that. There were a lot of young fellows going up and a lot of old-timers going back down. It made a balanced team. When I first went into that league Connie Mack's son was managing at Moline. There were any number of old-timers pitching there. A couple of old pitchers who had been in the big leagues were there, although I can't remember their names. Mordecai Brown pitched there the year before. [We chat about other Indianans like Vic Aldridge and Edd Roush. I mention that I have an appointment to see Roush later this very week in Oakland, Indiana. Miller picks up.]  You know down in St. Petersburg every year, the week before spring training begins, we have a game between National League old-timers and American League old-timers, and Eddie has been playing there for the last seven or eight years. But he had a stroke a couple of years ago. I talked to him a long time last March, but he wasn't able to put on a uniform.

Q. Is there anything you can suggest that I ought to ask him about when I see him, besides why he was a perennial holdout?

A. Yes, ask him if he remembers hitting against "Lefty" Miller in spring training. Every year when I was with Cleveland, 1925, 1926, and possibly 1927, coming north from spring training, we'd stop in Cincinnati and play on a Saturday and Sunday. Then we'd have Monday off and then come back to Cleveland to get ready to open the season. We'd play them Saturday and Sunday games and I'd always pitch against him.

Q. Now could you go over again how Cleveland got you?

A. They must have had a working agreement with Terre Haute by this time because they sent a number of players out there. And they also had a couple of players they farmed out to Peoria. If one club couldn't take them all they would farm the overflow to another club. Because the Three-Eye League was a good one then.

Q. What was the ballpark like in Terre Haute?

A. Oh, it looked like old League Park here in Cleveland. Old wooden building, wooden frame. Not a very good groundskeeper. But the year I left Terre Haute, 1924, they built a brand new concrete stadium out there. The old one held about 2,000 people. Yes, we got some pretty good crowds out there. I remember on Decoration Day my roommate and I pitched against Bloomington and the place was jammed full. We beat them both games. They gave us $100 apiece for winning those games [chuckling]. We got a little extra money that way. The owner gave us the money. The team was going so good, we were leading the league, and I was about 7-2 and my roommate had won eight or ten games.

Q. What was his name?

A. "Dutch" Levsen; Emil Levsen.

Q. Emil Levsen!  The fellow who pitched the double-header for Cleveland in 1926 and won both games?

A. That's the one. He and I roomed together at Terre Haute and then we roomed together in Cleveland, all the years he was with the club there... He was just a wonderful gentleman. He came from the area around Cedar Rapids, Iowa. He lived on a farm just as I had. He had a couple of brothers and sisters and they worked the family farm like we had. He went through Iowa State and was going to be a farmer, but he got to pitching out there in the Mississippi Valley League, with Cedar Rapids. He was scouted by old Cyril "Cy" Slapnicka, who was from Cedar Rapids. He discovered him and coached him along. Cy scouted for Cleveland so that's how Dutch got hooked up with the Cleveland organization. Dutch and I kept in touch with each other until he died about two years ago.

Q. Did he live out in Iowa after baseball?

A. No, he came to Cincinnati. Well, yes, he stayed out there for a long while. He married a girl from Maquoketa, Iowa. They settled there and then when she died he gave up the business. I think he sold insurance around Iowa for awhile and then came to Cincinnati and worked for that big government organization that handles wheat; I forget what they call it. He was buying wheat here in Cincinnati and then he moved to Minneapolis and that was where I met him again about ten years ago.

Q. Were you with him when he threw that double header?

A. Absolutely.

Q. How did that come about?  That's a rather unusual happening.

A. Well, Speaker was the manager and we must have been short of pitchers, I guess. It was 1926 and we finished second that year, by golly. We almost beat the Yankees out. But it was a hot day up there in Boston. That was in Fenway where they have that short left field fence, but Boston didn't have a real hot ballclub in those days. Dutch pitched the first game and it was so easy for him; he didn't even sweat any. And they didn't hit him very hard. I don't think we got him too many runs -- four or five maybe. And then when we settled down between ballgames to have a coke or a hotdog, somebody, I think it was George Burns, suggested to Speaker, "let's let Dutch start the second game."  I think Speaker probably asked Dutch, and he said "sure."

Q. Then it was a spur-of-the-moment decision?

A. Yes, it was not planned ahead of time, like in the morning or the night before. Speaker used to tell us the night before who was going to pitch the next day. I don't have the least idea now, I can't recall, who had been scheduled to pitch the second game. Usually, the second pitcher will stay in the clubhouse during the first game and not go out on the field and watch the game... No, it wasn't me. Dutch pitched the second game and I think he did a better job in the second game than he had in the first game.

Q. The plan probably was to just let him start and then see how far he could go and relieve him when it became necessary.

A. Yes, that was the idea. We got ahead in both games. You know it makes a difference if you get a two- or three-run edge; you pitch a little different and don't have to cut the corners so fine. He pitched two masterful games. About the only time that's been done in the century, I guess.

Q. Joe McGinnity did it way back when.

A. Yes, "Iron Man" Joe McGinnity. That's the guy I was trying to think of earlier. He pitched some out in the Three-Eye League when I was finishing up. They still talk about him out there. He pitched for Dubuque, I think.

Q. He had an amazing career. He won about 250 games in the majors and another 250 in the minors. I don't think anyone else has come close to that.

A. I met the "Iron Man" once. He came back and pitched a few innings, I think, some time out there in the Three-Eye League. At Danville we always played at the Old Soldiers Home and we always had a big crowd there because the old soldiers got in free. We played on their diamond. I met old "Uncle Joe" Cannon there.

Q. The Speaker of the House back in Taft's presidency. How would you rate Tris Speaker as a manager?

A. Well, I would say he was a little better than the average. He didn't bawl you out, but he didn't know the pitchers too well... Yes, his own pitchers. Whether he had too much on his mind with the rest of the club, or whether he was trying to set records with his own hitting -- I think he got over 3,000 base hits. And I think he got that hit right here in Cleveland and I don't remember a person saying a darn word about it. It must not have impressed us when we were playing on the same team.

Q. A lot of things, which seem to impress us today did not seem to impress in the older days.

A. Yes, he got his 3,000th in Cleveland. I remember when, in 1927, George Burns broke Speaker's records for doubles in one year. That just went by as if it was another double [chuckling]... No, when Dutch Levsen pitched that double-header there was not much attention paid to it. It was just one of those games.

Q. Can you manage a team very well from center field, like Speaker?

A. Cobb did. Of course, Cobb wasn't a good manager either. Now when I played with Speaker, in 1925 we didn't have a good club, but in 1926 we had a good club and should have beaten the Yankees. We let the lousy seventh and eighth place clubs beat us out. We could beat the Yankees, but we couldn't beat St. Louis. While the Yankees beat St. Louis twenty-one out of twenty-two times.

Q. Why couldn't you beat the Browns?

A. We couldn't build ourselves up for games with them, or else we just had a big series and then let down. That happens quite often in baseball.

Q. I hadn't realized you were that close in 1926. [The Yankees were 91-63=.847, while Cleveland was 88-66=.738 in 1926, the Indians three games behind.]

A. Oh, yes... We had George Burns, Joey Sewell, Luke Sewell, myself, Dutch Levsen, George Uhle, Carl Lind at second base. We had two second basemen and good ones, but they only lasted a year or so. Freddie Spurgeon was one and I don't remember if it was Freddie or Carl Lind in 1926; I think it was Carl. I can't recall who played third base.

Q. "Rube" Lutzke?

A. Lutzke was with us in 1925, but I don't remember if he was with us in 1926 or not. [It was Lutzke; he played 142 games at third base.]  In the outfield we had Speaker in center, Charley Jamieson in left field, and Pat McNulty and Homer Summa in right field. We had different right fielders, but Jamieson and Speaker were pretty steady. What got us through were Speaker, Jamieson, and Burns in hitting and Uhle's pitching. I think Uhle won twenty-six games that year. [He was 27-11.]... Yes, he had up-and-down years. A good one, then a poor one, then a poor one, and so on.

Q. I interviewed Uhle and he spoke of his up-and-down years.

A. You interviewed Uhle?  Did he mention the fact that Babe Ruth never hit a home run off of him?

Q. Well, I asked him about Ruth and the way he put it was, "The Babe never gave me much trouble." [We chuckle.]  He didn't say, though, that Ruth never hit a homer off of him. Uhle is most proud of his hitting. He is rather irked that he isn't remembered for his hitting. He was the greatest hitting pitcher in baseball, in my opinion.

A. Yes, he was a great hitter and he could pitch to Babe Ruth better than any pitcher I ever saw, for a right-hander. He had that splitting curveball, which broke straight down and Babe would just look sick trying to hit it. He'd swing over it every time. That's why I was thinking, here a month or two ago, Uhle gave a big interview for one of the local newspapers out in Fairview Park. It was quite an article and it said there that the Babe never got a home run off of him. I didn't know that and I still can't believe it. But anyone who pitched like he did -- for over twenty years -- and Ruth never got a home run off of him -- and Uhle won over 200 games -- he should be considered for the Hall of Fame. More than some of these other ballplayers who have gotten in.

Q. As I say, Uhle said the Babe never game him any trouble, but I don't think he made that point.

A. Well, he must have faced the Babe eight or ten games every year, and all the years he pitched, he must have faced the Babe a lot.

Q. But he did have those bad years, so he wouldn't have pitched to the Babe much in those years. He spent a lot of the time explaining to me how a medical doctor on the West Coast had treated his arm. That must have been quite a treatment he had.

A. He didn't happen to mention "Bonesetter" Reese did he?

Q. That may have been who it was.

A. Yes, that's who it was, but he never went to the West Coast. Every month or two we'd all pile into the car and go down to see Bonesetter Reese. He never had any formal medical training, but the state of Ohio gave him a license to be a chiropractor or an osteopath, whatever it was. He worked around the steel mills in Youngstown and helped so many people who were crippled and maimed. So they gave him a professional license to practice. [We chuckle.] Oh, he was well known back in the 1920s and early 1930s, my goodness.

Q. When did you actually move to Cleveland?

A. I lived with my brother right up until 1928, the year I got married. We lived in Parma part of the time. My father-in-law built a house and we lived in that. We went to Florida a few times in the winter. I worked several times during the off season in the engineering department of the city of Cleveland ... Yes, I was able to keep up in my profession as an engineer. I worked in the drafting department. In addition to working for the city one year, I worked for I. F. McDowell Sanitary Engineering, which was a private company. I worked for McDowell while he was county sanitary engineer, that's how that opened up, and when he left the county and opened up his own business I went with him.

Q. How did you meet your wife?

A. Well, she worked for a legal company, Reese Davis and Young in Cleveland and Reese Davis was city service director at one time, under City Manager Morgan, and a good friend of ours from Ohio State, Fred Young, was a partner in this law company, and my wife was working for him. He got interested in me because I was a baseball player and he knew my brother Edgar real well. I think they started their law office in 1921 and my wife was their first employee. She came from a little town over in Pennsylvania near New Castle. Her whole family grew up over there. Her dad was postmaster in that little town during Woodrow Wilson's administration.

Q. Did you move to the east side eventually to be near the ballpark?

A. No, we continued to live in Parma. Later, when I was through with baseball and we had two children, we moved to Cleveland Heights. That was because my job was out at the big pipe company right across from the Randall race track on

Miles Avenue. It was called the Universal Pipe and Concrete Company at that time... Yes, that was after baseball.

Q. Did you work most off seasons then while you were playing ball?

A. Well, after 1930 it was kind of hard to find a job. So I didn't do much then... No, I didn't do much hunting. My brother Russ, two years younger than me, he was a heck of a ball pitcher and one of the best hunters in the country. But I never got into hunting; I don't know why. Just two of my brothers were hunters; the rest of us didn't care much for it. We would go after squirrels and rabbits around the farm when we lived on the farm, but never went out with Speaker and the others to hunt moose all winter. I remember one year, Speaker, Cobb, and Buckeye -- oh, he was one of our pitchers in 1926, Garland Buckeye; when I used to drive to Minneapolis to visit my daughter, I used to always stop in Gary, Indiana, to see Buckeye. But he doesn't live there now. He's been in my position -- he's lost both of his wives and he's living up in northern Wisconsin now. He's got a summer home up in Sand Lake, way up in the northwestern part of Wisconsin.

Q. Wasn't he a great big man?  About six-feet and six inches tall?

A. No, he wasn't that big, but he was a big man. He was about my height [about six-feet and two inches], but he weighed around 250 pounds. He has trimmed down now and you would not recognize him compared to what he used to be.

Q. What was life like in the big leagues in those years?

A. It was such a nice life, a person hated to give it up... Big thrill?  Just playing baseball was a big thrill and having that terrific feeling after you win a game. I only won sixty or seventy games [he was 60-59 over a nine-year career], but every one you won made you feel like you were the best in the world. I always pitched well against the Yankees, Washington, and the Chicago White Sox, Boston, and even against the Athletics in 1929 and 1930 when they had those great teams. I enjoyed pitching against the Yankees for some reason or other, because Speaker used to tell me never to walk the Babe to get to Gehrig; you pitch to Babe because you've got his number... No, I didn't have too much trouble with Ruth; I pitched him sidearm and overhand curves. He took the mightiest swing and never come close to them.

Q. Was he a "guess" hitter?

A. No, he just swung at anything that came over the plate. But there were several of us left-handers who gave him a lot of trouble. Hub Pruett out of St. Louis, myself, and any number of others. Whitehill over in Detroit had that sweeping curveball which gave him trouble. He just seemed to swing right through the curveball. My curves seemed to go right around the end of his bat. I could not figure out why he missed them so often. I never walked Babe. Dutch Levsen pitched a game up at Yankee Stadium once and they only got one hit off of him. We got eight hits but no runs. He walked Babe to get to Gehrig and Gehrig hit a home run and beat him 2-0 and that was the only hit they got. Of course, Dutch was a right-hander, which made it easier for the left-hand hitters. We left-handers had it easier against Ruth and Gehrig both. I struck Ruth out a couple of times, in a couple of games, on six pitches, just throwing curveballs as fast as I could pitch them.

Q. Did you ever talk to Babe off the field about things like that?

A. No, you didn't have much chance to talk to him. You couldn't get into their clubhouse and out on the field they had a non-fraternization rule where you weren't supposed to talk to the other players. The only time we got to talk to the Babe was back in the early 1920s before they put in this rule about no fraternization. If Babe wasn't hitting that inning, he would walk over and sit in our bullpen, which was down the right field line. That was illegal, of course, but we would get to talk to him there a little bit. That's the only chance I ever had to talk to him. I was wondering if anybody ever told you -- did Charley Ruffing say anything about who autographed all the baseballs for the Babe? Well, if you ever talk to anyone who played with the Yankees, just find out who signed all those balls. We on the Cleveland club knew, or thought we knew, that he didn't sign more than 10 percent of them [chuckling]. He had one of the coaches, the third base coach, sign them. In Cleveland I remember, when the Yankees came to town, they brought boxes of new balls into the clubhouse for the Babe to sign. Our Yankee clubhouse boy said the Babe never signed any. Charley O'Leary, the coach, signed them. He could sign just as good as the Babe and you couldn't tell the difference [chuckling]. I've talked to a few of the old Yankees down in Bradenton and that's what they told me, too. I don't know any more than what they've told me. But I don't see how he would have the time to sign all those baseballs. Hank Aaron signed a lot of them and every time he got a ball to sign he used to say, "That Babe Ruth must have signed a lot of balls in his career."

Q. Well, I know one batter who had trouble with you -- Goose Goslin. Tell me about that, if you would?

A. [Chuckling]  Peck told you that, didn't he?  I knew he would.

Q. Yes, I was over to see Roger Peckinpaugh last night and I told him I was going to see you today and could he think of some good questions to ask. He said, "Ask him about Goose Goslin."

A. Oh, it was pitiful. Goose would stand up there and cut and slash and I would throw him a fast curve, then one a little slower, then one a little slower than that, and the slower you'd throw them the harder he'd swing [laughing].

Q. Peck said that before the game while you were warming up they would kid Goslin by calling to him, "Hey, Goose, look who's warming up."

A. And the funny thing, when we became good friends, Goose would always try to look me up to find out where he could get a good glass of beer. I used to take him out to some place over on West 25th Street, some kind of a German club where they had pretty good beer... Yes, we and few others would do that after a game in which I pitched against him... No, I wouldn't needle him about it. We wouldn't bring it up. Goose was a nice, easy-going chap. He was quite a ballplayer. He made the Hall of Fame, but it's too bad he died so quickly. Everybody liked him.

Q. How did you like Roger Peckinpaugh as a manager?

A. He was too good a guy to be a good manager. A lot of players took advantage of him. He's rather quiet and easy going and I don't think he had the spirit of a leader. But everybody liked Roger. As an infielder, he knew all about the game but he just didn't --

Q. How did he deal with discipline problems?

A. Only twice that I can remember did he have problems, and these were minor, I think. I don't know how he handled Uhle. Uhle used to be hard to handle at times, we thought. In training, I don't think he trained as hard as some of the rest of us. Maybe he felt he didn't need to, he had such a powerful arm. I don't know if he had any problems outside of training or not. Like the Babe was a roustabout, a holy terror, I guess. But the day after one of his binges, he would hit three home runs. He was a superman in that respect. I never knew Uhle that well enough to say that about him, but he was a Cleveland guy, and I wondered if after one of his good years, something might have happened there to make him slip a bit. Like Joe Vosmik, he was another local guy, and he had too many good times, I always thought. He came up later, but I knew Joe real well.

Q. So Peck was just too easy to be as tough as was needed?

A. Yes. And take Speaker, he didn't always know the names of the players. Even back in 1920 when they won the championship. Some of the old pitchers who came back and talked with us said he didn't even know their names. If he wanted some pitcher to go to the bullpen or to start the next day, he would just point to them, without knowing their names. I know one time he made a mistake with me. We were playing in Yankee Stadium; this had to be in 1925 or 1926. I was pitching in the regular rotation at the time. Buckeye started the game and in three innings they had him beaten, 8-0. Speaker pointed to me and said, "You go down to the bull pen."  I'd been pitching regular and I don't know if he thought I'd been out the night before and wanted to teach me a lesson, or what it was. I went out and pitched the next six innings and they never got a hit off of me. It's things like that you remember, which make you wonder if the manager was really serious about his job. It seems to me, as I remember, Speaker, Cobb, Johnson, Sisler, and any number of those famous men, they never became good managers. Hornsby was a lousy manager. My brother Russ played for Hornsby and Hornsby hardly ever knew him, he didn't know he was on the ballclub.

Q. It was the marginal players, the Gene Mauchs and Walter Alstons, that became good managers. Connie Mack wasn't much of a player.

A. Oh, he was a pretty good catcher. He knew baseball. You know what he called me, "Poison" Miller [laughing].  I didn't have much trouble with the Athletics in the first three or four years. Around 1930 they got a little troublesome.

Q. Who were some of the toughest hitters you faced?

A. Lazzeri was a tough one. He was a lowball hitter and I was a lowball pitcher and I couldn't seem to get the ball past him. He was the toughest right-hand hitter in the early part of my career. Later on, Simmons and Foxx were tough hitters. I never really had trouble with any left-hand hitter. I always felt I could handle them. I learned to pitch to the right handers after awhile  with the screwball. Mine was a sinker which broke down and away from right-hand hitters.

Q. The screwball is where you reverse the twist of your wrist, isn't it?  I would think that would be pretty hard on your wrist.

A. I tell you, a lot of left-handers have a natural sinker, they don't have to twist their wrist. I didn't have to. When I was at Terre Haute I used to pitch overhand all the time. Then I got a little kink in my shoulder and I went to Bonesetter

Reese. He got his knuckles in here [he demonstrates], pushed a little nerve over -- what I think he does is to set up a counter reaction. If you have a sore nerve he'll make another one sore right next to it and that first one will get well. But after I went to him that's when I developed that screwball and that sinkerball.

Q. Did someone suggest that you do this or did it just develop naturally?

A. Oh, no one suggested it; I just started to drop my arm down so the shoulder wouldn't bother me and pretty soon along came that sinker and then the screwball.

Q. Did you have a sore arm often?

A. Yes, I had many sore arms. I had sinus trouble most of my career. I would have times when I was pitching when my eyes got glazed and home plate would look like... If I could feel them coming ahead of time I would take a couple of aspirins. My eyes would clear up, but then my head would ache. I never had a real serious headache from my sinus, just that kind of glazing in my eyes. I can't really describe it. I had it a little bit yesterday when I was out in the yard raking leaves... Yes, I could still pitch that way. I could see the batter and the catcher and would pitch to the catcher. But I wasn't very effective, I can tell you that. I never told the manager or anybody about it. I had it in college. I remember when I was a sophomore I had that funny feeling in my eyes. I went to the doctor when I had one of these attacks and I went to other doctors and they couldn't detect anything. Later I heard it stated that migraine headaches were due to nerves and tension. I have trouble believing that.

Q. Did your arm get sore from the sinus?

A. No. I broke my ankle the first year I pitched -- 1926, my first good year -- and I came back and pitched in three weeks and I felt my arm tear a little bit in here. After that it was just off and on. I had a pretty good year in 1929, but I was in and out most of the time... Yes, I think that did shorten my career... The only thing I objected to in playing ball was trying to sleep after a game and trying to sleep on a train. I could never sleep on a train. And I never could sleep after I pitched a game, whether I won or lost. I must have keyed myself up so much... No, the night before a game never bothered me. I've often asked my son when he was playing basketball at Ohio State from 1951-1955, I know they had pep pills to pep you up and tranquilizers to slow you down. I just wish we had some of those back in the 1920s. I would like to have tried them out.

Q. On the trains at night, you would just thrash around or get up and walk around?

A. Yes. We had two private Pullman cars wherever we would travel. No upper berths. We had to take the media with us, they were in our cars. We didn't have to take the umpires with us; they had to ride in separate trains. That was fun to have your own Pullman to travel from St. Louis to New York, or from Chicago to New York, or from here to Washington. They were all overnight trips. The only day trip we had was from here to Detroit. That was fancy traveling in those days.

Q. What would you do on the trains to kill time?

A. Well, Uhle, Peckinpaugh, Luke Sewell, and Levsen were fanatics on bridge playing. They would always play bridge. Sometimes a poker game would get started; sometimes fan-tan. Those of us who didn't want to play cards just sat around. Some of us read. I did a lot of reading. I always like to read and still do.

Q. What are your reading interests?

A. History. I'm a nut on history. John, my son, majored in history for his Law degree.

Q. With Peckinpaugh playing cards with the players, was this a good thing; was it a natural relationship?

A. Oh, yes, it was natural. He was a good friend of the players. We did have an outfielder, Sam Langford, who disagreed with one of the coaches. The coach was a teammate of Peck's when he was with Washington and when he became manager of Cleveland he brought this fellow over as a coach. Sam had a disagreement with him about something and had to be disciplined... You remember Sam? I pitched against him out in the Three-Eye League in 1924 and he was a powerful hitter. When Cleveland got him I thought he would be a tremendous hitter for us. But you know what, when he came up they found a weak spot in his batting. If you threw a pitch across the letters he'd swing and then you'd pitch each successive pitch a little higher. Finally, strike three might be above his head and he just couldn't hold back. [Chuckling]... But that traveling was simply wonderful. Of course, nowadays the fellows all get, Lord knows, just $18-$20 a day as expense money -- they tell me. But in our time we had to pay our taxi cab bills, our laundry, our tips, and all those incidentals. Transportation to the ballpark. But we stayed in good hotels, as they do now, and it was a pleasure because in those days we'd play two four-day series in each town and one three-day series to make up the eleven games. And those hotels were real nice, dining rooms were nice; we ate most of our meals there, signed our checks. There were a lot of good shows in town.

Q. How were you treated in these places by the general public?

A. Wonderfully. In New York, Cleveland was one of the most popular clubs to come to New York. There would be as many people at the games cheering for us to beat the Yankees as there were for the Yankees. New York was that way in those days; it was a cosmopolitan town and the fans cheered the visiting ballclubs.

Q. Did you have any parks you liked to pitch in more than others?

A. I always liked to pitch in Boston even if they did have a short left-field fence. I always liked the old St. Louis park. Detroit was one of the nicest parks and still is. For hitting and pitching. I liked Comiskey Park, too. It was so big and I pitched pretty well there. Jimmy Foxx hit one off of me way up in the top of the left field seats; I think that was the longest one ever hit there. You see, I finished up with the White Sox in 1933.

Q. Yes, what happened to you in Cleveland. Was 1931 your last year there?

A. In 1931 they farmed me out to Indianapolis. I was having a bad year at Cleveland and I was thinking about retiring. My head hurt so from the sinus, I had migraine headaches and my arm didn't feel too good. I thought that since I was an engineer I might as well get on with my professional career. Almost before I even planned on it, Peckinpaugh told me I was being sent out to Indianapolis. I thought I'd go out there and finish the season, rather than tell the Cleveland club I was finished and wanted to retire.

Q. How did you do at Indianapolis?

A. Oh, I won about ten games, I think, and lost four. I don't remember the manager, but I'll tell you who was there that I didn't like, and that was Jack Hendricks.

Q. I wonder if there was anybody that liked him. [We chuckle.]  I think it was Elmer Smith who told me about Jack Hendricks. Smith and a couple of others.

A. Yes. I was trying to think of the manager who played first base. In fact, he went crazy and shot himself two years later. But I can't think of his name. He was a good first baseman; he hit well. Indianapolis was kind of low at that time and they wanted to finish high. Kansas City was leading the league. I went in there and won nine games and we finished second. We were kind of close to Kansas City and if the season had lasted longer we might have beaten them out.

Q. Did the White Sox buy you from Indianapolis?

A. No, the next year, 1932, I went into spring training with Indianapolis. I told them I was about to retire and they sent me over to Columbus. Rickey wanted me. He thought that the way I pitched over in Indianapolis I could help his St. Louis club. The Cardinals owned Columbus. So I trained awhile with Columbus and pitched a couple of games when I pulled a vertebrae in my sacroiliac and that ruined me. I layed around the rest of the summer and then quit until I got doctored up. Then they sent me to Toronto.

Q. This was what year now?

A. 1932. I was with Columbus and Toronto in 1932 and they released me. I went to spring training in 1933 with my back strapped up. I took several therapeutic treatments on it and went to spring training with the Cincinnati Reds.

Q. Did you contact them or did they contact you?

A. I used a little pull. Donie Bush was the manager and I had some good friends who knew Donie and they talked to him. So Donie let me train with the Reds and I came north with them. I pitched the last game of the exhibition season against Kansas City or Toledo. I didn't do very well so they didn't sign me up, but let me go. At the same time Pittsburgh came into Cincinnati to play and I knew a bunch of those guys -- old Grover Hartley, Hans Wagner, and some others. They said they had seen the Chicago White Sox play and that they didn't have any left-handers. So I called up the White Sox manager, Lou Fonseca, and he signed me up for the summer. He had been with Cleveland in 1929 and 1930.

Q. How did things go with Chicago?

A. Well, I beat Washington three games. I had a no-hit game going until the eighth inning in one of those games and Goose Goslin got the first hit off of me. [We chuckle.] I only won three or four games with them. [He was 5-6 with a 5.62 ERA. My arm was bothering me and I was still getting those migraine headaches. I kind of ached all over. I finished the season with the White Sox. Funny thing, we had a seventh place club and we played the Cubs in an intra-city series and beat them four straight. We beat Charlie Root and that bunch. They were winning pennants in those years. [I mention that I had interviewed Woody English, the Cub third baseman on those teams.] Oh, Woody and my brother Russ were good friends. They played together on those sandlots around Newark [Ohio]. They played for Heisy Glass back when the glass company was going good. [I mention that Woody's mother was still living, at the age of eighty-seven.] My mother died when she was ninety-six. That was the same year my first wife died in 1969. I have a sister who is ninety, my older brother would be eighty-eight, another sister who is eighty-seven. They just come right on down the line, eighty-seven, eighty-five, eighty-three, eighty-two, eighty, seventy-eight, and I'm seventy-six. My brother Russ passed away and one of the twin brothers passed away later. But there are still eight of us in the family going strong.

Q. Do you all get together very often?

A. No, it's hard to do. My brother in Detroit, Stanley, he used to pitch for Hamilton and Lima in the old Ohio State League. He's in Detroit and can't travel much. Then an older brother, Guy, the retired professor, he lives in Miami. I get to see him when I am settled in Venice, Florida, in the winters. It's kind of difficult for us to travel anymore and get together. My sister Martha is in the Eastern Star Home at Mount Vernon [Ohio], and the other sister, May, is at Cambridge, living alone.

Q. Do you own property in Venice?

A. No, I'm not going to buy any property. There's a little single house which I rent. John's father-in-law lives in a mobile home down there and my daughter's father-and mother-in-law live in Sarasota, so we have quite a colony down there... There are a lot of ballplayers down there. Early Wynn is near by and the old shortstop of John McGraw in in Sarasota --

Q. Fred Lindstrom?

A. Yes, Freddie, he's there. Lou Burdette. Wes Ferrell is in Sarasota some of the time. Wes was a good hitter, but not as good as Uhle.

Q. Peck said Ferrell had a terrible temper. He'd be mad at himself. He'd take him out of a game and he'd stomp around.

A. Yes, I don't know what was the matter with him; why he was that way? His brother Rick was a wonderful chap; he wasn't that way. I think there must have been something in that family. Another brother [probably George] was violent like Wes... Oh, yes, Wes took good care of himself. In all the years I knew him I don't think I ever saw him take a drink of beer. I don't think he ever dated a girl or anything like that... Oh, yes, he got married eventually. He married the daughter of the chap who ran the Bobby Jones Golf Course in Sarasota. I think she passed away sometime ago. You don't know where Hudlin is, do you?

Q. In Arkansas, I think. I'd love to interview him. Did you have any problems with umpires?

A. I never did. I only remember one umpire apologizing to me for making the wrong decision [chuckling].  That was Bill Summers. Remember him?  We called him "Anteater."  We used to tease him. Every once in a while the players would get together for a little conference and he would always come over and try to hear what we were talking about. That's where we got the name anteater for him because he was always sticking his nose in. Most of this was just for fun. But he was a good umpire. He called me out at first base once when I was past the base by three feet when he made the call. I never said anything about it. I used to complain once in a while, not to the umpire, but say to Babe Ruth. We'd give him a going-over now and then because we felt the umpire favored him... Yes, we did it in the umpire's hearing, but addressed our remarks to the Babe. But most of the time I left the complaining up to the catcher. I never complained about them. If I was having a good day I figured it didn't matter if one or two of the calls were in the wrong direction.

Q. Most umpires were pretty conscientious, was that your feeling?

A. Oh, yes. I respected them. I'll tell you another thing. After I was finished playing baseball I got a job with the government in relief work back in 1934 and 1935. In 1936, I knew the president of the American League and he got me a job umpiring out in the Northern League. So I umpired out there all that summer... Oh, yes, I knew Will Harridge. No, I never met Ban Johnson. I knew about him, of course, but I never met him. I played against all those buzzards. We played them a series in the Iron Range League. [He is speaking about the banished Black Sox.]

Q. What was "Swede" Risberg like?

A. He was a mean guy, but boy he could hit. They had a league up there and they were paying as much as $1,000 a month for anyone out of the big leagues who would come up there and play. They were outlaws who had jumped their contracts somewhere else. That's why the Black Sox came up there. They had a full team except for a couple of extra pitchers. Claud Williams [one of the expellees] pitched for them and I pitched against him once... Yes, I knew Joe Jackson, but "Buck" Weaver was the nicest of that bunch. Speaker said he never should have been outlawed. Maybe he should have been suspended for a year or two, but Landis was too tough on him. Maybe Risberg and that Gandil, he was a crook, should have been kicked out.

Q. It seemed to me that Jackson was victimized --

A. Yes, and Weaver was victimized... Yes, Gandil was the ringleader; I'm sure that's the way it was. If you could get ahold of Faber some time [I did and he was useless as far as supplying some inside information on the Black Sox], Ray Schalk and Nemo Leibold were also on that team. They were the clean ones and you might want to talk to them.

Q. I spoke to Leibold on the phone in Detroit last spring, but he wouldn't see me because it was mother's day. Why an eighty-four-year-old man couldn't see me on Mother's Day I couldn't figure out... What was the matter with "Pants" Rowland as an umpire?

A. He just missed too many. Honest to God, he was pitiful behind the plate. You never knew what he was going to do. He just missed them that's all. He didn't miss them intentionally, he just wasn't qualified, I guess. I know that for the umpire behind the plate, he's going to miss a few, but most of the calls will be so close that there won't be too much chance for an argument. Rowland would miss them when they were half a foot outside. Or some would come right down the middle and he would call them balls. I know because Luke complained about his calls, Speaker complained, we all complained. They didn't have any chief scout in those days; I don't know who looked after the umpires.

Q. Tommy Connolly was still umpiring, wasn't he?  But I guess Ban Johnson handled all the umpires directly.

A. Tommy was a prince. Yes, Ban did handle all the umpires. It wasn't until later that Tommy became the chief, the supervisor of American League umpires. Tommy was one of the best ever. I can remember back in 1925, the first year I went to spring training at New Orleans, and Charley Somers, who started the Indians ballclub in 1898 [actually 1901], I talked to him a little bit.

Q. He was the "financial angel" of the American League, wasn't he?

A. He certainly was... Yes, he did run into financial troubles and had to sell out to Jimmy Dunn. I don't know what he was doing that summer down there. He may have had an interest in the New Orleans club.

Q. Can you think of any outragcously funny or odd things happening on the ballfield during your career?

A. Well, I can't think of anything like that offhand. I just know it was a wonderful life. I just enjoyed it. Even after losing a game. By the next day you had almost forgotten about it and were looking ahead. In those days, with twenty-five ballplayers, all with different temperaments and different ideas about humor, some crazy things happened. Sometimes they'd go around and cut the rims of everyone's cap and when you put the cap on, the rim would fall off. Then they might have a spell of going around cutting neckties off about halfway down... No, I can't think of any real pranksters on the Cleveland club. Nothing like Nick Altrock and Al Schacht -- of course, they were legitimate comedians... No, I never met Germany Schaefer.

Q. Do you remember much about Eddie Morgan?

A. If he hadn't played football, and if he had taken care of himself, boy, he would have been a wonder. He could hit that ball!. He banged his shoulder up in football and had to throw awkwardly. No arm... Yes, he was a "playboy." That was one thing that surprised me. We'd get on the train down here at the old Union Depot at 10 or 11 o'clock and three or four of us would be carrying Eddie onto the train and Peckinpaugh would be standing right there and he wouldn't say a word. Nothing happened about a thing like that, at least to my knowledge.

Q. I remember he used to hit all those home runs and get an Elgin watch for each one.

A. Yes Elgin watches and then cases of Wheaties. [We chuckle.]  Yes, Eddie was probably the worst cut-up we had, at least, as far as I can remember.

Q. Not like Johnny Hodapp.

A. No, Johnny was a good boy. Bibb Falk was a good guy. Yes, he was quite a "bench jockey."  He nicknamed everybody on the club. And especially the umpires. He was one I was thinking of earlier. And every year on our first trip to Washington, Nick Altrock would come over to our bench and he'd pick out members for his ugly man's club. Of course, he'd always find somebody to pick on.

Q. Well, I guess we have taken up enough of your time.

A. I'm not doing much today, so that's all right. Pretty soon I will fix supper for my three grandchildren and do a little shopping. Tomorrow I've got doctors' examinations and the day after tomorrow I've got doctor's examinations. My kids will be here Sunday and I'm going to try to take off for Florida a week from tomorrow. I come back in the spring. And then these kids take a month's vacation in the summer and I come back and take care of the house. That's a real pleasure trip for me. I'm here all alone for two or three weeks.

Q. One final question about your career after baseball.

A. I worked as an engineering inspector for the PWA around Cuyahoga County and later on I traveled across southern Ohio from Steubenville to Portsmouth. I knew all the county engineers around there. I knew your old county engineer in Washington County [Marietta]. My sister who is now in Cambridge, lived in Marietta for fifteen to twenty years. Her husband ran one of those state farms down there, an experimental farm somewhere in that county. I worked for the government until 1940, then I got a job with the Universal Concrete Pipe Company out of Columbus. They had plants all over the United States. They had one here, one in Sandusky, one in Erie, and one in Youngstown. I worked in Columbus for awhile, then I transferred out to Sedalia, Missouri for a year, then I finally transferred here to Cleveland. That was it; I wasn't going to move anymore, so they left me here for twenty-some years. I became the superintendent, engineer, construction manager, and production manager for those five plants -- Cleveland, Sandusky, Erie, Youngstown, and one below Massillon. We kind of spun off of the main company. [He discusses in some detail how Universal Concrete kept buying companies and then in turn became part of Martin-Marietta, but the latter had to divest itself of some plants because of conflict with anti-trust laws. So he worked for a lot of different companies, but he remained in Cleveland for the rest of his working years until his retirement at age sixty-five in 1963.]

Q. Did you retain your interest in baseball in your retirement years?

A. Well, when I was working, I was working so hard I didn't have much time for baseball. I didn't go to the games here much. I was invited back to an old-timers affair in 1948 when the Indians won the pennant. They had a game between the 1920 champions and a bunch of us who played in the 1920s and 1930s. That was the only exhibition I played in. And I haven't seen many games since then. I do watch a lot of games on television. I read *The Sporting News* down in Florida; I don't get it up here.

* * *

At one point I asked him about his name because in some record books he is listed as "J. Walter" and in others as "Walter J." and his nickname in some places is "Jake." It turns out when one of his sisters took him in from the farm to enroll at Ohio State, she thought he should have a fancier name. So she put a "J." in front of Walter. "J. Walter Miller" was the way she enrolled him at Ohio State. The "J." had no meaning at all, but it stuck. He autographed a picture and my ball, "J. Walter Miller."... As for the "Jake," that was an entirely different situation. When he was with the Indians in 1925, Rube Lutzke saw him pitching over a period of time and didn't think he was working very hard at it. He pitched in an easy fashion and didn't seem to work up a sweat. So Lutzke yelled at him that he was "jaking it," which was apparently a phrase at the time for "goofing off" or "goldbricking." Then Gordon Cobbledick, the *Cleveland Plain Dealer*'s baseball writer, began referring to him as "Jake" and the term just caught on, although the nickname never enjoyed widespread usage... Miller struck us as a highly-educated, well-read gentleman, who enjoyed a very successful career outside of baseball, which owed nothing to his baseball career.

# Index